an introduction to

early childhood

Second edition

an introduction to

early childhood

A Multidisciplinary Approach

Second edition

Edited by **Tim Waller**

Los Angeles • London • New Delhi • Singapore • Washington DC

SAGE Publications Ltd
1 Oliver's Yard
55 City Road
London EC1Y 1SP

SAGE Publications Inc.
2455 Teller Road
Thousand Oaks, California 91320

SAGE Publications India Pvt Ltd
B 1/I 1 Mohan Cooperative Industrial Area
Mathura Road, Post Bag 7
New Delhi 110 044

SAGE Publications Asia-Pacific Pte Ltd
33 Pekin Street #02-01
Far East Square
Singapore 048763

Library of Congress Control Number: 2008931319

British Library Cataloguing in Publication data

A catalogue record for this book is available from The British Library

ISBN 978-1-84787-517-4
ISBN 978-1-84787-518-1 (pbk)

Typeset by C&M Digitals (P) Ltd, Chennai, India
Printed in Great Britain by TJ International, Padstow, Cornwall
Printed on paper from sustainable resources

Mixed Sources
Product group from well-managed
forests and other controlled sources
www.fsc.org Cert no. SGS-COC-2482
© 1996 Forest Stewardship Council
FSC

CONTENTS

ACKNOWLEDGEMENTS

The editor would like to acknowledge the contribution of all the authors, who completed their chapters for this book in addition to their 'normal' teaching and work commitments. Colleagues at the University of Wolverhampton, University of Northampton and Swansea University have been particularly supportive during the period of writing this book, and thanks go to our publisher Jude Bowen for her assistance.

Thanks also go to Amanda Bateman for her help with an early, initial literature review in preparation for Chapter 2.

On a personal level, I am once again very grateful to my family: Janet, Rachel, Amy and Jack, Ashley and Harri for giving me the time and space to complete this project.

Tim Waller
Wolverhampton
June 2008

The book is dedicated to our children and grandchildren.

ABOUT THE AUTHORS

Celia Doyle is a Senior Lecturer at the University of Northampton, teaching child development, welfare and protection in the Schools of Health and Education. Formerly, she specialized in childcare and protection, initially as a local authority social worker then as an NSPCC team member. She has published extensively on childcare and protection and has recently published the third edition of *Working with Abused Children*. The focus of her PhD thesis was on emotional abuse in childhood. A key theme of her current research is on how children, especially those experiencing emotional distress, can be helped to communicate their experiences, emotions, opinions and wishes.

Gill Handley is a Senior Lecturer in the School of Education at the University of Northampton, teaching on the BA (Hons) Early Childhood Studies, Sure Start Foundation degree and Early Years Professional programmes. Her background is in social work, having over 20 years' experience working in a variety of adoption and child protection roles, most recently as a manager in the Children and Family Court Advisory and Support Service representing the interests of children in court proceedings. She has also taught on the Open University social work programmes and acted as a mentor and supervisor for post-qualifying awards in social work. Her research interests include adoption and post-adoption support as well as children's rights, particularly their rights in relation to court decisions about their future care and contact with family members.

Denise Hevey is Professor of Early Years and Head of the Division of Early Years and Education Studies in the School of Education, University of Northampton. Professor Hevey joined the School of Education in November 2005 after 18 years at the Open University and a series of central government posts. Her background includes the production of distance-learning materials in areas such as child abuse and neglect and in working with children and young people. In addition to longstanding involvement in the field of early years, Professor Hevey has extensive experience of vocational and professional training, occupational standards and qualifications design across a wide area. She also has particular knowledge of relevant legal and regulatory frameworks and government policy relating to children's services from recent experience at a senior level in Ofsted and the Department for Education and Skills.

Christine Hickman is a Senior Lecturer in Education at the University of Northampton. Her academic background is in both art and special educational needs, with autism as a specialism. She has taught in both primary and secondary schools, and has been an advisory teacher for Leicester City LEA. Christine is also School of Education Art Coordinator. She teaches on all Initial Teacher Training (ITT) courses, coordinating and teaching the art modules, including art specialism modules. Christine has an interest in creative and therapeutic approaches, especially in the fields of art and music. She is involved with various international educational link programmes, and has research interests in the field of international perspectives, interactive play and gallery education.

Kyffin Jones is a Senior Lecturer in Education (SEN and Inclusion) in the School of Education, University of Northampton. Before working at the University of Northampton, Kyffin was a senior advisory teacher for Leicester City special needs teaching service. He has taught in both mainstream and specialist educational provision. His experience includes work in the USA and France. Kyffin is module leader for the undergraduate modules 'Children in Society' and 'Current Issues in Special Education', together with a number of other courses with a focus on inclusion and diversity to both undergraduate and postgraduate students. Kyffin is the Year 2 Coordinator for the BA Early Childhood Studies degree and accompanies students on a field trip to Sweden with a focus on inclusive educational Practices. Recent research projects include an evaluation of interactive approaches for children with autism and the role of volunteer mentors in schools.

Eunice Lumsden is the Course Leader and Admissions Tutor for the BA (Hons) Early Childhood Studies degree, in the School of Education at the University of Northampton. She also teaches on the Early Years Sure Start Foundation degree and contributes to other courses across the School of Education and University. Prior to joining the University of Northampton, she had over 20 years' experience as a social work practitioner in the statutory and voluntary sectors. The focus of her work was predominantly safeguarding children and adoption. She is also a practice teacher in social work. She has contributed to a number of research projects with subjects including outdoor play, Sure Start evaluation, interagency work and adoption.

Tania Morris is a Senior Lecturer in Mental Health in the School of Health at the University of Northampton; she also works one day per week in clinical practice at her local Child and Adolescent Mental Health Service as an Associate Therapist. Tania's clinical speciality is children's eating disorders, eating distress and self-harming behaviours. Tania is currently undertaking a PhD study; exploring if the emotional wellbeing of 'hard to reach' children in mainstream education can be positively influenced by their teachers and teaching assistants adopting strengths-based communication strategies.

Jane Murray is Senior Lecturer in Early Years Education and Course Leader for the BA (Hons) Early Years Education (QTS) degree at the University of Northampton. Following 20 years as a primary and nursery school teacher, as well as a primary and early years music consultant, during which time she gained an MA in Education, Jane moved to work in higher education in 2003. Since moving to the higher education sector, Jane has achieved the National Professional Qualification for Headship (NPQH) and has published a number of times within the fields of early childhood and the philosophy of education. Currently, Jane is engaged in writing for several publications covering both fields, as well as studying towards a PhD which is exploring young children as researchers in early years, settings.

Sharon Smith is a Senior Lecturer in Early Years and Child Health at the University of Northampton. Sharon has a varied background in child health, trained as children's nurse and health visitor. She has a BSC (Nursing), RGN, RHV, and PGCE and obtained a Masters degree in Public Health Care, prior to joining the School of Education in 2005,

Sharon was course leader for the Health Visiting course within the school of health was course leader for the Health Visiting course within the School of Health. She aims to promote the importance of child health and an holistic approach to working with children, within education programmes. Her research interests include child nutrition, mental health and children's emotional well-being.

Ros Swann teaches in the School of Education at the University of New England, New South Wales, Australia. She was formerly Course Leader on the Early Childhood Studies degree at the University of Gloucestershire and the University of Northampton. Formerly an early years teacher in Bristol, she has also taught in Canadian and American schools. She taught at the University of Gloucester for 10 years on undergraduate and postgraduate courses. In addition, Ros has taught on initial teacher education courses in America, Australia, Canada and Finland. Her research interests include the professional identities of early years teachers and the impact of an Early Childhood Studies degree on the training of Foundation Stage teachers.

Prospera Tedam is a Senior Lecturer in Social Work and the Course Leader for the BA (Hons) in Social Work at the University of Northampton and was formerly a Principal Social Worker in Northamptonshire. She has also worked in Milton Keynes and Ghana and is a member of the British Association of Social Workers (BASW) and General Social Care Council. Prospera has completed a number of research projects concerning health and human rights and in addition to her teaching is currently studying for a PhD.

Tim Waller is Reader in Early Years Education at the University of Wolverhampton. He was formerly Director of Postgraduate Studies in the Department of Childhood Studies at Swansea University. Previously, he taught in nursery, infant and primary schools in London and has also worked in the USA. His research interests include ICT and social justice, outdoor learning and equality. He has been investigating the use of computers by young children for over eight years and completed his doctoral thesis on scaffolding young children's learning and ICT. Since September 2003, he has been coordinating a research project designed to investigate the promotion of children's well-being through outdoor play. Tim has also recently edited a book with Margaret Clark entitled *Early Childhood Education and Care: Policy and Practice*, published by Sage in 2007.

Jane Waters Trained as a primary teacher, Jane has experience both as a class teacher in multicultural inner city schools and as a tutor for the PGCE (primary) Course in a university education department. On completion of a Master's degree in Education, she became an academic tutor for a BSc Early Childhood Studies programme at Swansea University and a commissioned researcher/consultant for funded research projects. Her current teaching includes an early childhood education module at level 1 undergraduate, an outdoor play and learning module at level 2 and a module focusing on teaching and learning in the early years classroom at level 3. Jane's doctoral studies, concerning child-initiated interaction in early years settings – indoors and outdoors – are ongoing. Jane has recently received an award from Swansea University for her outstanding teaching and has been appointed as lecturer in the University's Centre for Child Research.

KEY FOR ICONS

Chapter objectives

Case study

Reflection

Discussion point

Questions for reflection and discussion

Recommended reading

Recommended websites

Summary

INTRODUCTION

Tim Waller

We were delighted to be asked to write this second edition of *An Introduction to Early Childhood*. The first edition was published at a time of unprecedented change in early years provision and early childhood has come to occupy an increasingly high profile on the policy agendas of both governments and international organizations (Moss, 2006). Since the first edition was published soon after the *Every Child Matters* (ECM) agenda (DfES, 2004e) was introduced, we welcome the opportunity to reflect on the success of a policy which has involved promoting a more child-centred focus and both a culture of integration and a legal requirement for service providers to work together. Also, the children's workforce development strategy (HMG, 2006b) and the Integrated Qualifications Framework (CWDC, 2008) have been instigated. Recently, the *Children's Plan* (DCSF, 2007a) was introduced to reinforce the principles underpinning ECM and focus on supporting and involving parents and families.

Clearly, there is much to celebrate but, despite these welcomed initiatives, a number of challenges remain. There is continued concern and debate about the availability, cost and quality of care and education for young children, provision for children under three, local involvement and control of childcare and achieving a balance between the needs of children and the needs of parents. The early years workforce also remains poorly qualified. In addition, there have been a number of recent reports that have identified new concerns about the health, well-being and lifestyle of children in the UK (*The Good Childhood Inquiry.* The Children's Society, 2007a and UNICEF, 2007). In particular, there are concerns about the number of children living in poverty and vulnerable groups, such as looked after children and refugee children.

It is also important to note that, as a result of devolved government, there are growing differences in early childhood education and care (ECEC), children's services and many of the policies that impact on young children and their families, between England, Northern Ireland, Scotland and Wales. Therefore, it is misleading to consider the UK as a whole in these matters, as Clark and Waller (2007) point out. One clear example of the variation across the UK in ECEC can be found in the different curricula. In England, the *Early Years Foundation Stage* (EYFS) became statutory for all settings with children from birth to five years (DfES, 2007a) in September 2008. Also, in Wales, the new play-based *Foundation Phase* framework for children aged 3–7 (DCELLS, 2008) began rollout in September 2008. In Northern Ireland, changes have already been made to the curriculum for 3–4 year olds since 2006 (DENI, 2006) and the rolling out of a new primary curriculum for 5–11 year olds started in September 2008 (CCEA, 2006). Draft curriculum guidance in Scotland for ages 3–18 (*A Curriculum for Excellence*, Scottish Executive, 2005) was introduced and an ongoing process of review and evaluation implemented in April 2005.

Early childhood (usually described as the period from conception to eight years of age) has continued to develop as an area of study and now has its own QAA benchmark statements. Early Childhood Studies (ECS) degree courses remain popular and a number of universities have recently introduced new masters' courses in early childhood. Students of early childhood are fortunate in that they are able to draw on perspectives from a number of disciplines including, for example, anthropology, biology, education, health, history, psychology and sociology.

Much of the recent literature concerning early childhood has contested traditional perspectives of childhood – in particular, it has been critical of the central role of 'child development' in explaining children's lives (see Penn, 2005, for example). One of the reasons conventional views of childhood are problematic, is that they relate to a particular type of childhood that is presented as universal for all children. Also, many past studies have not considered the child's perspective. The authors of this book are therefore concerned not to promote an exclusive, Western view of childhood that mainly relates to economically advantaged children in wealthy parts of the world such as Western Europe, the USA, Canada, Australia and New Zealand.

This book was written as a result of working with ECS students since 1999. A significant number of these students are experienced early years practitioners, most are highly motivated to learn about early childhood and collectively their commitment and achievement have been an inspiration to the authors of this book. All the authors are themselves experienced early years practitioners in the field of education, health or social care. The multidisciplinary theme of the book is reflected in their collective understanding of working with young children and their families, and of teaching at undergraduate and postgraduate levels. The book also introduces readers to the possibility of multiple, but complementary, perspectives on the study of early childhood.

THE AIM OF THE BOOK

The purpose of the book is to provide a contemporary, holistic and multidisciplinary early years reader which covers the theoretical background relating to significant aspects of current international debate regarding early childhood. The book is based partly on the popular curriculum for the Early Childhood Studies degree at the University of Northampton. While the aim is to introduce students to some of the key areas, it is also hoped that the ideas presented will challenge students' thinking and encourage reflection, further reading and study. Through a consideration of multidisciplinary perspectives, the book is intended as a complement to other recent texts in the field – although, inevitably, it has not been possible to give attention to all aspects of modern childhood and the chapters in this book refer to a selection of possible topics, drawing on the strengths and interests of the authors.

CONTENT

The content is designed for a broad range of readers, in particular those with little previous opportunity to study early childhood. The introductory coverage and emphasis on core ideas make it an appropriate text for students who are new to the field and also students wishing to develop their understanding of contemporary issues in the early years.

The following themes underpin and frame discussion in each of the chapters:

- respecting and protecting children's rights and individuality
- equality of opportunity
- family and community experience and support
- multiprofessional and multidisciplinary collaboration
- opportunities for reflection on the reader's own experience and learning.

This second edition of *An Introduction to Early Childhood* has been expanded to include five new chapters – Well-being, Outdoor Play and Learning, Understanding Diversity, Working with Families and Professional Work in Early Childhood. Each new chapter concerns an aspect of childhood that reflects recent developments (above) or was identified as a perceived gap in the original edition. We are grateful for student feedback and the comments of reviewers in this respect.

As the number of chapters has increased from nine to fourteen, the book has been re-organized into three sections comprising: Theory, Values and Principles and Practice, in order to give the text a clear structure and aid conceptual understanding. Each of the original chapters has been revised to discuss recent and current research, literature, policy and legislation, as appropriate.

The first five chapters in Part 1 provide a theoretical foundation for the book. In Chapter 1, Tim Waller gives an overview of the current international literature and research which underpin the study of early childhood. Much of the recent literature has been critical of the central role of 'child development' in theory concerning young children. In order to provide a contemporary account of the young child, Chapter 1 identifies and critically discusses five key tenets of modern theory. Jane Waters explores the concept of well-being in Chapter 2. The chapter promotes an holistic perspective of well-being and the concept is viewed here as a complex construct that consists of a number of aspects including: the physical, psychological (emotional), cognitive, social and economic. In the chapter, Jane highlights the need for practitioners to attend to children's involvement levels during activity and consider the dispositions that children display within the setting in order to assess the levels of well-being the children are experiencing.

The focus in Chapter 3 by Tim Waller and Ros Swann is on how children learn. The chapter opens with a brief overview of traditional theories of learning and then considers learning relationships and sociocultural perspectives in detail. In particular, the chapter discusses how children's play and sensitive adult interaction and 'scaffolding' can contribute to successful learning. This chapter also provides a synopsis of recent theories of learning, including the work of Gardner, Rogoff and Vygotsky. The chapter concludes with a consideration of the potential of an 'emergent curriculum' (Jones and Nimmo, 1994) where children and adults work together on areas of mutual interest. Chapter 4 concerns outdoor play and learning. Tim Waller gives an overview of recent literature in the field and discusses the reasons why opportunities for outdoor play have become restricted in early childhood. This chapter also provides a critical review of the positive benefits of outdoor play for young children's health, risk-taking and well-being. Recent UK policy initiatives in relation to outdoor play are outlined and findings from an ongoing outdoor learning project are discussed in relation to some recent literature and research in the field. In Chapter 5, Tim Waller discusses international perspectives of early childhood. The chapter reviews a range of findings from recent international comparisons of early childhood education and care. A number of significant similarities and trends are identified. However, it is recognized that wider evidence is needed to represent a world view of early childhood education and care. Reference is also made to the emerging differences within the British Isles (Clark and Waller, 2007). The chapter provides an overview of early years policy and provision, commenting in more detail on diverse curricula and notions of 'quality'. Two examples of internationally renowned approaches to early years provision (Reggio Emilia in Italy and Te Whãriki from New Zealand) are briefly summarized to introduce students to the critical insights that can be developed through comparison. The chapter concludes with a consideration of the notion that 'children's services' should be replaced by 'children's spaces' (Moss and Petrie, 2002).

Four chapters focusing on Values and Principles form the second part of the book. Chapter 6 by Gill Handley outlines the impact of recent legislation, including the United Nations Convention of Rights of Children (UNCRC), the Children Act (1989), the Children Act (2004) and debates around the 'Every Child Matters' framework and agenda. Also, the recent OECD (2006) report is considered alongside contemporary literature concerning the principles and practice of children's participation across a range of integrated services for children. The chapter discusses the difficulty of defining children's rights and draws attention to the fundamental conflict between participation rights and protection rights. The final part of the chapter reviews the implications for early years practice in relation to children's participation and examines how children's rights to participation might be advanced. Celia Doyle writes about protecting children in Chapter 7. Readers should be aware that they may find some of the material in this section of the book emotionally demanding. The chapter provides an introduction to some of the key concepts involved in child protection, considering children who might be subjected to a range of abuse and neglect. The main emphasis of the chapter is on abuse by people who are responsible for the care of the children, particularly parents. An appreciation of the obstacles to recognition is given and the impact of abuse on victims is outlined with particular reference to the 'Stockholm syndrome' which results in children showing loyalty to and affection for their abusers.

In Chapter 8, Prospera Tedam discusses a range of contemporary literature and research concerning diversity and inclusive practice in the early years. Concepts such as diversity, equality and social justice are explored and the role that professionals, parents and the wider community have in encouraging and supporting young children in understanding issues of diversity in contemporary society is considered in detail. An overview of current national and international legislation and policy frameworks which underpin diversity is given and the implications for early years practice are outlined. The chapter also reflects on the barriers to equal opportunities for children, families and early years practitioners, and explores ways of removing barriers to offer equality of service. Chapter 9, by Chris Hickman and Kyffin Jones, introduces readers to inclusive perspectives in early childhood. In particular, this chapter includes an overview of the theory involving children with special educational needs in the early years. The definition and philosophy of inclusion is considered within an analysis of the historical and legislative context. The main focus of the chapter is on educational perspectives, although the importance of a multi-agency approach is acknowledged. The chapter also includes a discussion of 'Aiming high for disabled children: better support for families' (DfES, 2007b) and the Every Disabled Child Matters campaign.

In the third section of the book, the emphasis shifts to Practice. In Chapter 10, Jane Murray examines the contexts and rationales for the study of children's spaces and actions in Western society. The chapter discusses the domains in which knowledge and understanding about children are developed, the construction of childhood, and reasons why practitioners need to know and understand about the spaces and actions of young children. The chapter then focuses on more practical aspects concerning how the information about children might be gathered and used. Chapter 11 by Eunice Lumsden considers the development of interagency collaboration and the reasons why working outside professional boundaries still remains problematic. The chapter intends to provide the reader with a greater understanding of professional collaboration by clarifying the language of working together and the ingredients of effective communication. It also considers the role of initial training for early years practitioners in developing the key skills required by professionals working under the current legislation and policy such as *Every Child Matters* (DfES, 2004e), cross-referenced to the wider debate on professional development in Chapter 14.

Working with families is the focus of Chapter 12 by Eunice Lumsden and Celia Doyle. This chapter introduces readers to a range of literature concerning the diversity of children's home lives and recent policy initiatives in relation to children and their families. The chapter encourages readers to critique the relationship between the statutory and the private, voluntary and independent sector in the work with families, with a special focus on collaborative practice. An understanding of the importance of home–school school/setting liaison is promoted with the intention of assisting readers to develop a grasp of the complex relationships and partnerships between parent/carer school/setting. In Chapter 13, Sharon Smith and Tania Morris discuss the state of child health in the UK. The chapter takes an holistic view of child health and consequently explores children's physical, emotional and mental well-being. The chapter outlines relevant social policy, and socio-economic influences are considered, including the recent National Service Framework for Children (2004). Case studies and practice examples are used throughout to illustrate the implementation of health programmes. In Chapter 14, Denise Hevey provides a detailed consideration of recent literature and policy concerning professional work in the early years. A critical overview of the history of training for work in the early years is given with detailed discussion of recent key developments. Concepts of professionalism are explored in relation to the new Early Years Professional Status (EYPS) and its relationship to other established professions such as teaching, social work and health visiting in the UK and in relation to the concept of the social pedagogue. The difference between a graduate-level professional status and a fully registered and regulated profession is discussed together with the contrasting approaches to professional registration of early years workers in England, Scotland and Wales.

HOW THE BOOK IS ORGANIZED

This second edition of *An Introduction to Early Childhood* also includes the addition of new and enhanced pedagogical features. Each chapter is intended to provide a detailed review of current literature and research and, where possible, reference is made to developments and policy across the UK. All chapters clearly identify the objectives from the outset and end with a concise summary. In most cases, chapters also include case studies with reflection and discussion points to illustrate theory and conceptual issues. Further reading, recommended websites and key points for reflection are identified to promote critical thinking about early childhood. At the end of the book readers will also find a glossary of key terms.

Once more – welcome to the study of early childhood!

SECTION 1

THEORY

1

MODERN CHILDHOOD: CONTEMPORARY THEORIES AND CHILDREN'S LIVES

Tim Waller

Chapter objectives

- To review recent literature and research underpinning the study of early childhood.
- To outline the main features of contemporary childhood and children's lives identified by the literature.
- To critically examine the role of child development in our understanding of children's lives.
- To consider a range of perspectives on early childhood.
- To develop and discuss five key tenets of modern theory about early childhood.

This chapter provides an overview of current international literature and research which underpins the study of early childhood. Much of the recent literature has been critical of the central role of 'child development' in theory concerning young children. In order to provide a contemporary account of the young child, the chapter identifies and critically discusses the following five key tenets of modern theory:

1. There are multiple and diverse childhoods.
2. There are multiple perspectives on childhood.
3. Children are involved in co-constructing their own childhoods.
4. Children's participation in family, community and culture makes a particular contribution to their lives.
5. We are still learning about childhood.

> Childhood may be defined as the life period during which a human being is regarded as a child, and the cultural, social and economic characteristics of that period. (Frones, 1994: 148)

Drawing from a range of recent sources (for example, Corsaro, 2005; Dahlberg et al., 2007; Kehily, 2004; MacNaughton, 2003; Maynard and Thomas, 2004; Penn, 2005), this chapter identifies five features of contemporary theories about children's 'development' and discusses their relevance to modern childhood. The explicit purpose of the chapter is therefore to explore alternative, contemporary views and not to repeat traditional texts (of which there are many) that consider children and childhood mainly from a psychological point of view.

Brown (1998), MacNaughton (2003) and Robinson and Diaz (2006), for example, remind us of the importance of equity and the need to examine and question our own assumptions about children and childhood. It is common for adults to underestimate children. It is generally acknowledged that children are unique individuals, live in a social world, and that there is no such thing as 'normal' development (Donaldson, 1978; Dunn, 1988; Rose, 1989).

Moving towards a contemporary view of the child, the terms 'child' and 'child development' and the whole concept of childhood have been questioned. Drawing on a range of perspectives, including the emerging sociology of childhood, the concept of childhood and the social history of children are examined and discussed and an holistic view is promoted. The chapter considers issues of equality and how they affect children and also focuses on children's participation in the family and community (equality and diversity are discussed in detail in Chapter 8). Insights offered by recent research into early brain development are also evaluated.

THERE ARE MULTIPLE AND DIVERSE CHILDHOODS

A contemporary view acknowledges that childhood is not fixed and is not universal, rather it is 'mobile and shifting' (Walkerdine, 2004). This means that children experience many different and varied childhoods. There are local variations and global forms, depending on class, 'race', gender, geography, time, etc. (see Penn, 2005 for a detailed discussion of alternative childhoods). Until recently, most of the published research and writing about children, childhood and child development have focused on individual development as a natural progress towards adulthood. This natural progress is conceived as the same for all children regardless of class, gender or 'race' (see MacNaughton, 2003: 73). Much of this considerable body of work, written from the perspective of psychology and developmental psychology, has promoted what Walkerdine (2004: 107) suggests is an 'essential childhood'. This is a traditional, Western, developmental view of the child, which is used to categorize all children throughout the world (Dahlberg, 1985; Walkerdine, 1993). Penn (2005) cites Rose (1989), who makes the point that a 'normal' child is a:

> curious mix of statistical averages and historically specific value judgements. The most striking aspect of the 'normal' child is how abnormal he or she is, since there is no such person in reality and never has been. The advantage of defining normality is that it is a device that enables those in control or in charge to define, classify and treat those who do not seem to fit in. (Penn, 2005: 7)

Over 95 per cent of this literature originates from the USA (Fawcett, 2000) and much of it has been written by men, or from a male perspective. Walkerdine (1993: 451) argues that so-called 'scientific' psychological 'truths' about child development 'have to be understood in terms of the historical circumstances in which the knowledge was generated'. For Walkerdine, therefore, this knowledge has been generated in a patriarchal society and the story of child development is one that has been dominated by a male view. She argues strongly that relying on psychology to explain child development 'universalizes the masculine and European' (1993: 452).

Recently, due to the growing influence of a new sociology of childhood, cultural and anthropological studies, an alternative view which argues that childhood is an adult construction that changes over time and place has been put forward (see, for example, Gittins, 2004; James et al., 1998; Mayall, 2002; Prout and James, 1990). For MacNaughton (2003), the development of the child is not a fact but a cultural construction. When we describe a child's development, we are describing our cultural understandings and biases, not what exists in fact (Dahlberg et al., 2007).

As Penn (2005: 97) reminds us, 'the situation of most of the world's children is very different from those we study in North America and Europe'. The circumstances of the 80 per cent of the children who live in other parts of the world are significantly different in terms of wealth, health and culture (see Penn, 2005: 98–108).

1 in 6 children is severely hungry

1 in 7 has no health care at all

1 in 5 has no safe water and 1 in 3 has no toilet or sanitation facilities at home

Over 640 million children live in dwellings with mud floors or extreme overcrowding

Over 120 million children are shut out of primary schools, the majority of them girls

180 million children work in the worst forms of child labour

1.2 million children are trafficked each year

2 million children, mostly girls, are exploited in the sex industry

Nearly half the 3.6 million people killed in conflict during the 1990s (45 per cent) were children

Of the 15 million children orphaned by AIDS, 80 per cent are African. (UNICEF: The State of the World's Children, 2004)

Further, the whole idea and usefulness of actually categorizing and studying something called 'child development' has recently been questioned (see Fawcett (2000) for a more detailed critique). Clearly, change and transformation happen throughout human life, but the argument is about how that change is understood and constituted. Dahlberg (1985) asserts that due to the central and dominant influence of developmental psychology, our view of the child has been constrained to a scientific model of natural growth. Typically, this model of the child defines development in terms of a relatively narrow range of psychological aspects such as social, emotional and cognitive or intellectual and physical development. However, as Riley (2003) points out, these interrelated aspects are complex and developmentalism does not fully account for the complexity nor explain how they operate together in an holistic way. Zuckerman (1993) also argues that theories which suggest regular and predictable patterns of development oversimplify the reality of children's lives and actually hinder our understanding of childhood.

Dahlberg et al. (2007) contend that development itself is a problematic term to apply to childhood because it produces oppressive practices. Walkerdine (1993) and Silin (1995) argue that our perspectives on the child have contributed to their oppression and exploitation in different ways because 'we are in a process of judging their differences to us as inadequacies or weaknesses rather than alternative ways of knowing' (Silin, 1995: 49). MacNaughton (2003: 75) discusses this point and cites Cannella (1997: 64) who asserts that 'child development is an imperialist notion that justifies categorising children and diverse cultures as backward and needing help from those who are more advanced'.

However, while there is an argument for the recognition of the social construction of childhood and the emerging sociology of childhood, as articulated above and in the section below, this is only one of multiple perspectives of childhood. Walkerdine (2004), for example, rightly questions the place of modern accounts of childhood that replace psychological understandings of individual development with sociological interpretations that focus on 'how child subjects are produced' (2004: 96). She argues that this 'dualism' replaces internal views of the child with external views and that child development has a place. Considering childhood as a simple progression through defined stages is, however, too simplistic. There are multiple and diverse childhoods and, in order to study childhood, one has to consider a range of perspectives.

THERE ARE MULTIPLE PERSPECTIVES ON CHILDHOOD

A number of alternative and multiple perspectives can be drawn on to explain contemporary childhood (Walkerdine, 2004). These perspectives are culturally influenced and change over time. As Kehily (2004) points out, different disciplines have for a long time developed different ways of approaching the study of children. Recently, however, a growing body of international work – from the perspective of sociology (Mayall, 2002; Prout, 2005), early childhood education (MacNaughton, 2003), critical theory and feminism (Walkerdine, 1993) and cultural studies (Cole, 1996) – has been critical of the place of developmental psychology in producing explanations of children as potential subjects, whose presence is only understood in terms of their place on a path towards becoming an adult (Walkerdine, 2004). A current understanding of children's development is, therefore, that it can be approached from a variety of perspectives and that these perspectives are culturally influenced and change over time.

James and Prout (1997: 8) identified the following key features of the 'new sociology of childhood':

- childhood is understood as a social construction
- childhood is a variable of social analysis
- children's relationships and cultures are worthy of study in their own right
- children are active social agents
- studying childhood involves engagement with the process of reconstructing childhood in society.

They suggest that 'the immaturity of children is a biological fact of life but the ways in which this immaturity is understood and made meaningful is a fact of culture'. For Cunningham (1995: 3), 'childhood cannot be studied in isolation from society as a whole'. In contemporary culture, childhood has become a formal category with a social status, and is seen as an important stage in development. This status has been given boundaries by our society's institutions: families, clinics, early years settings and schools, etc. Jenks (1982) and Hoyles and Evans (1989) infer that this analysis places 'childhood' within a social construct, rather than it being a natural phenomenon.

The idea of childhood as a separate state to adulthood is a modern one. Aries (1962: 152) argues that very little distinction between children and adults was made until sometime around the fifteenth century: 'in mediaeval society childhood did not exist'. From the fifteenth century onwards, children began to appear as children, reflecting their gradual removal from everyday adult society. Then, following the advent of compulsory schooling in the late nineteenth century (in Europe), the specific category of 'childhood' was produced, constructed (Aries, 1962) and institutionalized (Walkerdine, 1993).

Alternatively, Pollock (1983) suggests that it is mistaken to believe that because a past society did not possess the contemporary Western view of childhood, that society had no such concept. Even if children were regarded differently in the past, this does not mean that they were not regarded as children. However, he does acknowledge that the particular form of modern childhood is historically specific. Historical studies of childhood suggest that, in the UK, childhood was re-conceptualized between the end of the nineteenth century and the start of the First World War (Gittins, 1998). These studies demonstrate a significant shift in the economic and sentimental value of children. Over a fairly short period, the position of working-class children changed from one of supplementing the family income to that of a relatively inactive member of the household in economic terms to be protected from the adult world of hardship (Cunningham, 1995). Zelitzer (1985) argues that children's contributions to the family in Western contexts is 'economically worthless' but 'emotionally priceless'. Children's value lies in their ability to give meaning and fulfilment to their parents' lives.

Alwin (1990) points out that the distinct category of childhood arose out of attitudinal shifts that placed children in the centre of the family and encouraged an affectionate bond between parents and their children. Thus, for Alwin, childhood is defined by four criteria: protection, segregation, dependence and delayed responsibility. Further, Gittins (2004) argues that the development of childhood as a concept was class-specific, reflecting the values and practices of a rising European middle-class that increasingly differentiated adults and children, girls and boys.

Views of childhood, therefore, *have changed* and *are changing*. The main factors impacting on childhood are: economic, demographic, cultural and political. Since 1945, as a result of economic conditions in the West and the increase of compulsory schooling to the age of sixteen, a 'teenage' culture involving clothes, music, media and films has been constructed. Teenagers are defined by their potential spending power and targeted by advertising in the same way as adults. More recently, a further group of 'tweenagers' or 'tweenies' have been distinguished (*Guardian*, 2001). These are defined as seven-to twelve-year-olds who already show teenage tendencies – for example, seven-to twelve-year-old girls who currently shop for 'designer' clothes, wear make-up and own mobile phones.

As soon as they are born, many children across the world are immersed in a way of life where digital technology is used for a range of complex social and communication practices. These practices, which are constantly changing, include using a range of hand-held devices such as mobile phones, multimedia players (iPods) and games consoles, playing interactive games on digital and satellite television and accessing the internet to communicate images and text, hold telephone conversations and play games with participants across the world. Currently, social network websites (shared databases of photographs which facilitate group discussion) and blogging (contributing to online web diaries) are very popular, but as the technology develops, new and different communicative possibilities and practices will evolve (see Waller, 2008). Although there are concerns about children who are excluded from modern communicative practices and 'digital divides' (Waller, 2008), there is a growing recognition of the impact of ICT on many children's lives. For example, scholars in the USA (Labbo and Reinking, 2003), Australia (Knobel and Lankshear, 2007; Yelland, 2006) and the UK (Facer et al., 2003; Marsh et al., 2005) put forward the view that electronic media has a significant influence on childhood and suggest that children's early literacy and play experiences are shaped increasingly by electronic media. Marsh (2007) contends that young children are just as engaged in current digital communicative and social practices as the older members of their families and communities.

While Postman (1983) predicted that computer use would lead to greater divisions between children and adults, this has not appeared to be the case. Many children have become experts in using technology and are able to access and use information in different ways as a result (see Heppell, 2000; Luke, 1999). Yelland (2006), also, argues that we need to take account of the child's perspective of electronic media.

CHILDREN ARE INVOLVED IN CO-CONSTRUCTING THEIR OWN CHILDHOOD

While a child is clearly biologically determined as a young person, a 'child' is also socially determined in time, place, economics and culture. There is debate about the role of adults in this social construction of childhood and the agency of children in their own lives. Mayall (1996: 1), for example, has argued that 'children's lives are lived through childhoods constructed for them by adults' understanding of childhood and what children are and should be'. Currently, there is an acknowledgement of the significance of the dimension of power in relations between children and adults, and the impact of this relationship on our concept, study and understanding of children and childhood (Riley, 2003). As Connell (1987) points out, power sometimes involves the direct use of force but it is always also accompanied by the development of ideas (ideologies) which justify the actions of the powerful. Cannella and Greishaber (2001) argue: that adult/child categories create an ageism that privileges adults' meanings over those of children.

Alderson (2005) draws on gender studies to identify and emphasize the significance of these adult definitions and ideas in the lives of all children. The columns in Table 1.1 relate to what women and men were assumed to be like and Column 1 can also be applied to how children are perceived and presented in traditional child development literature and adult constructs of the child.

Alderson (2005: 131) argues that:

- children often seem weak and ignorant because they are kept in helpless dependence
- children who try to move to Column 2 may be punished
- children are not allowed to gain knowledge and experience
- it suits adults to keep Column 2 for themselves.

While there are many recent examples of literature that promote positive views of competent children, Alderson argues that there is a problem, especially with older approaches, that emphasize negative stereotypes of children (based on Column 1) because of their age.

A modern view of the child acknowledges agency, that is, children's capacity to understand and act upon their world. It acknowledges children demonstrate extraordinary competence from birth. 'Agency' and 'participation' are two key features of the new sociology of childhood, which have influenced policy and practice in early childhood education and care, as well as contemporary understanding. These are now discussed in turn.

Table 1.1 'Half people'

Column 1 – Women	Column 2 – Men
Ignorant	Knowing
Inexperienced	Experienced
Volatile	Stable
Foolish	Wise
Dependent	Protective
Unreliable	Reliable
Weak	Strong
Immature	Mature
Irrational	Rational
Incompetent	Competent

Source: Alderson, p. (2005: 129) 'Children's rights: an new approach to studying childhood'. In H. Penn, *Understanding Early Childhood: Issues and Controversies*. Reproduced with kind permission of the Open University Press.

Agency

'Agency' involves children's capacity to understand and act upon their world, thus demonstrating competence from birth (e.g. James et al., 1998; Mayall, 2002; Wyness, 2000). In addition, children are perceived as actively involved in the co-construction of their own lives. From this perspective, children are viewed as active agents who construct their own cultures (Corsaro, 2005), and have their own activities, their own time and their own space (Qvortrup et al., 1994). It seeks to understand the definitions and meaning children give to their own lives and recognizes children's competence and capacity to understand and act upon their world. This perspective, therefore, sees the child as actively participating in her own childhood in accordance with Malaguzzi's (1993) concept of the 'rich child' – the child who is 'rich in potential, strong, powerful and competent' (1993: 10). For example, a child who may start to walk unaided at 11 months old is seen as playing an important role in influencing the development of this skill in the particular context of experiences within her family and community from birth, as opposed to an alternative view which suggests that the new found skill is the result of 'normal maturation'. The new sociology of childhood has therefore been critical of the place of developmental psychology in producing explanations of children as potential subjects, which classify children and their abilities into boxes, according to their age (Corsaro, 2005), and where the child is studied and tested in an 'individual' way (Cannella, 1999: 37). Despite the fact that children's agency seems to be recognized broadly in the field, there is an ongoing debate about power and the role of adults in the social construction of childhood and the agency of children in their own lives. There is therefore a need for further discussion and illumination of the terms 'agent' and 'actor'.

The fact that children can express their feelings and emotions in their surroundings confirms their ability to act competently. Nevertheless, the term 'agency' embeds a more active role (Mayall, 2002). Children as agents can express not only their desires and wishes but they can also negotiate and interact within their environment causing change. However, Cannella and Greishaber (2001) argue that adult/child categories create an ageism that privileges adults' meanings over those of children. For example,

Wyness (1999) states that in practice the school system has failed to recognize the child either as a competent actor or as an agent. Also, Mayall (1996: 1) has argued that 'children's lives are lived through childhoods constructed for them by adults' understanding of childhood and what children are and should be'. Consequently, Mayall (2002) contends that children are best regarded as a minority social group and she locates children's agency within the restriction of this minority status. However, Hendrick (1997) makes an important point about the agency of the child. He contends that changes in the conception of childhood did not just happen, they were contested and not least important amongst the contestants were the children themselves, but in the context of joint interaction with peers and adults.

Participation

Following on from the acknowledgement of the significance of children's agency is the recognition that children have the right to participate in processes and decisions that affect their lives. Children's views of their own childhood are therefore particularly significant. In the UK, the Children Act (1989) and Every Child Matters (DfES, 2004e) established the right of the child to be listened to. An important aspect is children's own views of their daily experience (shared with peers and adults – Emilson and Folkesson, 2006). Qvortrup et al. (1994: 2) contend that 'children are often denied the right to speak for themselves either because they are held incompetent in making judgements or because they are thought of as unreliable witnesses about their own lives'. Thomas (2001) suggests that if there is presumption of competence, rather than incompetence, children often turn out to be more capable and sophisticated than they are given credit for. He argues that the advantages of working with a presumption of competence and respect for children and what they wish to communicate are apparent in both childcare work and social research (2001).

Central to developments in policy and services for children is a growing acknowledgement of the legitimacy and value of children's participation in research and decision-making processes. Increasingly, however, there are reservations about whether children's participation actually results in worthwhile changes and benefits for the children involved (Badham, 2004; Tisdall et al., 2004). Hill (2006), for example, discusses the problematic nature of the 'participation agenda', identifying the multiple and sometimes conflicting views of the purposes of children's participation. As Sinclair (2004) asserts, while in principle children's views should always have an impact, it is questionable whether children's views have persistently been allowed to influence the direction of research, policy and services. Hill (2006) argues that adults' views, including the underestimation of children's capacities and a desire to protect their position of power over children, are significant barriers to participation. A critical factor, therefore, is the possibility that adults have used and 'institutionalized' the participation process to keep and exert control over children (Francis and Lorenzo, 2002; Moss, 2002; Prout, 2003). As Clark and Statham (2005) point out, most 'participatory' research still has an adult agenda.

Notions of 'agency' are also contested by Jans (2004), Kjørholt (2002) and Vandenbroeck and Bouverne-De Bie (2006), for example. Vandenbroeck and Bouverne-De Bie (2006) analyse the construction of the participating child at both micro and macro levels. They argue that participatory research and practice may actually be exclusionary because, if children are constructed as a separate but homogeneous category, their age, gender, ethnic or cultural dimensions or inequalities are masked. Vandenbroeck and Bouverne-De Bie propose reconsidering children's agency with further emphasis on context (i.e. agency has differing forms in different contexts). A key challenge in promoting children's participation therefore is how to ensure children have the space to articulate their views and perspectives beyond the constraints of adult views, interpretation and agenda (see also Chapter 6).

MacNaughton (2004: 46) suggests that 'children make their own meanings, but not under conditions of their own choosing'. MacNaughton (2004: 47) identifies four 'conditions of power' that impact on children:

1. The power of pre-existing cultural imagery and cultural meanings.
2. The power of expectations.
3. The power of positions.
4. The power of the marketplace.

MacNaughton argues that children enter a pre-existing world in which each of these conditions of power is already accomplished. As an example, she discusses the children's entertainment and toy industry to show how global capital produces the material culture through which children construct their meanings. However, as Riley (2003) points out, children are powerful consumers in the multi-million dollar industry of childhood that is focused around clothes, toys, books and electronic and digital media (see Marsh, 2005).

In the UK, a public opinion poll published by the Children's Society (2008), as part of its ongoing *Good Childhood Inquiry* (see also Chapter 2), reveals a consensus among adults that increasing commercialization is damaging children's well-being. Eighty nine per cent of adults felt that children nowadays are more materialistic than in past generations. Also, evidence submitted to the inquiry from children themselves suggests that they do feel under pressure to keep up with the latest trends. Further, Professor Philip Graham (Emeritus Professor of Child Psychiatry at the Institute of Child Health, London and an inquiry panel member) believes that commercial pressures may have worrying psychological effects on children. Evidence both from the United States and from the UK (Schor, 2004) suggests that those most influenced by commercial pressures also show higher rates of mental health problems. Bob Reitemeier (chief executive of the Children's Society) said: 'A crucial question raised by the inquiry is whether childhood should be a space where developing minds are free from concentrated sales techniques. As adults we have to take responsibility for the current level of marketing to children. To accuse children of being materialistic in such a culture is a cop out. Unless we question our own behaviour as a society we risk creating a generation who are left unfulfilled through chasing unattainable lifestyles' (the Children's Society, 2008, online).

Thus, while there is some debate in contemporary literature about the effect of adult power on childhood, children are seen as actively involved in the co-construction of their own lives. A modern explanation of childhood therefore seeks to understand the definitions and meaning children give to their own lives and recognizes children's competence and capacity to understand and act upon their world.

CHILDREN'S PARTICIPATION IN FAMILY, COMMUNITY AND CULTURE MAKES A PARTICULAR CONTRIBUTION TO THEIR OWN LIFE

Much of the recent literature in the field of early childhood argues that there is a need to consider the wider political, social and cultural context of childhood. Bronfenbrenner (1977) acknowledged a range of contextual factors that impact directly and indirectly on the development of a child in his concept of ecological systems (see Berk, 2000 for a more detailed discussion). Ecological systems theory represents the child's development as multilayered and the benefit of this model is that it places the child and the child's experience at the heart of the process of development. While it is a useful framework, it can be used to imply that context is something that impacts *on* the child, rather than *with* and *through* the child's participation. It does not fully articulate agency and co-construction.

The recent influential work of proponents of the sociocultural or 'situative perspective', such as Rogoff (1998, 2003), will now be briefly considered (the social construction of learning is discussed in further detail in Chapter 3). The sociocultural perspective has adapted and enhanced the ideas of Vygotsky (1978, 1986) and provided valuable new insights into the collaborative nature of learning and the social construction of knowledge. It has been particularly influential in the field of early childhood. This perspective takes into account not just the child but the social, historical, institutional and cultural factors in which the child participates and co-constructs. It recognizes that human activity is heavily influenced by *context*, which includes artefacts and other people. The sociocultural approach also emphasizes the shared construction and distribution of knowledge leading to the development of shared understanding and common knowledge (Edwards and Mercer, 1987; Greeno, 1997; Lave, 1988; Rogoff, 1990). As a result, the child is not seen as an individual learner but as a participant in a range of meaningful and instructional social practices. Learning and development are inseparable from the concerns of families and interpersonal and community processes. This is a dynamic and evolving cultural context, in which it is meaningless to study the child apart from other people. Participation, as contrasted with acquisition, is therefore a key concept here.

WE ARE STILL LEARNING ABOUT CHILDREN AND CHILDHOOD

If children are active participants in dynamic and evolving cultural contexts, as argued above, it follows that we will always be learning about children and childhood. In addition, changes in technology and new methods of investigation and research can also generate new areas of knowledge and understanding. One aspect of young children's progress that has received considerable attention over the last 10 years is early brain development. Following recent advances in computer technology leading to the development of brain imaging techniques, such as Functional Magnetic Resonance Imaging (fMRI) and Positron Emission Tomography (PET) scans, neuroscientists have been able to measure activity in the brain and map the growth of the brain (Blakemore, 2000; Goswami, 2004).

However, there has been considerable debate surrounding the implications of this neuroscientific research for education and care in the early years (BERA SIG, 2003) which has led to a number of misconceptions and 'neuromyths' (OECD, 2007). Bruer

(1997), for example, argued that making links between cognitive neuroscience and education is 'a bridge too far'. Alternatively, whilst Goswami (2004) views some of the popular beliefs about the potential of neuroscience for early education as 'unrealistic', she argues that new brain science technologies can complement rather than replace traditional methods of educational enquiry.

What the research has usefully shown is that there is a very rapid increase in the development of the brain for young children, especially those under three years of age (Riley, 2003). The brain appears as early as the third week after conception (27 days) and develops rapidly, so that by the end of the seventh month of pregnancy, the baby's brain has all the neurons of the adult brain and many to spare (Catherwood, 1999). Crucial are the synapses – the connections between cells (neurons) where information is exchanged. Most of the development of synapses occurs after birth, however, at birth, the neonate has approximately half the number of synapses of the adult brain. Very rapid growth then occurs from 2–4 months, so that by 6 months, a baby has more synapses than an adult. Stimulation from the environment causes 'learning' either by stabilizing existing networks in the brain or by forging new ones. The ability of the brain to develop connections (or synapses) is known as plasticity. Recent brain research (Blakemore, 2000) has revealed that, after the age of three, plasticity continues at a slower rate until the age of ten.

Bransford et al. (2000) review the work of 16 leading researchers in cognitive science in the USA. Key conclusions from this evidence suggest, according to BERA SIG (2003), that learning changes the structure of the brain; learning organizes and reorganizes the brain, and different parts of the brain may be ready to learn at different times. Thus, although there are prime times for certain types of learning, the brain also has a remarkable capacity to change.

BERA SIG (2003: 19) also usefully summarizes evidence from brain research that matches with psychological research as follows:

1. Experience – everything that goes on around the young child changes the brain.
2. Everything the baby sees, hears, touches and smells influences the developing network of connections among the brain cells.
3. Other people play a critical role.
4. Babies and young children have powerful learning capacities.
5. Babies and young children actually participate in building their own brain.
6. Radically deprived environments may influence development.

OECD (2007) identified a number of 'neuromyths' where scientific findings are translated into misinformation about the benefits of neuroscience for education. In particular, the OECD report focused on myths around 'critical periods' for learning, when plasticity is greatest. The argument is that if children do not have certain experiences during these critical periods, they will forever miss the opportunity to benefit from the experience and that the most effective educational interventions need to be timed with these periods (Goswami, 2004). For this reason, some writers (such as Brierley, 1994; Sylwester, 1995) advocate 'hothousing' – for example, starting to teach music to children under three, because the brain is so receptive to learning early on (see Blakemore, 2000).

It is now argued that while there are optimal 'windows of opportunity' for the development of synapses in the first three years, the brain is extremely flexible (OECD, 2007). An individual's capacities are therefore not fixed at birth, or in the first three years of life (Bransford et al., 2000). Blakemore and Frith (2005) assert that research on plasticity suggests that the brain is well equipped for lifelong learning and adaptation to the environment, and that there is no biological necessity to rush and start formal teaching earlier and earlier. As a result, OECD (2007) contends that there are no 'critical periods' when learning must take place, but there are 'sensitive periods' when an individual is particularly primed to engage in specific learning activities. Further, it is increasingly recognized that efficient learning does not take place when the learner is experiencing fear or inappropriate stress (Goswami, 2004), and the technology used in neuroscience has helped to demonstrate the effect that inappropriate stress has on both physiological and cognitive functioning. For Blakemore and Frith (2005), the main implication of the current research findings on sensitive periods is that it is important to identify and, if possible, treat children's sensory problems (such as visual and hearing difficulties), because the findings suggest that early sensory deprivation can have lasting consequences. However, they also suggest that even after sensory deprivation, it is possible for recovery and learning to still take place.

There is, therefore, much further research still to be done in the field of neuroscience, and the OECD (2007) has identified a number of priorities for additional educational neuroscientific research. These involve the optimal timing for different forms of learning, emotional development and regulation, how specific materials and environments shape learning, and the continued analysis of language and mathematics in the brain. There is also some continued scepticism in early childhood about the limited currency of biomedical explanations of learning. Wilson (2002), for example, discusses how neuroscientific research has provided the impetus for the introduction of early intervention programmes targeting groups who are considered to be 'at risk'. She argues that 'the factors impacting on childhood outcomes are complex and cannot be reduced solely to biomedical explanations. A more effective way to tackle child health and welfare problems would involve a multidimensional approach and include the elimination of poverty and the scrutiny of all public policy' (2002: 191).

We also have much to learn about children's lives and childhood across the world, although despite the continued paucity of published research about children from developing countries, we are now much better informed about their (often tragic) circumstances due to the publication of *The State of the World's Children* (UNICEF). This is a detailed report on the lives of children published every year by the United Nations Children's Fund (UNICEF). *The State of the World's Children 2005* focused on children's rights and argued that the promise underpinning the UNCRC 1989 already appears broken, as poverty, armed conflict and HIV/AIDS threaten children's survival and development. The report calls on all stakeholders – governments, donors, international agencies, as well as communities, families, business and individuals – to reaffirm and recommit to their moral and legal responsibilities to children.

Since 2005, the reports have shifted focus to make recommendations for action to improve the lives of children that are related to the Millennium Development Goals

(MDGs). The MDGs are eight targets to be achieved by 2015 that respond to the world's main development challenges:

Goal 1: Eradicate extreme poverty and hunger
Goal 2: Achieve universal primary education
Goal 3: Promote gender equality and empower women
Goal 4: Reduce child mortality
Goal 5: Improve maternal health
Goal 6: Combat HIV/AIDS, malaria and other diseases
Goal 7: Ensure environmental sustainability
Goal 8: Develop a Global Partnership for Development

The MDGs are drawn from the actions and targets contained in the Millennium Declaration that was adopted by 189 nations and signed by 147 heads of state and governments during the UN Millennium Summit in September 2000 (United Nations Development Programme, online).

The State of the World's Children 2006 concerned excluded and invisible children, including those living in the poorest countries and most deprived communities; children facing discrimination on the basis of gender, ethnicity, disability or membership of an indigenous group; children caught up in armed conflict or affected by HIV/AIDS; and children who lack a formal identity, who suffer child protection abuses or who are not treated as children. The report focused on the actions that those responsible for their well-being must take to safeguard and include them. *The State of the World's Children 2007* investigated the discrimination and disempowerment women face throughout their lives – and outlined action that should be taken to eliminate gender discrimination and empower women and girls. *The State of the World's Children 2008: Child Survival* examined the global realities of maternal and child survival and the prospects for meeting the health-related Millennium Development Goals (MDGs) for children and mothers in each of the five main sub-regions of Africa. Consequently, UNICEF was moved to publish the inaugural edition of *The State of Africa's Children 2008* which identified the urgent need for large-scale investment in health care for Africa to help prevent the deaths of five million children every year.

UNICEF maintains that meeting the Millennium Development Goals (MDGs) and the broader aims of the Millennium Declaration would transform the lives of millions of children who would be spared illness and premature death, escape extreme poverty and malnutrition, gain access to safe water and decent sanitation facilities and complete primary schooling.

SUMMARY

This chapter has identified and discussed five key tenets of contemporary childhood. The tenets have articulated a complex model of childhood which is fundamentally different from a narrow 'developmental' approach. This model acknowledges that there are multiple and diverse childhoods. There are local variations and global forms, depending on class, 'race', gender, geography and time. This model also acknowledges that while there are multiple perspectives on childhood, it would be wrong to ignore or disregard developmental insights. Views of childhood have changed and are changing. Students of early childhood need to understand how and why child development theory is a product of certain historical, cultural and economic conditions. Some theoretical perspectives are particularly suited to explaining certain aspects of growth and change over time but the complex and interlinked nature of children's 'development' needs to be recognized. Developmental psychology should be studied alongside sociological, historical and anthropological accounts of childhood.

However, a critical difference between contemporary and traditional views of childhood is that the former recognizes the differing contexts of children's lives, children's agency and the significance of children's involvement in co-constructing their own childhood through participation in family, community and culture.

After 150 years of recognized child study, we are still learning about children and childhood, the power of adults and the ability of children to determine their own future. Greater recognition of children's perspectives, the impact of new technology on children's lives and research methods will lead to further insights that will strengthen understanding and articulate new theories of early childhood.

 QUESTIONS FOR REFLECTION AND DISCUSSION

1. How do children shape their own development?
2. How does change occur?
3. How do children become so different from each other?
4. How can you find out?
5. How should we deal with theories that do not recognize multiple and diverse childhoods and the power relationships between children and adults?

Recommended reading

Corsaro, W. A. (2005) *The Sociology of Childhood*, 2nd edition. Thousand Oaks, CA: Pine Forge Press.
Dahlberg, G., Moss, P. and Pence, A. (2007) *Beyond Quality in Early Childhood Education and Care: Postmodern Perspectives*, 2nd edition. London and New York: RoutledgeFalmer.
Penn, H. (2005) *Understanding Early Childhood*. Maidenhead: Open University Press.
Prout, A. (2005) *The Future of Childhood: Towards the Interdisciplinary Study of Children*. London: Falmer Press.

Recommended websites

UNICEF – *The State of the World's Children*: www.unicef.org/publications/index.html;

Good Childhood Inquiry: www.goodchildhood.org.uk

2 WELL-BEING

Jane Waters

Chapter objectives

- To introduce the concept of well-being as complex rather than simplistic.
- To encourage reflection on practice through the inclusion of practice scenarios.
- To exemplify aspects of well-being within UK policy context.
- To suggest links between young children's well-being in early years settings and ideas about children's learning dispositions and their involvement levels.
- To consider the implications of a focus on children's well-being for the early years practitioner.
- To consider measures of well-being – from a national scale to the scale of the individual child.
- To introduce international comparative literature and national survey data concerning the well-being of children in the UK.

WHAT IS WELL-BEING?

'Well-being' is a term occurring frequently in policy and practice relating to children, but as Pollard and Lee (2002: 62) suggest, 'well-being is ... inconsistently defined in the study of child development. A systematic review of the child well-being literature reveals that the definition of well-being is highly variable'. A generic definition as given by the *Oxford English Dictionary* (2002) presents well-being as 'the state of being comfortable, healthy or happy' (2002: 960), and this may reflect a general understanding of the term. When we come to consider how a concern for children's well-being relates to practice though, this is not enough. The initial section of this chapter aims to unpick some aspects of the concept 'well-being' in order to develop a deeper understanding of what the term may involve.

Historically, well-being has been linked to health – the World Health Organization (1948) refers to 'well-being' as a concept which defines the global health of a person: 'health is a state of complete physical, mental and social well-being and not merely the absence of disease or infirmity' (1948: 2). More recently, Pollard and Lee (2002) have suggested that there are five distinct domains of child well-being that appear in the literature:

1. physical
2. psychological
3. cognitive

4. social
5. economic.

The physical domain includes physical health, rates of growth and knowledge about eating healthily and staying safe.

The psychological domain includes mental health, anxiety levels and psychosocial aspects such as self-esteem, confidence and emotion.

The cognitive domain includes aspects that are intellectual or school-related; this may include how children feel about school and their academic performance.

The social domain includes sociological perspectives such as family and peer relationships, communication skills and the availability of emotional and practical support.

The economic domain includes family income and wealth, economic hardship, availability of and access to economic support such as government benefit systems.

Roberts (2006) considers emotional well-being and reports on Bird and Gerlach's (2005) description of emotional health and well-being as:

> ... the subjective capacity and state of mind that supports us to feel good about how we are and confident to deal with present and future circumstances. It is influenced by our emotional development and how resilient and resourceful we feel ourselves to be. (Roberts, 2006: 6)

Such an understanding of emotional well-being would place this within Pollard and Lee's psychological domain, though in literature related to early childhood we may be more likely to come across the term 'emotional well-being' rather than 'psychological well-being'.

As practitioners working with early years children, we may be concerned with some or all of these aspects of well-being; and clearly some domains will overlap and impact upon other domains – for example, a family support officer may be more concerned with the economic aspects of a child's well-being than the health visitor who may have the physical aspects of the child's well-being foremost in his/her mind. The early years setting practitioner may have social and cognitive aspects of the child's well-being as their primary concern. What is important is not to lose sight of the global, or holistic, nature of the concept of well-being, nor to assume that a positive or negative assessment in one domain necessarily means that the child's well-being as a whole corresponds to this assessment.

 Case Study

In this case study, a child enters the nursery class of her local school, following a home visit where the practitioner met the child and her mother. A relative was looking after the younger twins for the duration of the visit. The child was quiet during the visit but keen to show the practitioner the new clothes she was wearing. The practitioner noted that the

(Continued)

(Continued)

home environment was fairly sparse and the child's mother was anxious for the visit to be completed before her other children returned.

Tamsin entered her nursery class as a well-dressed, well-mannered 3-year-old of average height and build. She joined in with the activities of the nursery and, though quiet, appeared to be making positive relationships with other children in the setting. At an open day, her mother spoke to the practitioner of her concerns about Tamsin whom she reported to be uncooperative and stubborn at home, who hit her small twin brothers and could not be left alone in a room with them and who was reported to be hating school. Tamsin's mother also reported that she was very concerned about the cost of nice clothes for Tamsin to wear to nursery because milk and nappies for the twins were very expensive too.

 Reflection

Here, at face value, Tamsin appeared to be a child with a high level of well-being – her appearance suggested good economic and physical well-being, and her engagement with nursery activities suggested good levels of cognitive and social well-being. However, following the open evening, it becomes clear to the practitioner that Tamsin's home life may be potentially stressful. Her mother is clearly concerned that Tamsin must be well turned out for school and this is impacting negatively on the family's finances; the demanding nature of young twins may mean that Tamsin seeks attention at home by hitting her siblings and complaining about school. Tamsin appears to be managing her anxiety effectively in the nursery setting, but clearly any positive assessment of her well-being in general would need to be adjusted in the light of these issues.

 Discussion Points

As a response to the open evening, the practitioner might reassure the parents that old clothes (or simple play clothes) are best for children attending the nursery. She/he might adjust the play provision in the nursery to encourage play and exploration of the tension of living with younger siblings. The practitioner will attend to and monitor the various aspects of Tamsin's well-being through observation and interaction, intervention and the development of a close working relationship with Tamsin's family.

The concept of well-being is not, then, a straightforward one. However, as early childhood professionals and practitioners, it is important to consider how the setting in which we work considers the term well-being. We may ask of our policy and practice: does this reflect an *instrumental* or a *holistic* view of well-being?

The instrumental view can be reflected by considering well-being in terms of what children should know about and what skills they should have – for example:

- knowing how to keep safe
- knowing how to eat healthily
- knowing how to keep clean.

The holistic view can be reflected by considering well-being in terms of how children experience their lives – for example:

- feeling part of a community
- feeling valued
- having a voice.

Policies and practices adopting either view will impact upon the child's experience within the setting, and in the following sections we will consider the importance of being aware of the complex nature of well-being and the value of being willing to discuss such complexity within settings.

The generic definition cited above indicates that well-being is generally perceived as an individual or 'within-person' (Anning and Edwards, 2006: 55) characteristic. This means that well-being can be viewed as something one person has or lacks independently of the well-being of other individuals, family or community. This approach, prevalent in UK policy and literature, is not universally applied however. Some international perspectives appear to perceive well-being as a social concept – a characteristic of the group, rather than the individual. The bi-cultural early years curriculum document of New Zealand: Te Whariki (Ministry of Education, 1996) states that 'The well-being of children is interdependent with the well-being and culture of: adults in the early childhood education setting; whànau/families; local communities and neighbourhoods' (1996: 42). The curriculum emphasizes the need for all the early years staff to be knowledgeable about different child-rearing practices and Maori culture. Under the guidance given to practitioners who are working to ensure the well-being of young children, it is stated that 'Culturally appropriate ways of communicating should be fostered, and participation in the early childhood education programme by whànau, parents, extended family, and elders in the community should be encouraged' (Ministry of Education, 1996: 42). The implicit understandings of the concept of well-being within this document are therefore clear; well-being for a community is linked to the respect afforded the group and its practices by others; well-being, then, has strong social and cultural links. This sociocultural link and social understanding of the term well-being is also implied by the Norwegian Framework Plan for the Content and Tasks of Kindergartens (Kunnskapsdepartementet, 2006) for children aged 0–6 (see Aasen and Waters, 2006).

WELL-BEING AND POLICY DOCUMENTS

The term 'well-being' within UK policy is variously linked to other individual characteristics – health in particular; and, similar to the position described by Pollard and Lee (2002) when they reviewed academic literature, usually not clearly defined.

We can take the 0–3 frameworks and subsequent early education guidance materials in England and Wales as examples. Roberts (2006) reports on the emphasis that well-being has within the 'Birth to Three Matters' framework (Sure Start, 2002), where children's earliest relationships are seen to have a bearing on their well-being – 'a relationship with a key person at home and in the setting is essential to young children's well-being' (2002: 3). Well-being here is seen as an individual, holistic feature of the child. The Early Years Foundation Stage (DfES, 2007a) in England has as one of its stated aims to support, foster, promote and develop 'children's personal, social and emotional well-being' (2007a: 8). In order to achieve this, it sets out support for transitions and inclusion and aims for each child to become a valued member of their community so that 'strong self-image and self-esteem are promoted' (ibid.). Emotional well-being is described as 'knowing who you are and where you fit in and feeling good about yourself' (2007a: 28). This suggests that, as McGillivray (2007) asserts, the view of well-being as an individual, holistic feature of the child is extended in English early years policy from the birth to three matters documentation into the foundation stage guidance materials.

Flying Start was launched in Wales by the Welsh Assembly Government (WAG) in October 2005 as a programme for birth to age three targeted towards families in deprived areas. Wyn Siencyn and Thomas (2007) report that this programme 'sees the integration of childcare, early learning, parenting, and health services as one vision for promoting the well-being of children in Wales … [and has] … been welcomed as a cornerstone in the WAG's drive to combating child poverty' (2007: 146). Here, clear links are being made between a family's economic and cultural capital and children's well-being. The framework for children's learning for three to seven-year-olds in Wales (DCELLS, 2008) places well-being 'at the heart' (2008: 15) of the foundation phase. The term is linked with children learning about themselves and others, developing their own sense of self-esteem and 'cultural identity' (2008: 15) alongside developing a respect for that of others. The description for the area of learning – *personal and social development, well-being and cultural diversity* – firmly associates an awareness of Welsh cultural heritage with children's sense of identity and well-being. Again, Welsh policy places an emphasis on the cultural aspects of children's well-being – it might be argued that this interpretation of the term involves a consideration of the well-being of the collective group as well as the holistic individual.

Well-being can be considered on a national policy level as well as on a local policy level. On a national level, Walsh (2007) describes policy and practice relating to early years children, their families and education in Northern Ireland. She reports that 'there is growing concern within some areas of Northern Ireland about young children's health and well-being' (2007: 63). This is supported by research and statistical evidence of young children's high levels of ill-health, poverty, obesity and increasing levels of asthma and mental health issues. She outlines a number of policies that have been put in place to overcome such concerns in the hope that these will have the effect of raising children's well-being in the longer term. Such policies include: a political commitment to peace within Northern Ireland, school policies to address healthy eating and tackle sectarianism and racism, inclusive policies for early years classrooms to include children with special educational needs and children of minority groups, policy statements to include the voice of the child in decision making and policy formation. This suggests that the concern over children's well-being is being taken seriously at the highest levels of government. Walsh suggests that, in order to be effective, adult approaches to and understandings of young children may have to change (2007: 77), and it is this issue that is particularly addressed in sections three and four of this chapter.

On a local level, in any setting, it is important for practitioners to discuss and agree their understanding of the term well-being and how this relates to policies regulating their practice. Not to raise this issue, and to leave practitioners to work within their own subjective interpretations of the term, offers the prospect of different ways of working with the child within a setting, a lack of continuity of approach and a potential undermining of positive outcomes for the child. For example, Aasen and Waters (2006) suggest that 'if teachers interpret well-being differently this may lead to variations in classroom practice' (2006: 124), indicating concerns that the promotion of child well-being will be context-specific, influenced by the teacher's subjective understanding and perspective, rather than influenced by an agreed understanding of the term within the local early years community.

Such local discussion may be particularly important during times of transition in curriculum guidance. For example, in a Scottish setting, providers of local authority-funded education are required to observe the Curriculum Framework for Children 3–5 (Carmichael and Hancock, 2007; Scottish Executive, 1999) but implement the framework 'in a way appropriate to the needs of the children who attend' (Carmichael and Hancock, 2007: 119). In this document, the term well-being is linked largely with the physical health of children: 'They [children] should be encouraged to feel good about their growing range of physical skills and to enjoy the feeling of well-being that good health and physical play bring' (Scottish Executive, 1999: 37), and so may lend itself to an instrumental understanding of children's well-being. However, the planned Curriculum of Excellence in Scotland (Learning and Teaching Scotland, 2008) describes well-being as an holistic individual quality, valued because 'with a sense of well-being they [children] will be better able to deal with the unexpected and cope with adversity' (Developing the curriculum 1: health and well-being; Learning and Teaching Scotland, 2008). In order for such changes in interpretation of the term well-being to be fully implemented, open discussion and agreement at a local level would clearly be beneficial.

The third and fourth sections below suggest a possible mechanism for supporting the social, emotional and cognitive aspects of young children's well-being and may provide a focus around which practitioners may start to consider these aspects of well-being for the children in their care.

POSITIVE DISPOSITIONS

Self-esteem

Self-esteem is linked to self-concept – it relates to how children see themselves and how they behave as a result of their self-perception. As Schaffer (1996: 159) points out, self-concept derives from experience which if perceived as successful generates feelings of competence, and if perceived as unsuccessful generates feelings of incompetence. Roberts (1998: 161) argues that 'children's self-esteem is a key factor not only for their well-being but also for learning outcomes'. However, self-esteem is a complex concept. Brooker and Broadbent (2003: 33) make an important point about the self-esteem of young children:

> Self-esteem has been described as the value that a child assigns him or herself: attempts to measure or describe it have focused on the disparity between what a child would like to be like and that child's view of how he or she actually is. But in early childhood it principally reflects the value the child perceives he or she has in the eyes of others, particularly those 'significant others' whose opinions count most.

Curry and Johnson (1990: 5–9, cited in Roberts, 2002: 12) identify four areas of self-esteem:

1. Acceptance (between mother and child and other significant people including family and friends).
2. Control (exerting control over the environment and self-control).
3. Moral worth (developing the concept of good and bad, right and wrong).
4. Competence (the ability to solve problems and the resulting sense of competence).

Roberts (2002: 105) argues that the characteristic of acceptance is at the core of self-concept and that 'unconditional acceptance' is critical for positive self-esteem. She suggests that 'the sort of acceptance that babies need from parents and other important people is acceptance that is independent of behaviour; without reservations and without judgements' (Roberts, 2002: 5). Such an argument can be taken forward for the older early years child. Johnston-Wilder and Collins (2008), who consider self-esteem and how it develops alongside a child's sense of identity, suggest that such acceptance is particularly important because 'children can begin to become the people we think they are' (2008: 43). They report on the 'teacher-expectancy effect' (2008: 48) where children tend to behave in ways that reflect the expectation that teachers have of them or support the labels that have been assigned them (either formally or informally). Johnston-Wilder and Collins argue that 'practitioners need to be aware that labels are likely to have consequences' (2008: 49), and that in order to support the development of positive self-esteem, 'practitioners can help by working towards positive relationships that display high levels of warmth and low levels of criticism' (2008: 52).

Dispositions

Roberts (2006) suggests that 'we have seen an important expansion in the view of the curriculum [for early years children] itself, in which children's personal, social and emotional areas of development are all acknowledged' (2006: 143). Arguably, this expansion includes a focus on children's self-esteem in the early years. However, Roberts (2006) suggests that children's *learning dispositions* are not yet given such acknowledgement. Katz (1993) suggested that educators need to consider four types of learning goals: 'those related to knowledge, skills, dispositions and feelings' (1993: 1). She defines dispositions as 'habits of mind' (Katz, 1999: 2) or 'tendencies to respond to certain situations in certain ways' (ibid.). Examples of dispositions may be friendliness, shyness, curiosity, bossiness. Katz reminds us that not all dispositions are positive and suggests that practitioners need to attend to the dispositions they want to encourage in the children in their settings – identifying which dispositions are to be strengthened and which to be weakened (1999) and creating situations to support certain dispositions above others (Anning and Edwards, 2006). How a child learns is seen as equally important as what she learns (Riley, 2003: 17). Self-esteem clearly influences learning dispositions; as Anning and Edwards (2006: 59) point out, 'dispositions are rooted in our sense of our likely effectiveness'. Those dispositions that are seen as positive for children's learning can be viewed as *positive learning dispositions*. Research concerning learning dispositions suggests that fostering positive learning dispositions leads to children becoming more purposeful, successful and less likely to become disaffected (Brooker and Broadbent, 2003). Carr and Claxton (2002) have identified three positive learning dispositions that may be particularly valuable to strengthen in early years children: resilience, playfulness and reciprocity. Resilience is the disposition to persist with a task even after a setback, to tackle a learning challenge where the outcome may be uncertain and to persist, even when this is hard work. Playfulness involves the inclination to be creative in response to situations: to tend to notice, imagine and explore alternative possibilities. Reciprocity is the willingness to engage with others, ask questions, communicate ideas and to listen to and take on board the views of others (Carr and Claxton, 2002).

For Katz (1995: 63), some dispositions to learn (such as exploration) are inborn but these can be adversely affected and even destroyed by inappropriate learning experiences. She gives the example of the child who, having been drilled in the methods for decoding words, is able to read but lacks the disposition to do so – and is therefore not 'a reader'. Dispositions are influenced by early experience: Anning and Edwards (2006) suggest 'these habits of mind are shaped in young children's interactions with others and in the opportunities for being a learner that are available to them, particularly in their families and in early childhood settings' (2006: 55). High-quality early learning involves supporting and strengthening learning dispositions (Carr, 2001; Sylva, 1994a).

Attending to children's learning dispositions and their self-esteem in early years settings is a mechanism for supporting aspects of young children's well-being. Whether well-being is viewed as an intrapersonal trait or one that is socially mediated, supporting children's tendencies to respond positively to learning opportunities, their ability to respond with resilience to setbacks and their tendency to communicate effectively with others can be seen to be theoretically contributing to high levels of well-being. However, unless we can assess or measure well-being in the children in our care, then this link remains a theoretical one. It is to this issue that we now turn.

CAN WELL-BEING BE MEASURED?

In their review of literature, Pollard and Lee (2002) conclude that 'there is little agreement in the research literature on how to best measure child well-being' (2002: 66). They outline a wide range of measures that are employed throughout the research literature, including objective measures such as: child case history reviews, educational assessments, medical records and national statistics like rates of death, drug abuse and suicide. Subjective measures are also used, including participants being asked to respond to multiple separate measures such as self-esteem levels, depression and relationships. Pollard and Lee make the point that such measures, particularly those that focus on self-esteem and depression levels and claim that these are measures of well-being, do not *actually* measure well-being since they attend to only one aspect of this complex construct: the psychological/emotional aspect. We should similarly guard against looking for a straightforward or simple way to assess the well-being of children in our care. What we might look for are ways of gaining an insight into aspects of children's well-being and treating these insights as *indicators* rather than *measures* of 'how our children are doing' (terminology adapted from Laevers, 2000).

Laevers (2000) argues that we can gain an insight into how children are doing by considering the linked dimensions of 'well being' and 'involvement' (2000: 24) that children display when engaged in activity:

> When we want to know how each of the children is doing in a setting, we first have to explore the degree to which children feel at ease, act spontaneously, and show vitality and self-confidence. All this indicates that their emotional well-being is 'OK' and that their physical needs, the need for tenderness and affection, the need for safety and clarity, the need for social recognition, the need to feel competent and the need for meaning and moral value in life, are satisfied ... The concept of involvement refers to a dimension of human activity. Involvement is linked neither to specific types of behaviour nor to specific levels of development. (2000: 24)

He argues that children experiencing the highest levels of involvement demonstrate their well-being (Anning and Edwards, 2006) and are disposed to engage in 'deep level learning' (Laevers, 2000: 20). Well-being is described as 'feeling at home, being oneself and feeling happy' (Laevers, 1994: 5). Involvement concerns 'the intensity of the activity, the extent to which one is absorbed' (ibid.) and is linked to Csikszentmihayli's (1979) 'state of flow' – usually experienced, in young children, in play (Laevers, 2000).

Laevers argues that adult observation of children's activity can allow an evaluation of the extent to which a child is involved in their activity; this in turn provides an insight into 'how they are doing' or their well-being. Well-being is indicated by the following:

- openness and receptivity
- flexibility
- self-confidence and self-esteem
- assertiveness
- vitality
- relaxation and inner peace
- enjoyment without restraint
- being in touch with one's self.

The signals of involvement that the adults attend to during their observation of a child's activity include:

- concentration
- complexity and creativity
- persistence
- reaction time
- satisfaction
- energy
- facial expression and composure
- precision
- verbal expression.

Laevers has developed the 'Leuven Involvement Scale' (LIS) in order for the observer to 'measure' the levels of involvement (as indicated by the presence of the signals) displayed by any particular child at any time. The LIS is essentially 'a five point rating scale. At level 1 there is no activity. At level 5 there is total concentration' (Laevers, 2000: 25). This scale has been termed the 'Child Involvement Scale' by Pascal et al. (1997) and is used as a tool for self-evaluation and improvement for settings involved in the Effective Early Learning (EEL) Programme (Anning and Edwards, 2006). Use of such a scale may help avoid the contentious issues of 'measurement' of well-being highlighted by Aasen and Waters (2006: 124): 'Well-being is a ... complex construct that can be subjectively interpreted'. Laevers (2000) has reported positively on the inter-observer reliability in studies that have employed the Involvement Scale.

There are, however, also calls for the child's voice to be considered when evaluating children's well-being. An argument can be made for children's perspectives to be included in research concerning their well-being on two counts – one: children's subjective perspectives should be a part of this assessment as it recognizes childhood as a stage in itself and it also supports their human rights (Ben-Arieh, 2005; Ben-Arieh and Frones, 2007); and two: children's active participation in research has been found to promote their well-being (Clark and Moss, 2001; Thomas, 2000). Lancaster (2006) places such arguments within the Every Child Matters (ECM) policy framework and the 2004 Children Act. She considered that the resulting initiatives – to ask for, listen to and respond to the voice of the child – make 'a positive contribution in challenging some of society's unwritten values and norms such as children should be seen and not heard, they should do as they are told and adults know best' (2006: 63). She suggests that this policy context 'is a lever to not only think about listening to children as routine, but also implementing child participation as everyday practice' (2006: 63). Such policies do not go without a challenge to traditional understandings about adults' and children's roles within society. 'Our taken for granted views about children and childhood have the potential to hinder children from actually achieving the outcomes we are working towards' (Lancaster, 2006: 67).

Carr (2001) has worked on methods that consider assessments of the child's learning dispositions alongside their right to be heard and have a voice within such assessments in education or care settings. She views learning dispositions as situated in and interwoven with action and activity, not as an individual attribute like temperament. For Carr (2001: 21), learning dispositions are 'situated learning strategies plus motivation – participation repertoires from which a learner selects, edits, responds to, searches for and constructs learning opportunities'.

Carr developed a framework for assessing learning dispositions from multiple perspectives (including the child's perspective), which she termed 'learning stories'. 'Learning stories' are structured narrative documentation based on critical incidents of children's learning, including the child's own comments (see Carr, 2001: 96).

It may be that by considering such initiatives as Carr's participatory approach to assessment via learning stories and Laevers's concern with attending to 'how children are doing' using involvement scales, we begin to attend to the needs and voices of children within our care in a manner that genuinely places their well-being at the centre of practice.

Case Study

Joshua had been highlighted as a cause for concern by early years practitioners within his nursery setting. He appeared unhappy and agitated in the setting when group time was taking place; he made little contact with other children or adults. He appeared most content when engaged in construction play alone and became very distressed when not permitted to remain in this area. By the time Joshua entered the Reception class, he was very resistant to attending school and had been identified as having a developmental disorder on the autism spectrum. Joshua was assigned one support worker for two and a half hours every morning. The Reception class teacher, while very supportive of Joshua's inclusion in the setting and efforts to support him, privately felt that the busy classroom environment might prove to be too much for him and that alternative provision may be more appropriate.

The Reception class teacher used baseline assessments for all the children in her class upon entry and supplemented this information with measurements of children's involvement levels during free play and teacher-directed activity. Joshua's baseline assessment caused some concerns for the teacher. His involvement levels varied from 1 to 2 during teacher-led group activity (such as story time, news time, circle time, to 2 to 3 during teacher-directed activity (such as shape sorting, making shape pictures) and 4 to 5 during freely chosen play activities (in which he consistently chose to play in the construction area).

The teacher noticed that when she took her class into the school garden area, a weekly activity, Joshua appeared less distressed during group time. She used the involvement scale to measure Joshua's involvement when he was outside. Joshua consistently demonstrated higher levels of involvement when outside: 3–4 during group activities (such as listening activities), 4–5 during teacher-directed activity (such as a spider hunt) and during free play outside, Joshua was highly involved in solitary exploratory activity – exploring puddles with a stick, digging holes in the soil and collecting small seeds – and consistently scoring a level 5 over a number of weeks.

The teacher began to take the class outside on two or three occasions during the week and began planning for more curriculum learning outside. Joshua's learning assistant was also encouraged to take Joshua and a group of children from the class outside when possible to play and for directed learning activities.

Over the next term, Joshua settled well into this routine and showed significantly reduced anxiety when undertaking group activities indoors. At Joshua's annual review, the practitioners working with him were able to report on the many aspects of school that he enjoyed and Joshua's parents reported that his resistance to going to school had noticeably decreased.

∿ Reflection

Over the time that Joshua was with the Reception teacher, she used observation and measurement of his involvement levels to gain an insight into 'what worked' for this particular child. By attending to a measure that attended to Joshua's well-being, rather than separate aspects of his cognitive and social development, she was able to adapt her practice and routines to cater effectively for him. Joshua's well-being appeared to increase as a result of these changes.

Joshua also appeared to be developing a more positive disposition to schooling in general, in that his resistance to attend had reduced. He began to demonstrate a strengthening disposition to explore his environment, to be curious. It was hoped that in time, and by providing for, encouraging and developing Joshua's enthusiasm for being outdoors, a level of reciprocity may be developed, within the bounds of his disorder. The positive behaviour and progress noted by the teacher enabled her to re-assess the expectations she had of Joshua and as a result her relationship with him was warmer and more positive. This may, over time, protect and help support Joshua's sense of self-esteem.

WELL-BEING IN THE UK

UNICEF (2007b) carried out an assessment of the well-being of children in rich countries. Child well-being was given an 'implied definition' (2007b: 3) within this study that was 'guided by the UN Convention of the Rights of the Child' (2007b: 2). Child well-being was measured in 40 separate indicators across six dimensions in order to compare how children were doing in the rich countries of the world.

These six dimensions were:

- material well-being
- health and safety
- education
- peer and family relationships
- behaviours and risks
- young people's own subjective sense of their own well-being.

Among the key findings was the fact that the UK ranks among the worst in the developed world for children's well-being. This is a shocking headline and bears further scrutiny; across the six dimensions, the UK ranks higher in the child health and safety dimension than in others (12th out of 21), with the educational well-being and material well-being dimensions being ranked above the bottom four (17th out of 21). The UK ranks very poorly in terms of the quality of children's relationships with their parents and peers (bottom of the table), behaviour and risk-taking (bottom of the table) and subjective well-being (20th out of 21). Similarly, the *Good Childhood Inquiry* (The Children's Society, 2007a) reports that 'children's well-being, particularly mental well-being, is lower in the UK than many other European countries' (2007a: 5).

The Children's Society commissioned the *Good Childhood Inquiry* to look at people's views about what constitutes a good childhood. Over 700 5–17-years-olds responded to the Children's Society's call for evidence and through different routes, the voices of thousands of contributors were used by the society to provide summaries on the following aspects of childhood: friends, family and learning (other aspects to follow from them). The 'friends' summary (The Children's Society, 2007b) reports that 'from the second year onwards, friendship is very important for children, both for their social and emotional development and for their own sense of well-being' (2007b: 3). Children's voices are included in this summary, for example: 'you can't have a good childhood without friends; every child needs friends' (2007b: 4). This summary serves as a reminder to practitioners that children's friendship experiences may be those that, to children, are the most important aspects of what happens in their education and care settings.

The second summary is that concerning 'family' (The Children's Society, 2007c). This summary begins with the statements that 'at the heart of the family is the precious relationship between parent and child, which is closely linked to child well-being' (2007c: 2) and 'families are the most powerful influence on children's lives' (2007c: 3). Children's voices support such statements: 'It's just a family that loves each other and as long as they do that's a happy family' (2007c: 4). These reported voices make no reference to material possessions or family circumstance, suggesting that love and respect within the family are what are valued by contributors. However, the summary also states that 'poverty remains one of the most significant predictors of children's well-being, causing material and emotional disadvantage and limiting aspiration' (2007c: 3).

The third of the summaries, 'learning' (The Children's Society, 2007d), makes no explicit link between children's well-being and learning, but states that 'our evidence shows that many children are ambitious. They want to succeed and dislike being held back by disruptive pupils. Children want their classes to be structured and clear. They want their teachers to be interesting and fun. Most of all, they want to learn' (2007d: 2). Children also reported feeling pressurized by a primary and secondary school structure that values external testing as a measure of progress. Arguably, children's cognitive well-being is best served by considering such evidence and the concerns raised by children themselves. And given that 'the student–teacher relationship is at the heart of learning' (2007d: 3), this means considering the ways that, as practitioners, we meet the needs of curriculum requirements in ways that support, encourage and value the child's autonomy, ability and innate worth. On the topic of participation, the Children's Society (2007d) reports: 'adults need to understand that children can form and express their views in coherent ways. Their inclusion should not be seen as 'cute': something that the media often presents ... We must continue to promote participation as a right not a gift' (2007d: 7).

Given the poor placing of the UK within international well-being tables, it may be that a focus on the core themes of a 'good childhood' is needed within UK society as a whole and within local communities and early years settings in particular if we are to help contribute to children's well-being though our early years practice.

SUMMARY

This chapter considered the concept of well-being as a complex construct that consists of a number of aspects including: physical, psychological (emotional), cognitive, social and economic. Policy documents may focus on one or two specific aspects of well-being or may be more holistically focused; they may consider well-being as an intrapersonal characteristic or one that is associated with the social or cultural group. When practitioners attend to the well-being of the children in their care, they are encouraged to consider which aspects their policy documents attend to and to avoid taking an instrumental view of well-being rather than a holistic view. It is suggested that attending to children's involvement levels during activity and considering the dispositions that children display within the setting helps with assessing the levels of well-being the children are experiencing. The chapter concludes by noting that international comparison tables place the UK poorly with regard to levels of child well-being. It is suggested that in order to improve such a placing, all those working with young children need to attend, thoughtfully and pro-actively, to the holistic well-being of children in their care.

QUESTIONS FOR REFLECTION AND DISCUSSION

1. What do you understand by the term 'well-being'? Try to come up with your own definition and compare this with a partner's definition. In what ways are the terms similar? How do they differ?
2. What interpretations of the term 'well-being' have you seen in practice? Try to ask a number of early years practitioners what they understand by the term. Compare and discuss the responses you get.
3. Discuss within a small group how you might define 'well-being' and how this might influence what you would plan, do and record in an early years education/care setting.
4. Given the evidence from the *Good Childhood Inquiry* (you can find the remaining reports from the end of 2008 on the website below), what should practitioners attend to in early years settings to ensure children experience a 'good childhood'? Do you think this is enough to ensure children's well-being? Why?/ Why not?

Recommended reading

Collins, J. and Foley, P. (eds) (2008) *Promoting Children's Well-being: Policy and Practice*. Bristol: The Policy Press.

Laevers, F. (2000) 'Forward to basics! Deep-level learning and the experiential approach', *Early Years*, 20 (2): 20–9.

Pollard, E. L. and Lee, P. D. (2002) 'Child Well-being: A systematic review of the literature', *Social Indicators Research*, 61: 59–78.

UNICEF (2007) *Child Poverty in Perspective: An Overview of Child Well-being in Rich Countries*. Innocenti Report Card 7. Florence: UNICEF Innocenti Research Centre.

Recommended websites

1. The Children's Society – *Good Childhood Inquiry*: www.childrenssociety.org.uk/all_about_us/how_we_do_it/the_good_childhood_inquiry/ 1818.html – from this site, you can access all the information and publications about the *Good Childhood Inquiry*.
2. Te Whariki, New Zealand: www.minedu. govt.nz/index.cfm?layout=document&document id=3567&data=l – from this site, the New Zealand Early Years curriculum guidance and support materials are available as downloads.

3 CHILDREN'S LEARNING

Tim Waller and Ros Swann

Chapter objectives

- To provide a brief overview of traditional theories of learning.
- To consider learning relationships and dispositions in detail.
- To discuss a synopsis of recent theories of learning from a social constructive perspective.
- To examine the role of children's play and sensitive adult interaction to support successful learning.

This chapter provides an introduction to theories of learning, which is defined as how children make sense of reality and make meaning in a social world. The chapter briefly considers well-known models of learning that focus on individual construction of knowledge (Skinner and Piaget) and then discusses more fully the view of the child as an active co-constructor of knowledge (Bruner, Donaldson, Rogoff, Vygotsky, etc.). The chapter also discusses recent literature on learning relationships, dispositions and play. Learning is considered generally, not in terms of school curricula (see Dowling, 2005; Siraj-Blatchford, 2004). However, the ideas about learning introduced in this chapter do have implications for learning and teaching in schools and readers are encouraged to reflect on this afterwards. Also, there is not scope within the chapter to give a detailed consideration of how children learn language, but it should be remembered that most children in the world are bilingual or multilingual (over 70 per cent). The ability to understand and speak more than one language can be a considerable benefit to learning in general (see Brooker, 2005; Brown, 1998; Gregory et al., 2004).

Learning can be defined in a relatively straightforward way as the process of coming to know something, the acquisition of knowledge and skills. As Smidt (2002: 2) points out, in physiological terms, learning can be very precisely demonstrated as when 'connections between cells are laid down and strengthened'. Bennett et al. (1984, cited in Moyles, 1997: 16), for example, offer a more extensive model. They put forward the view that learners demonstrate the ability to:

- acquire new knowledge and skills
- use existing knowledge and skills in different contexts
- recognize and solve problems

- practise what they know
- revise and replay what they know in order to retain it in the memory.

However, while acknowledging that learning leads to changes in understanding resulting in new knowledge and skills, recent literature and research in early childhood has focused on a wider view of learning involving context and relationships. As David (1999: 10) argues, learning is embedded in familiar contexts and in experience – it involves dispositions and relationships, including attitudes to learning and to oneself as a learner. Contemporary writing about learning has therefore highlighted the social nature of learning, viewing the child as an active and equal partner in the social process (for example, Radford, 1999: 107), but also recognizing the importance and significance of self-esteem (for example, Laevers, 1994; Roberts, 2002).

TRADITIONAL IDEAS ABOUT LEARNING

Most writing on childhood (for example, Kehily, 2004) identifies two central underlying themes that have influenced and continue to influence our view of the child and a child's learning. These ideas originated from philosophers writing during the 'Age of Enlightenment' in the late seventeenth and early to mid-eighteenth centuries (MacNaughton, 2003). First, the Romantic view or discourse, influenced by the work of the French philosopher Rousseau (1712–78), claims that children are naturally innocent and pure, and only contaminated through exposure to the outside world. Rousseau believed that hurrying children into adult ways of thinking risks harming the child and that a young child under seven has a natural disposition to play that should be celebrated and protected. Second, the alternative discourse stems from the ideas of Locke (1632–1704) who argued that children are born as tabula rasa, 'blank slates' or empty vessels, passively waiting to be educated and filled with 'knowledge' by adults. Childhood, including learning in childhood, is seen essentially as a period of preparation for adult life. From a contemporary perspective, the significant weakness of both these views is that neither seems to allow the child any agency in his own learning. Also, they do not fully acknowledge the context of learning, learning relationships and the relations of power between adults and children (for example, Silin, 1995; Walkerdine, 1993).

However, these underlying themes have an enduring influence on our understanding through 'common-sense' views, on theories of child development and on early years practice. Riley (2003), for example, discusses how the Romantic view has led to a sentimental perspective of the child. As MacNaughton (2003: 17) points out, Romantic beliefs are still popular as demonstrated by 'common-sense' views such as 'early experiences determine our future', 'the developing child is an incomplete adult and is different from adults' and 'we all progress through stages to adulthood'. Further, Locke's ideas still influence views of childhood through such examples as 'we can determine our own future', 'people of all ages learn in the same way' and 'effective learning is orderly and structured'. Despite their age and philosophical grounding, the theories of Rousseau and Locke had considerable influence over the supposedly 'scientific' understandings generated by developmental psychology. Woodhead (2003) has argued that in the early twentieth century, developmental psychology became established as the dominant paradigm for studying children (see Chapter 1). Essentially, this involved documenting the transitions and stages of Western childhood (Kehily, 2004).

MacNaughton (2003: 15) argues that the maturationist view of Gesell is directly influenced by Romantic ideas of innocence and the important stimulus of nature. Gesell's view was that children progressed naturally towards adulthood through genetically pre-programmed structures. For example, early physical development frequently characterized as developing from sitting up (around 6 months), to crawling (6–9 months) and walking (12–15 months). However, the maturationist view does not fully acknowledge individual and cultural differences. Cultures around the world vary in how much and in what ways babies are carried about by adults or older children and this will impact on the sequence of physical development described above (see Smith and Cowie, 2003). Also, the behaviourist theories of Watson and Skinner were, for example, influenced by Locke (see Berk, 2000). Behaviourists believe that development is determined by the child's physical and social environment and that a child is more likely to repeat a behaviour if adults or the environment reinforce it. As MacNaughton (2003: 26) points out, behaviourism has had a powerful influence on child development and many early childhood educators' views of learning. Many child development books, especially those written in the USA, are still from this perspective (see Chapter 1). However, as Hargreaves and Hargreaves (1997: 30) point out, behaviourist theory cannot fully explain more complex learning and behaviour that the child originates without apparent reinforcement, such as empathy and the generation of language. A memorable example of this is provided by the author's daughter Amy when, aged three years and two months, she commented on a particularly heavy downpour in terms of:

'It's chuckling it down.'

'Do you mean chucking it down?'

'No, it's chuckling it down because it's funny rain.'

MODERN IDEAS ABOUT LEARNING

This section now provides a brief overview of Piaget's work to acknowledge the significant impact and influence of his views. However, a detailed account is not given because his work is well known and there are many good sources of information about Piaget, such as Penn (2005), Riley (2003) and Arnold (2003). Attention is then concentrated on contemporary perspectives of the learning process.

Constructivism

Piaget (1954, for example) focused on how children acquire knowledge. Piaget has had an enduring influence on our understanding of early learning (see Penn, 2005: 40, for an overview). For example, many early years practitioners in the UK have been influenced by Athey's work on children's 'schemas', which was derived from Piaget's ideas. 'Schemas are patterns of repeatable actions that lead to early categories and then logical classifications' (Athey, 1990: 36). Arnold (2003) provides an interesting discussion of the schemas exhibited over a number of years by one particular child (Harry).

It is also important to acknowledge that the results of many of Piaget's ingenious experiments have been challenged and disputed because they did not take into account the context of children's learning (see Donaldson, 1978). Donaldson (1978, 1993) emphasized the need for embedded learning – that is, learning embedded in the context of meaningful experiences for children. When children are involved in tasks that are meaningful to them, they achieve greater success. When children are involved in 'disembedded' tasks that are not meaningful, the process of learning is significantly more difficult, as with many school-based tasks (1993: 19).

One of the most significant aspects of Piaget's work was the identification of stages on the way to becoming a logical thinker. For Piaget, the child is an active enquirer trying to make sense of their world, constructing an intellectual map for themselves. Children gradually structure their minds, described by Piaget as a series of major changes or stages in development:

- the *sensori-motor stage* (0–2 years): learning is from and through physical (or motor) action
- the *pre-operational period* (3–7 years): learning is intuitive in nature
- the *concrete operational stage* (8–11 years): learning is logical but depends on concrete referents (real experiences)
- *formal operations* (12–15 years): learning and thinking involve abstractions, generalizing rules from experience.

As an example, Piaget's theory could be applied to the game of chess. In the sensori-motor phase, the child would play with the pieces and in the pre-operational stage, learn to move the pieces. During the concrete operational phase, the moves and strategies would be learned from the experience of playing and in the formal operations stage, players are able to think several moves ahead and try to work out their opponent's strategy in advance. Of course, many children learn to play chess well before the age of 12, although Piaget did not see the stages as being fixed and static (see Smith and Cowie, 2003). While the stages of learning (or cognitive development) identified by Piaget are associated with characteristic age spans, they vary for every individual.

Piaget (Piaget and Inhelder, 1969) argued that learning consists of a constant effort to adapt to the environment in terms of assimilation and accommodation. Learning takes place through the processes of adaptation: assimilation and accommodation. Assimilation involves the interpretation of events in terms of existing cognitive structure, whereas accommodation refers to changing the cognitive structure to make sense of the environment. An example would be a six-month-old child playing with a beach ball. The child initially tries to put the ball in her mouth (as with most other things) and is unable to do so because the ball is too big. The child assimilates this knowledge and accommodates it by adapting her behaviour to lick the ball instead.

Following Piaget, Bruner (1990) also viewed learning as an active process in which learners construct new ideas or concepts based on their current and past knowledge (see Hargreaves and Hargreaves, 1997). Drawing on the work of Piaget, he developed a theoretical framework that views learning as three increasingly powerful ways of representing the world:

- *enactive representation:* thought based only on actions
- *iconic representation:* where the child can form and use images of objects without the objects having to be present
- *symbolic representation:* where the child can use and think in terms of symbols such as words.

For Bruner, the learner selects and transforms information, constructs hypotheses, and makes decisions, relying on a cognitive structure or framework to do so. This mental model gives meaning and organization to experiences and allows the individual to 'go beyond the information given'.

Multiple intelligence

Gardner (1983) argued that people learn in different ways and that there are different types of intelligences. He suggested that everyone possesses each type of intelligence to varying degrees. Gardner identified the following seven different types of intelligence:

- bodily kinaesthetic
- linguistic
- logical and mathematical
- musical
- visual and spatial
- social (inter-personal)
- personal (intra-personal).

A key element of Gardner's theory is that learning and intelligence is not fixed. It can and does change throughout each individual's lifetime. Measuring only one aspect of intelligence, such as a single IQ measurement, is therefore meaningless. As Gardner (1983: 70) points out, 'these intelligences are fictions and most useful fictions – for discussing processes and abilities that (like all of life) are continuous with one another'. Gardner is critical of schooling because he feels that it recognizes and promotes a limited view of intelligence (especially logical–mathematical). One of the strengths of his theory is that multiple intelligence draws attention to the uniqueness of the learning of each individual child and recognizes the culturally diverse patterns of learning. As Penn (2005: 54) points out:

It is clear that in different societies different kinds of intelligence are valued. Euro-American societies (over) value linguistic and logico-mathematical intelligence. Other societies, for instance some communities in northern India or West Africa, may value musical and kinaesthetic intelligence very highly — for example the praise singers of Mali and Senegal.

Metacognition

Metacognition is 'thinking about thinking' – it involves children's ability to reflect on their own thinking and learning. This aspect of learning has recently received greater attention and Brown (1987), for example, shows how metacognitive experiences involve the use of strategies or regulation. They include knowledge about the nature of a task as well as the type of demands that the task will place upon the individual. These processes help to regulate and oversee learning, and consist of planning and monitoring cognitive activities, as well as checking the outcomes of those activities. As David (1999: 5) rightly points out, children under the age of seven are unlikely to have fully developed mental strategies such as rehearsal and organizing their thoughts and will develop these through adult modelling and scaffolding (see below). The point about metacognition is that it does not suddenly develop in later childhood – it is founded in early learning relationships. For example, Hudson (1993) discusses the scripts and scenarios that children use to inform themselves about a particular experience. Children have to learn these in order to know how to act in different social situations. They learn what behaviour is expected of them and can predict what others are likely to do (see Merry, 1997).

Clearly, children will hold views about their success as learners. Dweck and Leggett (1988) conducted research into the views children hold about their approach to learning. They identified two possible learning dispositions: 'mastery' (where children approached new tasks enthusiastically, were determined to succeed and took responsibility for their learning) and 'helpless' (where children showed little interest in new tasks, gave up easily and tended to rely on others to help them). Dweck and Leggett emphasize the importance of 'mastery' learning dispositions in children (see Chapter 2 for further discussion on dispositions).

Social constructivism

For Rogoff (1997: 269), 'learning' is a process of improving one's participation in systems of activity, particularly social systems: from a sociocultural perspective, developmental processes are not just within individuals but also within group and community processes. Hence, individual children are not regarded as developing with everything else static.

Rather than equating the notion of 'culture' with the ethnicity or nationality of individuals, Rogoff conceptualizes culture as a dynamic process that is continually developing and adapting to changing circumstances. She describes 'culture' as the 'routine ways of doing things in any community's approach to living' (2003: 3). These 'routine ways of doing things' will inevitably impact on the expectations of children both over time and from community to community.

> A cultural approach notes that different cultural communities may expect children to engage in activities at vastly different times in childhood, and may regard 'timetables' of development in other communities as surprising or even dangerous. (Rogoff, 2003: 4)

Rogoff uses as an example the age at which children are considered responsible enough to take care of others. In the UK, it is against the law to leave a 'child' under 14 years of age without adult supervision, however she cites an example of a six-year-old Guatemalan girl who is both skilled and competent at taking care of her baby cousin. The Aka children of Central Africa are able to cook themselves a meal on the fire by three to four years of age (Hewlett, 1991 in Rogoff, 2003).

The impact of these differing expectations of children can be illustrated in the experience of a colleague of the author, a head teacher of a nursery school who had a policy of allowing children access to small-scale, real carpentry tools. A group of visiting Japanese teacher educators were both intrigued and horrified to see three- and four-year-old children using these tools. The visitors were, in fact, so focused on the potential dangers of the use of such tools that they failed to notice that the children were able to use them both competently and without mishap (see Chapter 4 for a wider discussion about attitudes to children's safety).

Rogoff warns of the dangers of researchers making assumptions or generalizations about the practices of other communities based on 'research or everyday life from the researcher's own community' (2003: 30). Since the UK is an increasingly multicultural society, Rogoff's perspective is particularly relevant for practitioners working in early years care and education:

> Variations in expectations for children make sense once we take into account different circumstances and traditions ... people's performance depends in large part on the circumstances that are routine in their community and on the cultural practices they are used to. (2003: 6)

Rogoff's view is one that gives much greater recognition to the importance of social interaction and support for the learner than Piaget's 'lone scientist' (1954) and proposes the learner as a social constructor of knowledge. Vygotsky (1978) asserted that a group working together can construct knowledge to a higher degree than can individuals in that group working separately. The knowledge is dependent upon the group interaction. Individuals working alongside more knowledgeable others can 'borrow' their understanding of tasks and ideas to enable them to work successfully (see Wray and Medwell, 1998: 8). For example, consider how a parent/carer may support a child's early literacy development during a 'bedtime story'. Importantly, the context is one where the child is comfortable and expects to succeed. For Rogoff (1990: vii), 'children's cognitive development is an apprenticeship – it occurs through guided participation in social activity with companions who support and stretch children's understanding of and skill in using the tools of culture'.

Scaffolding

Wood et al. (1976) were the first to use the term 'scaffolding' as a metaphor for the process by which an adult assists a child to carry out a task beyond the child's individual capability. Through the process of 'scaffolding', the adult guides and supports the child's learning by building on what the child is able to do (Bruner, 1978; Tharp and Gallimore, 1991; Wells, 1987; Wood et al., 1976). Bruner (1978) links 'scaffolding' explicitly with Vygotsky's concept of the 'zone of proximal development' (ZPD). ZPD is Vygotsky's model for the mechanism through which social interaction facilitates cognitive development. It resembles an apprenticeship in which a novice works closely with an expert in joint problem solving in the zone of proximal development (ZPD). The novice is thereby able to participate in skills beyond those that she or he is independently capable of handling.

Originally, little attention was paid to the means by which the transfer of responsibility from the adult to the child was accomplished. However, more recent discussions of the term scaffolding have shifted from an emphasis on relations in which the adult is directing to an emphasis on mutuality (Stone, 1998). Mutuality describes the degree of emotional intimacy and intuitive understanding involved in 'joint activities'. It concerns the way in which adult utterances tend to respond directly to, and to extend, the communicative intent of the children. What the adult does and says in these situations is therefore based on, and responsive to, the state of understanding achieved by the child (Lepper et al., 1997).

Rogoff (1998: 698) criticizes the specific linking of ZPD with scaffolding because much of the early writing and research about scaffolding located the power and control with the adult. Berk and Winsler (1995) develop a conception of scaffolding where there is a focus on joint problem solving and inter-subjectivity. They assert that: 'inter-subjectivity creates common ground for communication as each partner adjusts to the perspective of the other' (1995: 27). As Jordan (2004: 33) points out, Rogoff (1998) distinguishes between the function of scaffolding, where an expert assists a child, and ZPD, where participants mutually contribute to learning. Jordan (2004: 32) discusses a significant difference between scaffolding, where the adult or teacher is seen as an expert and co-construction, where there is equal partnership between the adult and child. The emphasis in co-construction is on the child as a powerful player in her own learning. The partnership between adults and children therefore focuses on forming meaning and building knowledge with each other. Jordan argues that when children are involved in co-construction, they become full members of their communities of learning through accepting greater responsibility for their own learning (Wenger, 1998). Rogoff (1998: 690) described this as a 'transformation of participation'. She identifies three interwoven levels or planes – the personal, the interpersonal and the community/institutional as sites for this transformation. For Rogoff, development is 'a process of transformation of participation where individuals participate and contribute to ongoing activity' (1998: 695). Learning and development are therefore inseparable from the concerns of families and interpersonal and community processes.

Learning as a relationship and a disposition

The relationships children develop with their mother and 'significant other' people, including family and friends and themselves, form the basis of their social world and are extremely significant in shaping and supporting their learning. Bruner (1986) argued that most learning in most settings is a communal activity – a sharing of the culture. As Anning and Edwards (2006) point out, the learning path followed by many children from birth to eight is one of a gradual shift from interdependence to independence, from a focus on personal meanings to public meanings. In many Western childhoods, this means moving from family and community to the early years setting and formal schooling.

Trevarthen (1977) conducted research with infants of only a few weeks old and identified a sharing, democratic character of early interactions between children and parents. Gopnik et al. (1999: 32) also argue that 'babies understand that there is something special about other people and that they are linked to other people in a special way'. Trevarthen's concept of 'motherese' is important here as the rhythm and melody of the mother's voice helps to encourage a partnership of shared interest (see Arnold, 2003: 70). Rogoff (1990: 12) also acknowledges the value of parental involvement: 'parents routinely adjust their interaction and structure children's environments in ways consistent with providing support for learning'.

This 'intersubjectivity' is crucial to learning for two significant reasons. First, 'the child is using other people to figure out the world' (Gopnik et al., 1999: 34). Second, it is in this physical and psychological space between participants that the participants develop strategies to tune into each other (Trevarthen, 1993) and the disposition to learn (see Anning and Edwards, 2006).

For Schaffer (1992), learning occurs through interactions with objects. Objects may be used in different ways in different communities. Schaffer (1992) paid particular attention to the 'joint involvement episodes' where adults and children pay joint attention to and act on an object. In these everyday exchanges, the quality of the interaction influences the quality of learning. The variable quality of interaction between children and adults was evident in a study by Tizard and Hughes (1984). They recorded the conversations of 30 four-year-old girls with their mothers at home and their nursery teachers at school. Their findings suggested that children's learning was significantly more useful and challenging at home because it was embedded in meaningful contexts and involved conversations initiated by the child.

The Effective Provision of Pre-school Education (EPPE) research in the UK has identified a range of practice in early years settings that has a strong influence on children's learning. In settings which were assessed as 'excellent', children and adults were more likely to be involved in 'sustained shared thinking'. According to Siraj-Blatchford (2004: 147), sustained shared thinking involves 'episodes in which two or more individuals "worked together" in an intellectual way to solve a problem, clarify a concept, evaluate activities or extend narratives, etc. During a period of sustained shared thinking, both parties contributed to the thinking and developed and extended the discourse'. Supporting children's sustained shared thinking has recently become a focus for practitioners, and the Early Years Foundation Stage (DfES, 2007a) is predicated on the adult's awareness of the child's interests and understandings and the adult and child or children developing an idea or a skill together.

Dowling (2005) identifies seven principles in the provision of appropriate contexts for children's thinking:

- scope to become involved in activities and situations that interest and intrigue them
- access to a rich range of provision that is continuously available
- space inside and outside to move, make and do things without disturbing others
- time to practice and apply what they have learned, explore and experiment in depth, follow through their interests and decisions, even if they don't work, and make connections
- scope to link their home experiences with experiences in the setting
- opportunities to have their thinking made visible, through records of their ideas, in words and images
- opportunities to think which are embedded in their culture and language.

Dowling further identifies a repertoire of 15 possible interactive responses from the adult: tuning in, showing genuine interest, respecting children's own decisions and choices, inviting children to elaborate, re-capping, offering your own experience, clarifying ideas, suggesting, reminding, using encouragement to further thinking, offering an alternative viewpoint, speculating, reciprocating, asking open questions and modelling thinking (see Dowling, 2005: 6).

Underpinning the sustained shared-thinking approach is the recognition that while young children's thinking is still in the process of developing, it is nonetheless powerful and worthy of respect. The process is that of actively engaging with children to discuss real issues that are meaningful to all participants.

PLAY AND LEARNING

It is recognized that play is important for both children and adults. Play is recreative and gives individuals the opportunity to step outside the world of work and relax, or focus their attention on something different.

For young children, however, play is more than recreation – it is the foundation for all learning (Bruce, 2001; Moyles, 2005; Wood and Attfield, 2005). While the understanding that play is central to early learning is one of the fundamental principles of the care and education of young children in the UK, play is, in fact, hard to define. Perceptions of play and its importance in early cognitive development will depend very much on cultural and social constructs of children (Sayeed and Guerin, 2000; Wood, 2007).

Wood and Attfield (2005) identify two fundamental questions in seeking a workable definition of play:

1. What is play?
2. What does play do for the child?

Play can be both purposeful and concentrated or trivial and apparently lacking in purpose, and it can be characterized by focused, motivated and creative behaviour or seemingly aimless 'pottering'. As Wood and Attfield point out, however, 'ambiguities surrounding the definition of play have done little to substantiate claims that children learn through play or that a play-based curriculum is the best or only approach to supporting early learning (2005: 2). They add that play is also contextual and may not always be a positive experience for the very young child in school faced with a large and threatening tarmac playground full of much larger children. 'Play' or 'playtime' can become a traumatic and negative experience.

In answer to their second question, Wood and Attfield (2005: 6) summarize the experiences that play can offer the child:

- Play is personally motivated by the satisfaction embedded in the activity and is governed neither by basic needs and drives nor by social demands.
- Players are concerned with activities more than goals. Goals are self-imposed, and the behaviour of the players is spontaneous.
- Play occurs with familiar objects, or following the exploration of unfamiliar objects. Children supply their own meanings to play activities and control the activities themselves.
- Play activities can be non-literal.
- Play is free from rules imposed from the outside, and the rules that do exist can be modified by the players.
- Play requires the active engagement of the players.

Should the overarching principle here be that of children owning their play? As Wood and Attfield point out:

> In the urge to explain and categorise play, we may be in danger of overlooking the fact that children define play themselves. They often establish mutual awareness of play and non-play situations. They create roles, use symbols, redefine objects, and determine the action through negotiation and shared meanings play is not just about fantasy. It doesn't have a life of its own which is divorced from reality. Children continuously weave in and out of their play their knowledge and understanding gleaned in other areas of their lives. (Wood and Attfield, 1996: 85)

While there are often generally agreed features that we use to describe play, these are not always consistent characteristics. For example, play is often described as active, but this is not always the case as play can involve apparent inactivity. Play or playfulness can be identified though by a number of different criteria, one of the most significant being that it is self-chosen.

The centrality of play in the early years curriculum has long been, and still is, the subject of much debate both in political and educational contexts. Early years practitioners and theorists, particularly those concerned with pre-school settings, have defended the role of play since the late nineteenth and twentieth centuries, and the principles of play-based learning are now enshrined in the Early Years Foundation Stage document

(DfES, 2007a). More recent observational studies (Broadhead, 2004; Nutbrown, 1999, 2006) have given us greater insights into how children's social and cognitive development takes place during play, and social constructivist theories such as those of Vygotsky (1933; see Smith and Cowie, 2003) have reinforced our understanding of the importance of play. In addition, recent neuroscience research on brain development in young babies (Perry, 1996 in Mustard and McCain, 1999) confirms the essential role of play in aiding the forming of neuron synapse connections in the brain, and the impact of the emotions on cognitive development is now more clearly understood (see Chapter 1).

It is recognized that young children are active learners (minds as well as bodies) who find it easier to learn through concrete experiences and materials and for whom a simple transmission model of teaching is inappropriate (Donaldson, 1978). It is also recognized that young children are powerful if inexperienced learners who will need both the skills and tools for learning that they can access through play (Moyles, 2005). It is important to remember, though, that as well as providing the opportunity to develop those skills, play provides the context in which children can develop the dispositions of perseverance, collaboration, problem solving, responsibility and independence.

THE ROLE OF THE PRACTITIONER AND THE EMERGENT CURRICULUM

If indeed children do own their play, is it appropriate for adults to become too involved? The process of embedding a play-based philosophy into the Early Years Foundation Stage curriculum has opened up a new area of debate within the sector – the extent to which educators should shape and control children's play. Inevitably, since practitioners will organize the learning environment for the children in their setting, play will be shaped by the constraints of space, time and resources, both human and physical. At what level of involvement though are adults in danger of 'hijacking' children's play?

A set of rules for their teacher devised by a group of Swedish children between the ages of four and five were written up by their teacher and offer an interesting insight into the children's perspective:

The first rule states 'Don't interfere with our play'. (Dagis, 2006)

Wood and Attfield (2005: 46) argue however for the role of parents and carers as children's first 'co-players' and advocate a central role for practitioners in enriching and extending children's thinking. They identify seven principles underpinning the role of the adult when interacting with children in their play:

- support and respond to children's needs and potential
- support children's skills as players and learners

- enrich the content of their play
- support their own ideas and provide additional ideas and stimuli
- enable children to elaborate and develop their own themes
- be responsive to the level of play development
- remain sensitive to the ideas that children are trying to express.

Wood (2004: 19) contends that the sociocultural model of teaching and learning equally supports the development of a 'pedagogy of play' defined as: 'the way in which practitioners make provision for playful and play-based activities, how they plan play/learning environments and all the pedagogical techniques and strategies they use to support or enhance learning through play'. Further, Wood and Attfield (2005: 159) suggest that the early years educator has an important role to support children's development and learning through play in contexts 'where play is likely to be a leading form of activity'.

Dockett and Fleer (1999) identify a continuum of the ways the adult's role can be classified in the support of young children's play: the indirect, as a manager (where the focus is on organizing resources, space and time), the direct, as a player (where the focus is on playful interaction and mutality) and the intermediary roles of facilitator and mediator (where the focus is on interpreting children's play themes).

At this point, readers may find it useful to refer to the case study below and consider what would be the most appropriate response for Laura to make in the light of Dockett and Fleer's classification.

 Case Study

Four-year-olds Dominic and Ben were busy in the construction play area and had constructed a complex system of roads and buildings which extended their play beyond the mat serving as the boundary for the area. They had become completely absorbed in the construction element of their play and were more interested in developing it across the floor than introducing the cars and lorries still in the basket beside them. Their discussion centred around the directions that their roads were following and the creation of junctions and roundabouts. In their conversation, both children were reflecting some early knowledge of the highway code and the rules of safe driving. 'We have to put traffic lights here 'cos we have four roads together, you have to stop in a car if it's red.' 'Yes, an' if there are shops, people have to cross here, you have to look.' The boys were also discussing how they walked to the centre every morning. 'We have to cross a big road, by the park. There's lots of cars and mum makes me hold her hand.'

Sally, the room supervisor, noticed that the boys' intense concentration on their play had left them completely oblivious to play areas close by and their construction was beginning to interfere with other children's activity. Some of the children were beginning to accidentally tread on the Duplo buildings and Dominic and Ben were becoming frustrated. She motioned to Laura, a first-year student on placement, to prevent the brewing argument.

 **Reflection**

Ben and Dominic were engaged in a complex level of play which was clearly encouraging them to reflect on their own understanding and experience of road traffic and a knowledge of local landmarks. They were using collaborative, cognitive, problem-solving, linguistic, physical and geographical skills in this positive play experience.

 Discussion Points

How should Laura respond to the situation? What should be her first priority?

- Prevent an argument by instructing Ben and Dominic to 'tidy up' their construction and move it back to the mat?
- Ask the other children to move out of the way so that Ben and Dominic can continue extending their construction?
- Sensitively involve herself in the boys' play so that she can deflect the tension and encourage them to continue developing their ideas?
- How might Laura achieve this without 'hijacking' the children's play and controlling its development?

Vivien Gussin Paley's (1990) approach to play tutoring is one that, while it supports an adult engagement in play, does not direct the action. The children dictate their own stories, which are recorded by the adult and then acted out by the children. The authors of the stories have control over their own stories, deciding on who takes on the roles and the direction of the action as the practitioner reads the story. Payley's approach not only reflects a commitment to play and the support of children's communication and exploration of ideas, but also offers the practitioners some rare insights into their children's thinking.

The emergent curriculum (Jones and Nimmo, 1994 in Fraser, 2000) is a form of child-centred curriculum which emphasizes adults and children working together on shared interests and ideas.

> In early childhood education, curriculum isn't the focus, children are. It's easy for teachers to get hooked on curriculum because it's so much more manageable than children. But curriculum is what happens in an educational environment — not what is rationally planned to happen, but what actually takes place. (Jones and Nimmo, in Fraser, 2000: 122)

An emergent curriculum then begins with observations of the children's play and a recording of their current preoccupations. In discussion with the children, the practitioner selects a number of ideas that have been identified as of interest to the children.

The planning is based on these shared discussions and on the understanding that the curriculum should be driven by the children. The practitioners who have adopted this approach have found that it is more responsive to the children's interests and allows for greater flexibility and creativity than planning a theme beforehand. An example of how a practitioner might follow this approach is in the next case study below.

Case Study

Narinder (3.11 years), Louise (3.10 years) and Jim (4.1 years) were outside playing in the sandpit on a sunny day. Narinder picked up a bucket, stood up and then began to walk out of the sandpit. As she moved, she said, 'Look, there's a black shape on the ground.' Louise stood up and walked to her and asked her where it was. Jim then stood up and as he moved towards them, cried out, 'Look there, it's there, I know … it's a shadow!' All three children then moved out of the sandpit and invented a game of chasing and jumping on each other's shadows. Claire, a first-year student on placement, heard the laughter and went over to the children who asked her why the shadows were following them.

Reflection

The children were already demonstrating some understanding of cause and effect by their game of chasing and jumping on each other's shadows. They understood that the shadows were 'theirs' but had not made a connection with the sunshine and shadows.

Discussion Points

What could Claire have done to help the children understand the connection and how could she build on the children's excitement and interest in the shadows?

1. Could she have joined in the children's game and commented on her longer shadow?
2. Could she have joined in the children's game and commented on the places in the sunny garden the children did not make shadows?
3. Would it have been appropriate for Claire to develop a series of focused science activities for the children exploring the properties of shadows?
4. Would some planned art experiences perhaps involving shadow puppets have been appropriate?
5. Could Claire have provided opportunities to extend the children's play by introducing further resources to support the integration of other aspects of developmental domains, for example cognitive or linguistic development?

SUMMARY

In summary, this chapter has identified a number of theories on how young children learn and how these theories impact on our practice. We have considered the role of play in the early childhood curriculum and acknowledged the fact that there is no complete consensus within the early years care and education sector as to what constitutes best practice. Our beliefs will be influenced by our own personal histories, culture and experience. What is clear, however, is that the personal ideologies of practitioners will be reflected in their practice: in the way that resources and the environment are organized, the amount of time that is allocated to any particular activity, the way the content of the day is planned, the nature and extent of the interaction between adults and children and ultimately the children's experiences of the early childhood settings.

 QUESTIONS FOR REFLECTION AND DISCUSSION

1. How do the views of Piaget and Rogoff differ in relation to children's learning?
2. Can you think of any aspects of children's learning that may be naturally scaffolded by parents/carers?
3. Can you think of particular activities where children benefit from supporting each other's learning?
4. Why are relationships seen as so important to learning?
5. What are the implications of your discussion for teaching and learning in early years settings and schools?

Recommended reading

Bodrova, E. and Leong, J. (2007) *Tools of the Mind*, 2nd edition. Colombus, OH: Pearson.
Dowling, M. (2005) *Young Children's Personal, Social and Emotional Development*, 2nd edition. London: Paul Chapman Publishing.
Rogoff, B. (2003) *The Cultural Nature of Human Development*. New York: Oxford University Press.
Wood, E. and Attfield, J. (2005) *Play, Learning and the Early Childhood Curriculum*, 2nd edition. London: Paul Chapman Publishing.

Recommended websites

General information on Piaget, Bruner and Vygotsky: www.trackstar.hprtec.org;
Centre for Brain and Cognitive Development Research: www.psyc.bbk.ac.uk

4 OUTDOOR PLAY AND LEARNING

Tim Waller

Chapter objectives

- To provide an overview of recent literature on outdoor play and learning.
- To discuss the reasons why opportunities for outdoor play have become restricted.
- To consider the benefits of outdoor play and learning.
- To outline recent UK policy in relation to outdoor play and learning.
- To report on findings from an ongoing Outdoor Learning Project.

We should feed children's natural desire to contact nature's diversity with free access to an area of limited size over an extended period of time, for it is only by intimately knowing the wonders of nature's complexity in a particular place that one can fully appreciate the immense beauty of the planet as a whole. (Hart, 1997: 18, cited in Casey, 2007: 9)

Currently, there is a great deal of interest in the use of outdoor environments in early years education in the UK, and many practitioners and parents would empathize with Hart's beliefs above. Also, the curriculum in Scotland (A Curriculum for Excellence 3–18) and Northern Ireland (CCEA, 2006; DENI, 2006), the Foundation Phase in Wales (Welsh Assembly Government (WAG), 2003) for children aged 3–7, and the new Foundation Stage in England for children from birth to five (DfES, 2007a) all emphasize the need for the provision of regular outdoor experience. However, a clear pedagogy for the use of the outdoors as a site for learning has not been established (Waller, 2007b) and, as Fjørtoft (2001) and Waite et al. (2006a) point out, there has been relatively little research on what actually happens in outdoor environments. Further, a number of writers have raised concern over the impact of a 'culture of fear' on children's outdoor play (for example, Furedi, 2002; Tovey, 2007). This chapter considers what counts as outdoor play and learning and provides a critical overview of the positive benefits of outdoor play for young children's health, risk-taking and well-being. Recent UK policy initiatives in relation to outdoor play are outlined and findings from an ongoing outdoor learning project are discussed in relation to some recent literature and research in the field.

CONTEXT AND RATIONALE

There has been a growing interest in the use of outdoor spaces for play by young children over the last decade or so, and for many parents and early years practitioners, outdoor play is seen as a natural and significant part of a child's healthy development (Clements, 2004). Outdoor play and learning is used here as an 'umbrella' term to cover a range of children's experiences in different outdoor locations. As Waite et al. (2006a) point out, outdoor learning is not a single entity but comprises many different sorts of activity with distinct purposes. For young children, attending an early years setting in the UK, these opportunities may include:

- play in outdoor areas within the setting
- visits to natural, wild environments, community parks and play spaces
- Forest School

As with Fjørtoft (2004), natural, wild environments are defined as environments not designed or cultivated by humans – typically, woods, forests, beaches or riverbanks, etc. Forest School involves activities (including traditional games and woodcraft) usually organized and directed by trained Forest School teachers. Forest Schools originated in Scandinavia in the 1950s as a way of teaching about the natural world. By the 1980s, they became an integral part of the Danish early years programme and significantly influenced the development of the Forest School movement in the UK in 1993 (Maynard, 2007a; Murray, 2003). Currently, a number of local authorities in the UK organize Forest School programmes for children from the age of three onwards.

At the present time, there is considerable justification for turning our attention towards outdoor environments as a site for learning. As discussed in Chapter 1, the changing place of childhood in many countries is widely acknowledged within the sociology of childhood (James and Prout, 1990). A significant aspect of recent changes to childhood in many countries (Fjørtoft, 2004; Holloway and Valentine, 2000) is that facilities for outdoor play and opportunities for free play outdoors are declining. Opportunities for outdoor play have become much more restricted over the last three generations due to a rise in traffic, greater institutionalization of childhood (breakfast and after school clubs, etc.) and parents' safety concerns (Burke, 2005; Valentine and McKendrick, 1997). At the same time, access to the outdoors for children has become limited with far greater use now of adult-controlled and structured space – for example, the significant rise in the number and use of private and commercially run play spaces in pubs, theme parks and shopping centres (Tovey, 2007).

There is growing statistical evidence that children spend increasing amounts of time inside the home, which may be at the expense of time spent playing outside. Research cited by Learning through Landscapes (2005) found that nearly half of seven to twelve-year-old children in the UK spent more than three hours watching television per day. Much of the recent literature concerning outdoor play is in no doubt about the reason for the decreasing amount of time many children spend playing outside. Children's participation in the public domain has been restricted in an attempt to keep them safe from risk, thus leading to an erosion of opportunities for independent play in outdoor spaces (Harden, 2000). This risk anxiety and 'culture of fear' (Furedi, 2002) have led to a tendency to protect children 'from situations previously considered to be innocent and risk free' (Sharp, 2004: 91).

As Tovey (2007: 2) argues, 'the decline in access to outdoor spaces has been paralleled by an unprecedented rise in the level of anxiety for children's safety. It appears that parental anxiety and fear of abduction or "stranger danger" has had the most persuasive effect on children's play (Valentine and McKendrick, 1997)'. Evidence from a number of recent surveys (Barnardo's, 1995; Gill, 2007; Maudsley and Smith, 2005) shows that not only are few parents happy for their children to play outside without an adult present, but also that many children are concerned about the danger of abduction or murder if they play outdoors.

This 'culture of fear' does not, however, reflect the reality that incidents of child abduction (although tragic) are extremely rare and have remained largely unchanged over the last 30 years or more. As Hope et al. (2007) report, in an average year, between seven and nine children are abducted by strangers in Britain: a figure that's stayed exactly the same for the past 30 years.

Hope et al. (2007: 326) report a survey carried out by Barnado's (1995) which reflects this 'culture of fear' and expresses concern about erosion of children's freedom and also the influence that this could have on their overall development and independence. The number of unaccompanied activities taken by junior-aged school children at weekends halved between 1971 and 1990 (Hillman, 1993). As Hope et al. point out, this figure is probably much lower now as local streets and parks are perceived as areas of risk. Moorhead (2007) poses an important question here: why is it that many parents appear gripped by mass hysteria about the dangers of their children being taken from outdoor spaces and playgrounds by abductors? The net effect of this fear on children's lives is that it minimizes both their world outside home and school and their confidence to operate in this world (Tovey, 2007). Sharp (2004) argues that this 'culture of fear' has also permeated early years provision. Maynard and Waters (2007) report that reception teachers involved in a study that explored their use of outdoor space with their children stated that concerns about safety were a limiting factor in their provision of outdoor experiences. Recently in the UK, a minority of early years practitioners have also declined to organize visits outside the setting because of the perceived possibility of litigation if any children were involved in an accident. A 'culture of fear' is also apparent outside the UK and Clements (2004) discussed three studies from Canada, England and Japan that demonstrate this concern.

WHERE DO CHILDREN PLAY?

Maudsley and Smith (2005) conducted a survey in the south-west UK of children's preferred places for play. When asked to indicate where they play, children identified the beach (72 per cent) and the park (71 per cent) as their highest responses. (However, as Maudsley and Smith note, the high response to beaches could be due to the fact that the information was collected from children living in the south-west who might have a higher than average access to beaches). Fifty-seven per cent of children said they played in their garden and 46 per cent said they played in or around the home. Eighteen per cent of the children surveyed played in the street, 13 per cent by the shops and

7 per cent in the city. This evidence presents a similar pattern to that discussed previously but suggests, as with Barnardo's and Transport 2000 (2004), that children believe speeding, dangerous driving and busy roads stop them from playing outside. Their report also suggests that traffic is a major reason why parents don't allow their children to go outside to play. Forty-six per cent of the children surveyed played in woodland and even less near fields, rivers or hills, perhaps indicating that play in highly natural areas (wild spaces) is relatively uncommon. Maudsley and Smith (2005: 57) concluded that:

> Parks, as widespread features, are particularly good starting points for encouraging outdoor play ... Other wild spaces are less intensively used for children's play, e.g. woodlands and rivers, resulting in a corresponding paucity of naturalistic kinds of play such as den-building and tree climbing. Streets and areas near heavy traffic are not considered safe for play either by children themselves or parents, and motorised traffic is acknowledged as a significant barrier to outdoor play.

As a result, Clements (2004) argues that it has become apparent over the last few years that childhood, society and the use of the environment have changed significantly, resulting in fewer and fewer children playing outdoors in woods, community parks and back gardens, etc. with increasing numbers in private and commercially-run play spaces such as theme parks. For many children, opportunities for naturalistic play – play in natural environments (Hart, 1997; Wood, 1993) – have therefore become evermore valuable and significant.

WHY OUTDOOR PLAY IS SIGNIFICANT

Tovey (2007: 37) cogently argues that some learning can only happen outdoors and summarizes the *unique* opportunities that outdoor play provides as:

- the space and freedom to try things out
- an environment that can be acted on, changed and transformed
- a dynamic, ever-changing environment that invites exploration, curiosity and wonder
- whole-body, multi-sensory experiences
- the scope to combine materials in ways that are challenging and problematic
- the opportunity to make connections in their learning
- a rich context for curiosity, wonder, mastery and 'what if' thinking
- the space to navigate and negotiate the social world of people and friendships, and to experience disagreement and resolve conflicts with peers
- the opportunity for giddy, gleeful, dizzy play
- the potential for mastery, a willingness to take risks and the skills to be safe
- a wide range of movement opportunities that are central to learning
- experience of the natural world and their place within it
- opportunities for learning in all areas of the curriculum.

For Tovey (2007: 38), few of these benefits can be realized in open, windswept, asphalt-surfaced playgrounds and outdoor play is about *potential* – the potential of outdoor spaces to support, enhance and engage children's imagination, curiosity and creativity and foster their health and well-being.

Health and outdoor play

In terms of young children's health, there is a direct relationship between physical activity and health. A lack of regular outdoor play from an early age is likely to impact negatively on children's health – and they are less likely to take up sporting activities when older. It will also impact on their physical competence and children who are physically able and confident tend to be popular (Waters and Begley, 2007). Children need physical activity in order to thrive and levels of activity impact directly on health, for example on blood pressure (Malina and Bouchard, 1991), on bone health (Bailey and Martin, 1994) and on mental health (Mental Health Foundation, 1999). Guidelines produced in the UK recommend that children need a minimum of 60 minutes of accumulated moderate-intensity activity per day for optimal health (Hope et al., 2007). However, Macdonald et al. (2005) have raised concerns that many children are currently undertaking much less physical activity than that recommended by the guidelines.

Also, as Hope et al. (2007) point out, there is mounting evidence of a relationship between a lack of physical activity and a significant rise in obesity. In the UK, Zaninotto et al. (2006) found, in a report for the Department of Health, that in 2006 nearly 20 per cent of children aged two to ten were described as overweight or obese, representing a dramatic increase over a 20-year period. Further, children from poor backgrounds and those living in urban areas are more likely to be obese than those from more wealthy backgrounds living in suburban or rural areas. Nevertheless, Hope et al. (2007: 326) caution us against a simplistic view of the discourse 'obesity epidemic'. They argue that there are issues over the measurement and definition of obesity for children using the body mass index (BMI) which take no account of age, sex, ethnicity or level of fitness. There is however common agreement in the literature that regular physical activity is good for promoting a longer and better quality of life and that good habits in terms of physical exercise start in childhood. For example, Fjørtoft (2001) investigated the impact of children's play in the natural environment on their motor ability. Her research found that there was a significant relationship between the diversity of the landscape and the affordance of play. The natural environment offers a much greater diversity, thereby offering the child much more in terms of play. For Fjørtoft, children using the forest landscapes performed better in motor skills than those children playing in the playground. The Mental Health Foundation (1999) also found that a lack of opportunity for outdoor play impacted on the mental health of children and families.

In this context, opportunities for play in outdoor environments are evermore valuable and significant; they provide countless opportunities for healthy development (Bilton, 2002); they are essential for all aspects of development, especially social and well-being (Durant, 2003); and they have positive effects on all children, but some children in particular (Rickinson et al., 2003). Further, it is interesting to note that in the survey conducted by Maudsley and Smith (2005), there was a high response to the use of local parks, highlighting the value of these public green spaces for children's play. Maudsley and Smith also show that 40 per cent of users visit parks every day and 70 per cent get there by walking. Here, a clear link between good health and the use of outdoor spaces is demonstrated.

Positive risk-taking and 'staying safe'

Attitudes, discourse and practice around safety vary culturally and over time. For example, early years practitioners in Sweden may be happy to encourage five year-olds to climb trees several metres high, or play in the forest out of sight of an adult, while many practitioners in the UK would not consider either activity an acceptable risk on the grounds of safety. Also, currently, practitioners in England would be expected to conduct a formal 'risk assessment' exercise following a detailed procedure laid down by the local authority in order to take children out of a setting. In Sweden, this would not be needed and has only recently been deemed necessary in England.

As previously discussed, there is no doubt that the effect of the 'culture of fear' (Furedi, 2002) has been to limit many children's opportunities for outdoor play recently and as Smith (1998) points out, there appears to be a common assumption that risk is a negative concept that must be avoided and reduced. In the UK, much of the current discourse around children's safety in outdoor spaces is from this perspective. Once more, the apparent fear is not borne out by the evidence. As Ball (2002, cited in Tovey, 2007: 107) reports, the majority of playground accidents are little more than bruises or cuts and children are many times more likely to be seriously injured in a road traffic accident or an accident in the home than in outdoor play.

A contrasting view of risk is, however, adopted here (following Tovey, 2007; Waters and Begley, 2007). This perspective recognizes the positive benefits of risk-taking behaviour. Tovey (2007: 102) summarizes this perspective as follows: a safe environment 'is one where safety is not seen as safety from all possible harm, but offers safety to explore, experiment, try things out and take risks'. This perspective does not seek to be complacent about the possibility of accidents but argues that the danger of creating risk-free environments is that adults' expectations remain low and children do not have the opportunity to develop and demonstrate competence and confidence (Tovey, 2007).

At this point, an important distinction between 'hazard' and 'risk' in children's outdoor play should be made (see Lindon, 1999; Tovey, 2007). 'Hazard' is taken to mean an activity that may cause serious injury or death. A judgement has to be made based on whether challenges constitute hazards or risks. For example, taking children to play and explore in the forest may be seen as a positive risk with many benefits. However, occasionally, on days when there is a strong or gale force wind, the possibility of a tree falling becomes a hazard and therefore unacceptable. Also, 'what is challenging for one child may be a hazard for another because of the developmental range of skills and abilities' (Stine, 1997 in Stephenson, 2003: 39).

Stephenson (2003) argues that children naturally and regularly seek out and enjoy physical challenges in their play, as a matter of course. Further, Stephenson identified a number of components which she believed were significant in four-year-old children's physical risk-taking: 'attempting something never done before, feeling on the border-line of "out of control" often because of height or speed and overcoming fear' (Stephenson, 2003: 36). We have to consider the negative consequences if children do not confront and conquer risky physical activities. As Smith (1998) points out, for young children, risk-taking in the physical domain is the starting point for taking risks in other domains (emotional, social, intellectual). Children therefore need the opportunity to take acceptable risks and the question is how we juggle the requirement for safety with the need for children to have physical challenges.

Waters and Begley (2007) assert that children facing such physical challenges and tak-ing physical risks in their play can be viewed as engaging in positive risk-taking behav-iour. There may be links between risk-taking and the development of a disposition to persist in the face of difficulty. As Stephenson (2003: 41) points out, there may be 'a fun-damental link between a young child's developing confidence in confronting physical challenges, and her confidence to undertake risks of quite different kinds in other learn-ing contexts'. This has important implications for the development of self-esteem and confidence. Success and mastery lead to self-esteem and confidence – if you are suc-cessful as a risk-taker, this may be a transferable skill (see Chapter 2).

There are further long-term implications arising – making a space hazard-free can lead to a risk-free environment. As Little (2006: 151) suggests, the early childhood set-ting may need to consider how to provide:

> a safe learning environment in which children feel secure enough to take the risks and make mistakes as necessary for learning. At the same time the environment needs to elim-inate opportunities for negative risk-taking behaviours such as misuse of equipment as a result of insufficient challenge or boredom.

Children will become bored and this may lead to apparatus being used in truly dan-gerous ways as children try to create challenges! Ofsted (2006) have identified good practice in terms of health and safety in early years settings. This guidance does not suggest risk and challenge are removed from early years settings. It highlights exam-ples where children undertake 'risky' behaviour in a 'controlled and supportive' envi-ronment. For example, 'a child using a rake was given help to use it safely without his fun being spoilt' (Osfted, 2006: 10).

Well-being and outdoor play

Every Child's Future Matters (Sustainable Development Commission, 2007: 6) makes a strong case for the need to consider sustainable development as a fundamental require-ment underpinning children's well-being: 'Children's environmental well-being – their daily experience of living and learning in the environment around them, and their options and opportunities for experiencing a healthy environment in the future – is a critical factor in their overall well-being.' This is a statement which many early years professionals will relate to from their own experience of what constitutes high-quality learning experiences for the children they are responsible for. Opportunities to play outdoors every day, to engage with the environment in all weather conditions and to build an understanding and appreciation of the natural world are experiences which all young children are entitled to.

This is especially the case in natural, wild, outdoor environments, which are complex and diverse environments for play. They afford different play and learning opportunities. Children perceive them as their own domain, where there are numerous possibilities to construct and re-organize play. Titman (1994) notes children's preference for outdoor play because of the realness of the physical attributes. 'The rough surface provides movement challenges, and topography and vegetation provide a diversity of different designs for playing and moving' (Fjørtoft, 2004: 22). In addition, as Rivkin (1995) suggests, outdoor settings often incorporate the symbolism and images that can make an environment magical. Natural environments can also provide spaces that enhance social interactions and promote a 'sense of belonging' leading to place attachment (Hart, 1979). Significantly, outdoor environments can provide different opportunities to creatively express and articulate children's values and perspectives through play (Rickinson et al., 2003).

 Case Study

Ashleigh is aged three years and six months and attends her local nursery school every morning. She is an only child and is looked after by her grandmother before and after school and during the school holidays. When Ashleigh started at the nursery, it was her first experience of an early years setting and she appeared very reserved, quiet and shy. Although appearing happy to participate in many of the nursery activities, she rarely chose to speak to other children or adults in the nursery. Both her mother and grandmother reported her spoken language to be 'no problem at home'. Ashleigh has frequent bouts of illness and has regularly been absent from nursery since she started in September.

In the following January, the school started taking the children to a local country park for one day per week. Ashleigh participated in the first visit but missed the second visit due to illness. She asked her grandmother to take her to school on the day of the visit even though she was not well. As a result, her grandmother promised to take her to the country park when she was better. Ashleigh's grandmother reported to nursery staff that she was amazed that Ashleigh seemed to make a quick recovery from illness and was very keen to go to the country park the next day. Not only did Ashleigh give her grandmother some directions to the park (which were generally correct), but also gave her a guided tour of the park, speaking at length about playing on a special tree and looking for rabbits in the woods. Her grandmother reported that she was surprised at how much knowledge of the park Ashleigh already had after just one previous visit and also how well she was able to articulate this experience.

 Reflection

Clearly, both girls and boys may demonstrate positive dispositions in outdoor contexts. This case study also shows how important it is to give children the experience of wild, outdoor environments and also to elicit their experiences of the environment.

Discussion Points

1. Why do you think Ashleigh was so keen not to miss her visit to the park?
2. Why might Ashleigh feel more inclined to talk about her experiences in the outdoor spaces?
3. What aspects of the outdoor environment might she particularly enjoy?

RECENT POLICY INITIATIVES IN THE UK

As Waite et al. (2006a: 3) acknowledge, the use of the outdoors as a site for learning is long established in the UK, in both early years practice and in settings with older children. Recent interest in the potential of outdoor learning is also evident in policy across the UK. For example, outdoor play is firmly enshrined in the new Foundation Phase curriculum in Wales for children aged three to seven years (WAG, 2003). Wyn Siencyn and Thomas (2007) point out that the main focus of the Foundation Phase is the child's personal, social development and well-being, which is placed at the centre of the curriculum and is viewed as fundamental to young children's learning. Outdoor learning is also considered integral to the curriculum in each of the seven areas of learning in the Foundation Phase and activities are to be organized in both the indoor and outdoor learning environments. The Foundation Phase document suggests a requirement to view the outdoors as an holistic part of the day-to-day environment where all aspects of the curriculum can be experienced (ACCAC, 2004). Also, the first national play policy in the world was developed in Wales by PlayWales (WAG, 2002).

In Scotland, an outdoor education programme was initiated in 2005 led by Learning and Teaching Scotland (LTS). Following large-scale research, 'Taking Learning Outdoors: Partnerships for excellence' (LTS, 2007) was published. The vision promoted by the document is one where outdoor learning is embedded in the curriculum (A Curriculum for Excellence 3–18) and it argues that children and young people must be offered core outdoor experiences 'regularly and routinely, through their transition from pre-school education to adulthood' (2007: 1). It also aims to stress the 'considerable benefits of outdoor learning as opposed to the disproportionate emphasis on risk' (2007: 1).

In England, the government launched an 'Education Outside the Classroom Manifesto' (DfES, 2006a). At the launch, then Education and Skills Secretary Alan Johnson argued that: 'Learning outside the classroom should be at the heart of every school's curriculum and ethos' (DfES, 2006a, online). This recent ministerial commitment to children's play is consistent with the ethos of ECM and the Children's Plan (DCSF, 2007a). This commitment was further supported by a consultation on children's outdoor play in the community with the aim of establishing the first national Play Strategy in England (DCSF, 2008a). At the same time, it was announced that £235 million was going to be invested in children's play in the community.

Outdoor play is also seen as significant within the Early Years Foundation Stage (EYFS) (DfES, 2007a). One of the four principles informing the new EYFS is 'enabling environments'. The practice guidance document (DfES, 2007a: 5) recognizes that 'the environment plays a key role in supporting and extending children's development and learning' and goes on to suggest that effective practice involves ensuring children have 'opportunities to be outside on a daily basis all year round' (Practice card 3.3). However, following the publication of the EYFS (DfES, 2007a), concern was raised about why the government did not take the opportunity to ensure that all providers had an outdoor play area.

This chapter will now briefly report on an outdoor learning project as an example of the emerging research in this field.

THE OUTDOOR LEARNING PROJECT

The Outdoor Learning Project (OLP) takes place in two different early years settings in the UK, one in England and one in Wales. The project started in January 2004 in Setting 1 and expanded in September 2005 to include Setting 2. In the project, children aged 3–11 years are given regular opportunities to play and learn in natural, wild environments (such as woodland and river banks).

Setting 1

The project is based at a state nursery school located in a (mixed) housing estate on the outskirts of a large town in the English Midlands area of the UK. Children (aged three and four years) attend the nursery on a part-time basis (40 in the morning and 40 in the afternoon). The school adheres to the statutory Early Years Foundation Stage (DfES, 2007a). Children normally attend for one year and then transfer to the reception class of local primary schools. Staff includes a head teacher, class teacher, three nursery nurses and three learning support assistants. There is a base ratio of one practitioner to ten children and the children are organized into 'key groups' of around 14.

Outdoor learning is an integral part of the curriculum and the large garden area is open for the children to use freely for all but the very end of sessions when the children go into their key groups. The country park used for the project has elements of a 'natural, wild environment'. The park is built around an Edwardian reservoir and arboretum and below the reservoir dam is an area of approximately 52,000 square meters containing woods, open grassland, a purpose-built children's play area on sand, an amphibian pond and a butterfly garden. Visits to the country park are undertaken on one day per week (morning and afternoon), whatever the weather. The children are transported by bus to the park, with the journey lasting approximately fifteen minutes in each direction. The children are accompanied by practitioners and students allowing for a one to one, or one to two, adult–child ratio. A programme of visits is organized so that a small group of children (one 'key' group) are taken on each occasion. This allows for an appropriate level of interaction and support for the children at the park and is also designed to have a minimal impact on staffing at the nursery. Additional adults are also needed to support the collection of written observations, video and photographic evidence.

Setting 2

The project is based at a state primary school located in a community close to a town centre in south Wales. Initially, 25 children in a reception class (aged four and five) participated in the research. The class follows the statutory *Desirable Outcomes for Learning* (ACCAC, 2000). In 2006, the project was expanded to include all infants aged 4–7 and in September 2007 will involve the whole school. Staff currently involved in the project include the head teacher, four class teachers and four learning support assistants. The school is located in a large Victorian building on the side of a steep hill. There is a tarmac playground used by the children at break and lunch time. The playground is also built on a steep hill. In order to give the reception children more space in the playground, their morning and afternoon breaks are timetabled without the other children in the school (approximately 170 children aged 5–11).

The riverside woodland area used for the project has elements of a 'natural, wild environment' (as defined on page 48). The woodland is adjacent to a river and areas of open meadow and is situated immediately below the school. However, there is a main road between the woodland and the school. In order to get to the woodland, the children walk about 1 km on the pavement and about 0.5 km along a tarmac path to the entrance. This journey is made considerably longer because of the need to cross the main road in a 'safe' place. The woodland has open access and is not maintained by the local authority, resulting in some rubbish and waste being deposited there. The children are accompanied by practitioners and students, allowing for a one to one, or one to two, adult–child ratio. A programme of visits is organized for all children in the infant classes for one morning per week in term time.

A similar pattern was observed in both the settings. On the first visit, the children predictably tended to stay together with the adults, spending time exploring a relatively narrow area. After the first visit, the children tended to split into small groups immediately on arrival and go to different parts of the park or woodland. Once more familiar with the outdoor environment, the children recorded image-based data revealing an interesting range of both 'social spaces' and 'individual landmarks' (Clark and Moss, 2001, 2005). As the visits increased, the children re-visited and named familiar places – 'The Octopus Tree', 'Eeyore's Den', the woods, 'The Top of the World', 'The Giant's Bed' (of leaves), 'The Goblin's House' and 'Dragonfly Land' (Setting 1) and 'Morgan's Mountain', 'The Crocodile Tree', 'The Giant's Den', 'The Trampoline Tree' and 'The Troll Bridge' (Setting 2). Quite often, the children used the environment as a context for their imaginative play involving themes such as dinosaurs or goblins (Setting 1) and 'Swamp Monsters' (Setting 2). While both outdoor environments have open access to the public, on many occasions, especially in the winter months, there were no other visitors at the same time, allowing the children complete freedom of space.

Initially, a range of mostly qualitative and some quantitative information was gathered in the form of questionnaires, observations and video and photographic evidence, and an assessment of children's 'Involvement Levels' (Laevers, 1994) was undertaken. For example, Table 4.1 (below) shows a comparison of children's involvement levels in the nursery and the country park over the year, in this case 2006. At the school, each child is observed regularly and a judgement made about involvement levels every half term. The levels are based on the five-point scale devised by Laevers (1994) (see Chapter 2 for more information on Levels of Involvement). While it could be expected that children's levels of involvement would increase from autumn to summer as they settle in to nursery, the data shows that the involvement levels were consistently higher in the country park. For some individual children (in particular, several boys), they were significantly higher in the park.

Table 4.1   Children's involvement levels

Nursery	
Autumn term	3.22 (n = 84)
Spring term	3.32 (n = 87)
Summer term	3.76 (n = 87)
Country park	4.31 (n = 79)
(Mean Involvement Scores using Laevers's scale, 1994)	

Observations made at the park were also classified according to the areas of learning within the Foundation Stage Curriculum (DfEE and QCA, 2000). As can be seen in Figure 4.1 (opposite), the majority of the observations made at the country park are within the areas of knowledge and understanding and physical development. Practitioners revealed that they were pleasantly surprised by the relatively high number of observations recorded for maths, which is significantly higher than normally found at the nursery.

The study draws on the 'Mosaic approach' for listening to young children described by Clark and Moss (2001, 2005). The method uses both the traditional tools of observing children at play and a variety of 'participatory tools' with children. These include taking photographs, book making, tours of the outdoor area and map making. 'The Mosaic approach enables children to create a living picture of their lives' (Clark and Moss, 2005: 13). Also, part of the Mosaic approach is to involve adults in gathering information in addition to perspectives from the children (for further discussion, see Waller, 2005a, 2006).

The OLP has so far revealed a wealth of information about the children's views of the outdoor environment, including places they liked and their play with friends. Similar methods have been used in both settings. The initial findings from the project were reported by Waller et al. (2004). One feature of these findings was that involvement in the project promoted a high level of reflection on the benefit of giving children opportunities to create their own learning environments. The project therefore became more focused on eliciting children's views and perspectives. Further papers on the methodology and ethics (Waller, 2005a, b) and on young children's geographical literacy (Waller, 2005c) were given. Also, in Waller (2006), a critical discussion of participatory research methods is offered, while Waller (2007a) discusses the construction and development of children's narratives located around their outdoor experiences.

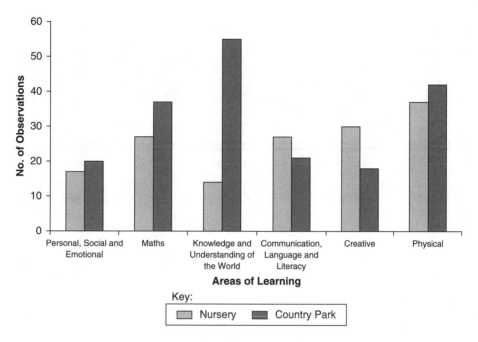

Figure 4.1   Observations of areas of learning

 Case Study   Archie's Den

Scenario 1
Children attending a reception class (aged four and five) had been visiting a woodland environment regularly and had discussed the possibility of making a den. On one visit, an adult suggested that a good place for the den would be deep in the woods next to a large pile of twigs and small branches that could easily be used for constructing a den. Thus, the den was constructed by children collecting twigs and passing them to the adult who placed them in position to organize a den in the conventional 'tent' shape. The children then developed a narrative around the theme of 'Eeyore's den' and returned to play in the den on subsequent visits. However, during a break from the visits, due to a school vacation, the den was dismantled and upon seeing this, some children became quite upset. The den was hastily constructed in the same manner and the children returned to their previous play patterns.

Scenario 2
The following year, the reception class contained a new group of children. Archie had been on several visits to the woodlands and back at school had discussed with practitioners his desire to make a den. They had encouraged him to plan out his idea and helped him to make a list of tools and equipment he might need to take with him in order to build the

(Continued)

(Continued)

den. Archie duly collected his equipment at school together in a rucksack and took it with him on his next visit to the park. It was the start of summer and the local weather had been dry for several weeks, so consequently the ground was very hard. Archie enlisted the help of a number of children and they went in search of a location for the den. Having found a location in the woods that they deemed suitable, the children (frequently directed by Archie) started to construct a den that involved placing sticks in the ground and joining them together with string. However, the ground was too hard and the sticks would not push in, nor could they be put in place with the use of a hammer. Archie asked the practitioner what to do and then tried to hammer the ground. The practitioner asked if he was trying to make the ground softer so that he could put the sticks in and then suggested he think what else might make the ground soft. Archie then picked up a water bottle and poured water into the hole for the sticks, thus enabling them to stay in place and complete the den.

 Reflection

These two different scenarios both involved the building of dens, although the first one was much more adult-directed and was constructed to look like a conventional den.

 Discussion Points

1. What are the different roles of the adult in the two scenarios?
2. How much assistance should adults give children in their play?
3. Does it matter if Archie's construction did not have the appearance of a den?

The OLP has evolved methods and tools for eliciting the perspectives of young children, aged three and four in educational settings, drawing on the Mosaic approach (Clark and Moss, 2001, 2005) and Learning Stories (Carr, 2001). This model demonstrates, firstly, that young children's views about their environment and experiences within that environment are crucial insights and, secondly, that these insights can help implement changes in practice. Evidence from the OLP also suggests that there are significant benefits when young children are given appropriate access to outdoor environments. This is because the outdoor environment affords the space, time and location for children's culture (Corsaro, 2005; Fjørtoft, 2004; Waller, 2006). Image-based data gathered for the project by the children revealed an interesting range of both 'social spaces' and 'individual landmarks' (Clark and Moss, 2001, 2005). Also, as the practitioners and children became more confident in the outdoor environment, increased opportunities for prolonged conversation and 'sustained shared thinking' (Siraj-Blatchford, 2004) with children occurred. Thus, the OLP found (like Clark, 2004b and Burke, 2005) that the process of using participatory tools increased our understanding of the children's lives (Waller, 2007a).

This ongoing project has helped to widen our understanding of the possibilities of participative approaches and the interrelationship between children's spaces, early years pedagogy and research. It has also started to demonstrate the significant benefits of outdoor learning for both adults and children. Overall, the main goals in the first four years of the project – to give the children an opportunity to interact regularly with natural surroundings and to develop their own independent learning paths and dispositions – were achieved. A further benefit has been the enhanced staff and student awareness of the potential of an outdoor learning environment, not least as a result of the construction of knowledge through shared reflection and collaborative enquiry.

SUMMARY

This chapter has presented an overview of current literature concerning young children's play and learning in outdoor spaces. Drawing on evidence from an ongoing project and the literature, it has also attempted to demonstrate the significant benefits of outdoor learning for both adults and children. In particular, concerns over the restricted opportunities for outdoor play due to risk anxiety and the 'culture of fear' (Furedi, 2002) have been considered and set against a much more positive approach which recognizes the significant benefits of outdoor play for health, well-being and risk-taking. It has been argued that all young children need regular physical activity outdoors to thrive and that their levels of activity impact directly on their physical and mental health. This involves giving children the opportunity to take acceptable risks in their outdoor play. Thus, the perspective taken in this chapter (Tovey, 2007; Waters and Begley, 2007) contends that creating risk-free environments is actually dangerous and inhibiting because children do not have the opportunity to develop and demonstrate competence and confidence in their play. Consequently, there are significant implications for the training of early years practitioners who also need to develop confidence in outdoor spaces in order to encourage children to benefit from the experience of taking positive risks in their play.

A number of recent UK policy initiatives in relation to outdoor play have been outlined and discussed alongside evidence emerging from current research. The significance of adult attitudes to outdoor play has been highlighted as one of the main factors in determining children's access (Waite et al., 2006b). Experiences of the Outdoor Learning Project (discussed above) suggest that early years practitioners should recognize the significant potential of outdoor learning and, in addition to developing outside play opportunities within their school grounds, they should also consider giving children regular opportunities to experience wild, natural environments. Children will of course benefit from the opportunity to play regularly in pleasant outside environments located within school grounds but the danger is that these spaces may become and adult-dominated in the same way as inside the classroom. In both these contexts, it appears that practitioners' attitudes and dispositions towards the shared construction of learning are key factors (Waller, 2007a). The outdoor environment is therefore viewed as a place which offers a range of distinctly unique opportunities and potential for play and learning (Tovey, 2007) rather than being purely a set of physical features.

QUESTIONS FOR REFLECTION AND DISCUSSION

1. How significant is the attitude of adults (parents and practitioners) towards giving children the opportunity for regular outdoor experience?
2. What is the difference between play and learning in outdoor spaces and indoors?
3. Why has Forest School become so popular in parts of the UK? Should all children be given the opportunity to experience Forest School?
4. What do children and adults gain from regular experience in 'wild' natural environments together?

Recommended reading

Casey, T. (2007) *Environments for Outdoor Play: A practical guide for making space for children.* London: Paul Chapman.

Education 3–13 (2007) Volume 35 Issue (4) Special Issue on Outdoor Play and Learning, November.

Lindon, J. (1999) *Too Safe for their own Good? Helping children learn about risk and life skills.* London: National Early Years Network.

Tovey, H. (2007) *Playing Outdoors.* Maidenhead: Open University Press.

Recommended websites

Taking Learning Outdoors: www.LTScotland.org.uk/takinglearningoutdoors/index.asp;
Education Outside the Classroom: http: publications.teachernet.gov.uk/

5 INTERNATIONAL PERSPECTIVES

Tim Waller

Chapter objectives

- To discuss findings from recent international comparisons of early childhood education and care.
- To provide an overview of issues around early years policy and provision in OECD countries.
- To consider diverse curricula and notions of 'quality'.
- To discuss two internationally renowned approaches to early years provision (Reggio Emilia in Italy and Te Whãriki from New Zealand).
- To introduce students to the critical insights that can be developed through comparison.

This chapter develops an overview of recent international comparisons of early years provision. Current issues and significant trends in early years care and education are identified and discussed. A number of significant similarities and trends are identified, however, it is recognized that wider evidence is needed to represent a global view of early childhood education and care (ECEC). It is not the intention to provide detailed statistics, although some are given, rather to enable students of early childhood to engage in critical reflection on the benefit of cross-national studies. The chapter concludes with a consideration of the notion that 'children's services' should be replaced by 'children's spaces' (Moss and Petrie, 2002).

Increasingly, the UK is taking note of early years care and education policy and practice in other countries – notably those within Europe and the OECD (Organization for Economic Cooperation and Development). This chapter explores the principles and practices adopted by a selected group of countries using the OECD thematic review as a framework. It aims to give students the opportunity to compare a variety of practices and consider possible outcomes and implications for children related to a holistic perspective. The chapter discusses both curricular and policy issues and encourages readers to critically analyse current policy and practice in early years care and education in the UK.

It is important to note, as Clark and Waller (2007) demonstrate, that for ECEC, children's services and many of the policies that impact on young children and their families, there are growing differences between England, Northern Ireland, Scotland and Wales as a result of devolved government. Therefore, it is misleading to consider the UK as a whole in these matters.

Recently, the range of information and knowledge about international aspects of early years care has increased due to the availability of online data and publications (see, for example, online early years journals such as *Contemporary Issues in Early Childhood* (www.wwwords.co.uk/ciec) and the *Journal of Early Childhood Research* (ecr.sagepub.com). However, it should be acknowledged that most of the online material is available in English and to a large extent concerns English-speaking countries and Europe, so it does not represent a world view and a complete picture of early childhood education and care (see Clark and Waller, 2007). As Moss et al. (2003) point out, one of the problems of limiting our attention to those countries with which we are similar is that we risk missing some of the most important reasons for doing cross-national study. There is a need for wider comparison through further data from a greater number of countries around the world.

CONTEXT

Contemporary international studies comparing ECEC include Anning et al. (2004) who discuss early years provision and research in three different contexts: Australia, New Zealand and the UK. Also, Boushel (2000) reviews childrearing across a number of different cultures and MacNaughton (2003) provides information on approaches to the early years curriculum from a range of countries across the world. Penn (2000) presents an overview of global early childhood services and Penn (1997) compares nursery education and policy in Italy, Spain and the UK. Penn (2005) includes a chapter with a comparative overview of early years practice in China, North America, Europe and transitional countries such as Russia. She also briefly discusses practice and children's lives in a number of Asian and African countries and draws attention to studies such as Tobin et al. (1989) who videoed life in nurseries in China, Japan and the USA. David (2006) also reports on studies undertaken in China (Vong, 2005). A number of other studies have drawn attention to the features of Nordic childhoods, such as Einarsdottir and Wagner (2006), while Cohen et al. (2004) compare England, Scotland and Sweden and Moss and Petrie (2002) dedicate a whole chapter to ECEC in Sweden.

In addition, a range of recent reports concerning ECEC have identified some similarities and trends that allow broad international comparison. They also identify a diverse range of views of children, concepts of childhood and traditions and policies for ECEC adopted by the countries involved.

Bennett (2001) reported the following demographic, economic and social trends relevant to early childhood:

- ageing populations, declining fertility rates, a greater proportion of children living in lone-parent families
- a sharp rise in dual-earner households, increased female employment rates
- paid and job-protected maternity and family leave, which are seen as essential for parental support and equity but the level of payment and take-up vary across countries
- a significant increase in the number of refugee children and families from areas of conflict around the world – policy and attitude vary across countries.

Also, Moss et al. (2003) reported for the DfES on evidence from 15 countries, which were grouped according to differences in welfare regime. These included four 'English-language' countries (Australia, New Zealand, the UK and the USA, four 'Nordic' countries (Denmark, Finland, Norway and Sweden) and seven 'Other European' countries (Belgium, France, Germany, Italy, the Netherlands, Portugal and Spain). The 15 countries were compared in terms of a number of demographic, employment, economic and policy dimensions, in relation to the welfare regime. Generally, there are strong similarities among the Nordic countries and among the English-language countries, with more variation among other European countries (paras 5.1–5.7). The key findings of this study, which generally concur with Bennett (2001), include:

- fertility rates are generally low (below replacement level except in the USA)
- the ageing of the European population
- English-language countries have high child poverty rates (defined as the proportion of children living in low-income households) and the Nordic countries have low rates
- the USA has the highest per capita national income, the highest child poverty and the lowest social expenditure and tax rates.

Moss et al. (2003: para. 5.5) also found that while women's employment is highest in the Nordic countries, part-time employment varies considerably. Employed women are most likely to work part-time in the Netherlands, Australia and the UK, and least likely to do so in Finland and southern European countries. There are considerable variations in leave entitlements between different countries within the three groupings, in terms of length and payment. Including paid maternity and parental leave entitlements, Nordic countries offer the most generous leave arrangements to employed parents. While taken overall (and including levels of payment), the English-language countries generally offer the lowest levels of paid leave.

The OECD provides a Thematic Review of Early Childhood Education and Care Policy [see www.oecd.org]. The first review, over the period 1998–2004, involved 20 countries, with expert teams evaluating each country's policy for children from birth to compulsory school age. A report covering the first 12 countries was published as *Starting Strong* (OECD, 2001). The second report, *Starting Strong II*, was published in 2006 and covers all 20 countries, also assessing progress in the original 12 countries. However, for any comparison involving the UK, one of the limitations of these reports is that much of the information given is either specific to England, or it is difficult to determine whether or not it applies to all four countries of the UK, as Clark and Waller (2007) point out. For example, the reference list cites no official sources other than those that apply to England. In Clark and Waller (2007), the differences between policy and practice in the various countries that make up the United Kingdom are clearly identified.

For Bennett (2001), *Starting Strong* shows that the countries involved have adopted diverse strategies to ECEC policy and provision. These strategies are deeply embedded in particular contexts, values and beliefs: 'Early childhood policy and provision are strongly linked to cultural and social beliefs about young children, the role of the families and government and the purposes of ECEC' (OECD, 2001: 38). For example, according to Anning and Edwards (1999: 13), the 'concepts of social responsibility and democratic decision making are high priorities in Danish cultural life'. In Denmark, there is a tradition of providing funding for the integrated care of children, managed by local communities. Ofsted (2003) compared the education of six-year-olds in England, Denmark and Finland. They found that the curriculum is more centralized and pre-scribed in England and that more importance is attached in Denmark and Finland to the way children develop as people. More is expected of English six-year-olds in terms of achievement in literacy and numeracy. In England, children were also grouped according to 'ability'. These factors and differences relate to cultural values and the way each country views children.

POLICY AND PROVISION

Bennett (2003) argues that ECEC is increasingly viewed as a key component of national policy and that due to changes in economic conditions and child-rearing patterns, most countries were prepared to invest in ECEC to facilitate employment and to promote children's cognitive, social and emotional development and life chances. The OECD (2001) report identifies the main focus of policy developments as:

- expanding provision to universal access
- raising the quality of provision
- promoting the coherence and coordination of policy and services
- exploring strategies to ensure adequate investment in the system
- improving training and working conditions
- developing pedagogical frameworks for young children
- engaging parents, families and communities.

Within the OECD countries, Bennett (2003) identified the following similarities and trends:

- most countries provide nursery education/kindergarten from three years
- there is a considerable variation in provision for 0–3
- there is a persistent division between education and care.

Curtis and O'Hagan (2003: 201) point out that in Europe there is a general agreement on the division between policy and provision for children aged 0–3 and 3 to school age. However, the responsibility for the provision and the age of starting school varies (see Table 5.1). Curtis and O'Hagan also argue that Europe is 'united' in making inadequate provision for children from birth to three (e.g. poor training, poor salary levels, poor career structure, etc.), with the exception of Finland and Sweden. In the UK generally, three key problems with provision for children under three exist: the variable quality of provision; the high cost of childcare; the lack of provision in some areas (see Clark and Waller, 2007). As Curtis and O'Hagan (2003) point out, legal entitlement to a place in childcare provision for children under three exists only in Sweden and Finland – in

Sweden from 18 months, and in Finland from birth. Both countries have excellent training provision for early childhood workers. Bertram and Pascal (2002) reported that few countries in the INCA survey had national curriculum guidelines for children under the age of three years. However, Bertram and Pascal argued that there was evidence of a general agreement that emphasis on individual children's developing interests and needs, dispositions and social and emotional well-being should be the focus of the curriculum for children under three years.

Most European countries have both private and state provision for 0–3 and 3–5-year-olds. Curtis and O'Hagan argue that this diversity sometimes leads to a lack of coordination in services provided. Across the UK, for example, despite the very welcome adoption of the National Childcare Strategy in 1998, Moss and Petrie (2002: 172) suggest that policy and provision for young children has been characterized by a 'contract model' which has led to short-term funding requiring competitive bidding. The effect of this policy is to ensure central control through a standard approach (Gewirtz, 2000). Moss and Petrie discuss data from the Daycare Trust (2001), estimating that there were 45 different sources of funding for 'childcare services' in the UK. Bennett (2003) also stressed the importance of not leaving early childhood provision at the mercy of the market and Ball and Vincent (2005) demonstrate the difficulties and divisions caused by this policy in England. Also, Scrivens (2002) distinguishes a tension between market-driven policies and a new culture of professional inquiry; an inclusive view of education and care and a tighter outcomes-focused view of policy and practice.

Penn (1999) and Bennett (2003) identify the major policy challenges as: (i) the need to ensure sufficient public funding and adequate coordination of the agencies involved, and (ii) the need to improve the supply of services for children under three to meet the demand and to improve the recruitment, training and remuneration of early years professionals (particularly for children under three).

Bennett (2001) and Penn (2007) acknowledged a range of common problems for the ECEC of children under three:

- local inequalities
- cash and funding
- fragmented and incoherent services
- responding to ethnic diversity.

OECD (2006) also found that access to ECEC for this age group is limited in most countries but that there is considerable variability of provision. In several countries, a majority of under-threes are in unregulated family daycare for at least part of the day. Access for under-threes is highest in Denmark and Sweden. Under-threes have a legal right to attend free school-based ECEC in Belgium.

CURRICULUM

Bennett (2003) shows that most OECD countries provide a curriculum framework for young children aged 3–6, but the frameworks differ greatly in terms of length, detail,

Table 5.1 Aspects of early years curricula across the study countries

Country	Organizing body	Ages	Types of curricula
Nordic Countries			
Denmark	Municipal	0–6	No formal curriculum
Finland	National	0–6	All providers' framework curriculum
Norway	National	0–6	All providers' framework curriculum – children's culture, activities worked out by environment and committee of parents/staff
Sweden	National	0–6	Publicly provided framework curriculum with democracy, citizenship, provision, local interpretation, environment, creativity (over 90 per cent of total). Welfare and education linked
English-speaking countries			
Australia	Territory	4–7	Public, private and expert-driven (variation from territory to territory)
New Zealand	National	0–5	All licensed providers; guidelines; local, bicultural, bilingual not compulsory, i.e. in receipt of different public funds, interpretation, broad, inclusive of principles and goals
UK (England)	National	3–6	Settings in receipt of expert, outcome-driven equal opportunities and government funding, respect for diversity to provide early education
US	State	4–7	Variation from state range – from expert-driven, conflict between state to state to local interpretation curriculum and some national programmes
Other countries			
Belgium	Umbrella	3–6	All providers' expert-driven programme; Flanders and Walloon – each community has own programme
France	National	3–6	Public provision and expert-driven through 'livret scolaire'
Germany	Land	3–6	Public and voluntary basic principles only; local interpretation
Italy	Regional	3–6	Public provision; guidelines; 'oriamenti' citizenship; creativity only at national level
Netherlands	Municipal	4–6	Programme even; kindergarten not school, some private
Portugal	National	3–6	All *jardins d'infancia*; guidelines, not a programme; many Ministry of Education pedagogical models

(Continued)

Table 5.1   (Continued)

Country	Organizing body	Ages	Types of curricula
Spain	National	0–6	All providers' broad general framework; allowance made for initiatives at language and culture – regional, local and e.g. Catalan. Pedagogical setting level principles for each curricular block

Source: Adapted from Moss et al., 2003: 8

prescription and pedagogical practice. Bertram and Pascal (2002) and Moss et al. (2003) also identify wide variations in how prescriptive the curricula are. Moss et al. found that leeway for local interpretation is common in the Nordic countries, and central specification strongest in England and France (paras 3.5–3.8). All curricula include the general goals of personal development, language and communication. Bertram and Pascal (2002) found that there was some variation in how the ECEC curriculum for children over three was defined: most countries used areas of learning, few used activities, and no country used disciplines or subjects. Many countries emphasized cultural traditions and aimed to enhance social cohesiveness through the ECEC curriculum. Only three countries emphasized early literacy and numeracy within the ECEC curriculum. Moss et al. (2003) also found wide variation in terms of detail and benchmarking on specific subjects, skills and competences (paras 3.5–3.8). They argued that each country in their report attempted to link curricula for early childhood services with entry to school in different ways. Only Sweden has a curriculum for out-of-school provision, though Finland, Spain, Sweden and France are developing curricula in this area (para. 3.12) (see Table 5.1).

The Qualifications and Curriculum Authority (QCA) in England commissioned an international review of the early years curriculum in 20 countries (Bertram and Pascal, 2002). The countries involved were Australia, Canada, France, Germany, Hong Kong, Hungary, Ireland, Italy, Japan, Korea, the Netherlands, New Zealand, Singapore, Spain, Sweden, Switzerland, England, Northern Ireland, Wales and the USA. Bertram and Pascal (2002: 7) identified the following five key areas of early childhood education and care as central to the debate:

1. The early years curriculum, viewed in its widest sense.
2. The issue of pedagogy (including staffing levels and the qualifications of staff).
3. The continuity of a child's experiences (within the setting, before arriving and after leaving the setting).
4. Definitions and measures of quality in early childhood settings.
5. Questions and key issues in the future development of early childhood education.

In their study, Bertram and Pascal (2002: 8) argued that there was 'almost universal promotion of an active, play-based pedagogy within the participating countries, where self-management and independence were encouraged. Delegates generally agreed that the role of the adult was to support, scaffold and facilitate rather than to overly direct. Some countries, such as Sweden, specifically discouraged a formal approach'.

Bennett (2004) and OECD (2006), however, identified two different approaches to the curriculum for ECEC, for children over three years. First, the 'social pedagogy' approach adopted by the Nordic countries (Denmark, Finland, Iceland, Norway and Sweden) and Central Europe – according to Bennett, the principle of this approach is a focus on the whole child involving a play-based, active and experiential pedagogy with an emphasis on the outdoors. A strong intergenerational and community outreach ethos is fostered. There is a short core curriculum to guide early education practice and local interpretation is encouraged. There is little systematic monitoring of child outcomes or measures, as this is the centre's responsibility. As Einarsdottir and Wagner (2006, cited in Clark and Waller, 2007: 7) stress, Nordic people generally view childhood as important in its own right, not simply as a platform from which to become an adult. Furthermore, they begin formal schooling later than children in many other parts of the world, so Nordic children have both the time and freedom during their early childhood years to play and explore the world around them, unencumbered by excessive supervision and control by adults.

Second, the 'infant school' approach adopted by Australia, Belgium, France, Ireland, Korea, Mexico, the Netherlands, England (reception classes) and the USA – the focus of this approach is on 'readiness for school'. For Bennett, this approach is characterized by a restrained, teacher-directed, play-based pedagogy where attention is given to achieving curricular aims and to measuring individual performance. There is central specification of a detailed curriculum and parental and community involvement is underplayed except in 'at risk' situations. A disturbing trend noted by Einarsdottir and Wagner (2006) was that more formal and academic curricula are beginning to spread from other countries into the Nordic countries, leading to an emphasis where school readiness, teacher-directed learning and testing become the norm (see also Cohen et al., 2004 for a comparison of developments in early education and care in England, Scotland and Sweden).

Despite the recent, welcome increased attention given to the ECEC of young children throughout many of the wealthier countries of the world, Bertram and Pascal (2002), Bennett (2003) and Moss et al. (2003) identify a number of barriers to development. Continuity in children's early experiences from home to setting and between settings is seen as a key to effective ECEC. The separation of education and care and early years and primary education, with different zones of ministerial responsibility, separate budgets and professional cultures is one of the most significant barriers (see also David, 2006). Further aspects of ECEC which need urgent attention are the status, training and career progression of staff and the gendered workforce.

The OECD (2001) report signposted the way forward with the following 'Eight Key Policy Elements for Early Childhood Education and Care':

- a systemic and integrated approach to policy development and implementation
- a strong and equal partnership with the education system
- universal access and SEN
- substantial public investment

- a participatory approach to quality improvement and assurance
- appropriate training and working conditions
- systematic attention to data monitoring and collection
- a stable framework and long-term agenda for research and evaluation.

However, as Penn (2005) argues, while the OECD report provides useful comparative statistics and makes general recommendations, discussion is focused at the level of policy rather than practice. She makes the point that as with the EU, the OECD:

> argues that equality of access and quality of practice are important goals for services, but that they can only be achieved by adequate public funding and by a good infrastructure of planning, evaluation and training. By these criteria the USA performs very poorly, almost bottom of the class. Nordic countries do very well. It is ironic that the US model, which stresses individual improvement at programme level, is so enthusiastically adopted by the World Bank and other international donors. (Penn, 2005: 181)

Starting Strong II (OECD, 2006: 11) argued that 'these eight elements were intended to be broad and inclusive so that they can be considered in the light of diverse country contexts and circumstances, values, and beliefs. They should form a part of a wider multi-stakeholder effort to reduce child poverty, promote gender equity, improve education systems, value diversity, and increase the quality of life for parents and children'. The following ten recommendations for 'consideration by government policy makers and ECEC stakeholders' were made:

1. To attend to the social context of early childhood development (by organizing services to support parents in child rearing, provide opportunity for women to work, and help include low income and immigrant families in the community and society).
2. To place well-being, early development and learning at the core of ECEC work, while respecting the child's agency and natural learning strategies.
3. To create the governance structures necessary for system accountability and quality assurance.
4. To develop with the stakeholders broad guidelines and curricular standards for all ECEC services.
5. To base public funding estimates on achieving quality pedagogical goals.
6. To reduce child poverty and exclusion through upstream fiscal, social and labour policies, and to increase resources within universal programmes for children with diverse learning rights.
7. To encourage family and community involvement in early childhood services.
8. To improve the working conditions and professional education of ECEC staff.
9. To provide autonomy, funding and support to early childhood services.
10. To aspire to ECEC systems that support broad learning, participation and democracy. (OECD, 2006: 16–17).

QUALITY

While many countries have recently focused on expanding provision for young children, there has been at the same time a significant international trend to define and measure the effectiveness and 'quality' of that provision. The EU, for example, developed 'A Framework for Quality for Early Childhood Services' (see Penn, 1999) stating that:

> Equal access to good quality early years services is a goal of the European Union. Good quality services are a necessary part of the economic and social infrastructure. Equal access to these services is essential for equality of opportunity between men and women; for the well-being of children, families and communities; and for productive economies. It is a goal to be espoused at all levels — local, regional, national and European — and a goal for which all of these levels can and should work together. (European Commission Network on Childcare and Other Measures to Reconcile Employment and Family Responsibilities, 1996)

First, it is important to recognize that the need for definitions of quality come from a context of greater public accountability and expectations that services will provide 'value for money' (Elfer and Wedge, 1996) and the marketization of public services (Hill, 2003). Moss and Petrie (2002: 69) also discuss how the concept of 'quality' has been incorporated into ECEC from the commercial world. Second, as (Pascal and Bertram, 1994: 3) point out, 'quality is value laden, subjective and dynamic'. 'Quality' is not universal but is a relative concept, depending on cultural values and beliefs about the nature of children and childhood. Moss and Petrie recognize that in the field of early childhood, 'quality' is increasingly discussed as a relative term with the possibility of multiple understandings, and Raban et al. (2003) argue that acknowledging the complexity of measuring quality is actually desirable. (For a review of the debate about 'universal' or 'culturally specific' definitions of quality, see Raban et al., 2003 and Dahlberg et al., 2007 for a more detailed discussion of quality.)

As Penn (1999) points out, the notion of quality is meaningless unless there is clarity about values and beliefs that underpin a service. Elfer and Wedge (1996: 66) argue that 'quality is a misleading concept if it encourages the idea that we are all agreed on what we want for children before we have gone through a process to ensure that'. The difficulty is as Pence (1992) put it: who defines what is to be measured? Katz (1992) recognized three dimensions of quality: indicators, stakeholders, beneficiaries, and four perspectives: top-down, outside-inside, inside-out and bottom-up. Pascal and Bertram (1994) developed 10 dimensions of quality as part of their Effective Early Learning (EEL) project.

While there is recognition that a range of different interest groups such as children, parents, practitioners and stakeholders may all have different views of what quality means in terms of early childhood provision, there is an argument for developing common indicators of quality (Raban et al., 2003). Curtis and O'Hagan (2003: 169) discuss the guidelines for 'quality' early years provision that were developed by two international organizations: OMEP (the World Organization for Early Childhood Education) and ACEI (American Childhood Education International) in 1999 (see www.ecec21. org). These organizations agreed that effective early years provision involves 'a comprehensive network of services that provide:

- environment and physical space settings for children
- curriculum content and pedagogy
- early childhood educators and caregivers
- partnership with families and communities

- services for young children with special needs
- accountability, supervision and management of programmes for young children.

Within each area, special attention must be directed towards:

- services with equal attention to all children
- links between programmes and services
- recognition of the value of those who care for and teach young children including appropriate working conditions and remuneration
- intergenerational approaches whenever feasible
- empowerment of communities, families and children
- a mechanism for adequate and uninterrupted funding
- cost analysis, monitoring and evaluation of programme quality' (Curtis and O'Hagan, 2003: 169–70).

Different ways of describing quality are defined as 'quality frameworks', such as the Early Childhood Environment Rating Scale (ECERS) (Harms et al., 1998). This framework has been used in the USA and the UK to evaluate the day-to-day functioning within settings (e.g. social interaction, children's activities and physical facilities). These aspects are rated on a seven-point scale which is used as a diagnostic and longer-term monitoring tool. However, ECERS are generally used to provide a staff perspective and not that of children or parents. ECERS have also been used in research on early childhood (for example, Phillips et al., 1987; Sylva and Siraj-Blatchford, 2001). In particular, ECERS have provided data for the Effective Provision of Pre-school Education (EPPE) project funded by the UK Department for Education and Skills on the developmental progress of more than 2800 pre-school children in England (see www.ioe.ac.uk/cdl/eppe/).

'Quality' is a problematic concept and there is a real danger of focusing on a framework and on easily measurable standards such as space/size and not on qualitative aspects such as relationships and dispositions and the meanings constructed by those who use the setting. As Dahlberg et al. (2007) and Moss (2001d: 130) argue, 'quality is not neutral, it is socially constructed'. The concept of quality has created its own discourse (Centres of Excellence, etc.) and evaluating the effectiveness of early years provision through predetermined, standardized criteria, according to Moss (2001d: 131), leads to 'a pedagogy of uniformity and normalisation … and a definitive conclusion'. Dahlberg et al. (2007) and Moss (2001d) compare the 'discourse of quality' with an alternative 'discourse of meaning making' which 'recognises the negotiated and provisional nature of understanding and assessment' (Moss, 2001d: 132). The approach of the 'discourse of meaning making' therefore allows for judgements about the effectiveness of early years settings to be constructed, debated and disputed within a particular context based on data meaningful to the setting (for example, the use of pedagogical documentation in Reggio Emilia).

Starting Strong: Curricula and Pedagogies in Early Childhood Education and Care (OECD, 2004) discussed the following five curricula:

- *Experiential Education* – Effective learning through well-being and involvement (from Flanders and the Netherlands).
- *The High Scope Curriculum* – Active learning through key experiences (from the USA).

- *The Reggio Emilia Approach* – Truly listening to young children (from Italy).
- *Te Whāriki* – A woven mat for all to stand on (from New Zealand).
- *The Swedish Curriculum* – Goals for a modern pre-school system (from Sweden).

As Clark and Waller (2007: 172) note, this document on curricula and pedagogies raises several important issues concerning the role of play in young children's learning, and the relationship between play and learning and curriculum and pedagogy. It also questions whether there is currently a lack of, and need to develop, evaluations and assessments of curricular programmes for young children. In particular, concern is expressed with regard to assessment in that if only small details are evaluated, the whole idea of fostering young children's thinking and creativity may be lost.

Two of the above examples of internationally renowned early years provision are now discussed to encourage reflection and debate on international aspects of ECEC. For further details of the Reggio Emilia approach and Te Whāriki, see *Five Curriculum Outlines* (OECD, 2004).

TE WHĀRIKI

Te Whāriki, the early childhood curriculum framework developed in New Zealand in 1996, has received a great deal of worldwide interest due to its innovative holistic and emergent approach to the curriculum. Whāriki (or mat) is used as a metaphor to signify the weaving together of the principles and strands, as well as the diverse peoples, philosophies and services that participate in early education (Anning et al., 2004: 12). The view of the child is as 'a competent learner and communicator' and the approach fosters a holistic approach to curriculum planning and learning: 'The curriculum is founded on the following aspirations for children: to grow up as competent and confident learners and communicators, healthy in mind, body and spirit, secure in their sense of belonging and in the knowledge that they make a valued contribution to society' (MoE, 1996a: 9).

According to Podmore (2004: 152), widespread consultation culminated in an innovative bicultural framework, with the document partly written in Maori. Te Whāriki received strong support from practitioners. The framework identifies learning outcomes for children as: working theories about the people, places and things in learners' lives and as learning dispositions (MoE, 1996a). Te Whāriki invites practitioners to weave their own curriculum drawing on the framework of Principles, Strands and Goals. The focus is also on children's perspectives to define and evaluate (quality) practices in early childhood centres.

Te Whāriki has four central principles:

1. Empowerment
2. Holistic development
3. Family and community
4. Relationships

and five strands:

1. Well-being
2. Belonging
3. Contribution
4. Communication
5. Exploration.

The goals within each strand highlight ways in which practitioners support children, rather than skills or content, promoting a project-based approach drawing from the children's interests. Thus, the content emerges from children's interests which are tracked through the four principles. The guidelines apply to all children in all settings, including those with special educational needs who may be given an Individual Development Plan (IDP).

Local flexibility in content is seen as important to meet the needs of culturally diverse groups, including the Maori, within New Zealand. However, Anning et al. (2004: 12) argue that the strong free-play tradition within ECEC in New Zealand has meant that practice has been slow to move away from individual self-selection of activities to collaborative learning through projects. Also, as with many other ECEC programmes across the world, despite the principles of Te Whãriki, Anning et al. identify a problem with top-down pressure from the government for more literacy and numeracy content within the curriculum. Cullen (1996) also argues that the flexibility of Te Whãriki can lead to early childhood programmes of variable quality.

Anning et al. (2004: 11) describe early childhood services in New Zealand as 'primarily community based' with little shared history and few links between early childhood and primary education. However, since 2002, the New Zealand government has developed a 10-year strategic plan for early childhood (*Pathways to the Future: Nga Huarahi Aratiki* – MoE, 2002), with the aim to increase participation and quality of ECEC services and to promote collaborative relationships.

REGGIO EMILIA

Reggio Emilia has been internationally renowned for its early childhood programmes for over 40 years. Reggio Emilia is a city in the Emilia Romagna region of northern Italy with approximately 150,000 inhabitants. The region is one of the wealthiest parts of Europe. Since 1963, the municipality of Reggio Emilia has developed its own services for children from birth to six years of age, which have grown to include a network of 33 centres for young children. These are organized into *Asili Nido* (for children from three months to three years) and *Scuole del Infanzia* (3–6 years). The early childhood centres were established in close liaison with parents and the local community and children's rights are seen as paramount.

Loris Malaguzzi (1920–94) was the first head of municipal early childhood centres and significant influence on development of the Reggio approach. He advocated 'a pedagogy of relationships'. He held a positive and participatory view of early education and promoted a generous, optimistic view of human nature. For Moss (2001d), the significance of this positive approach is that it rejects the construction of the 'child at risk' or 'in need', not only because it produces a 'poor child', but also because it has chosen to move from the child as a subject of needs to a subject of rights.

Curtis and O'Hagan (2003: 217) summarize six principles of the Reggio Emilia approach as follows:

1. The study of child development as central to practice.
2. The importance of the teacher–child relationship.
3. The need for children's experiences to be taken into account when building the curriculum.
4. The importance of a rich environment in developing children's learning.
5. The importance of ongoing professional development for teachers.
6. The importance of the role of parents in the life of the school.

The main feature of the Reggio approach is that it advocates communication between adults and children and promotes collegiality and ethos of co-participation with families in the educational project (Nutbrown and Abbott, 2001: 1). Malaguzzi sees children as autonomously capable of making meaning from experience: 'Children's self-learning and co-learning are supported by interactive experiences constructed with the help of adults, who determine the selection and organisation of processes and strategies that are part of and coherent with the goals of early childhood education' (Malaguzzi, 1993: 9). As Rinaldi and Moss (2004: 2) point out, in this approach, 'learning is a process of constantly constructing, testing and reconstructing theories. Learning is a subject for constant research and must be made visible'. Knowledge is the product of a process of construction, involving interpretation and meaning making. It is co-constructed. Moss (2001d: 128) cites Rinaldi (a former pedagogical director of early years centres in Reggio): 'what children learn emerges from the process of self and social construction'. For Rinaldi, 'learning is the subjective process of constructing reality with others'. The practitioner is therefore not a transmitter of knowledge and culture but a facilitator in children's co-construction of their own knowledge and culture. The task of the practitioner is to offer a context in which the child can themselves explore and go deeper into a problem (Moss, 2001d: 129). Not only is the child viewed as a strong, powerful and competent learner, the child also has the right to an environment that is integral to the learning experience. Great value is placed on the whole environment as a motivating force:

> It is indisputable that schools should have the right to their own environment, their architecture, their own conceptualization and utilization of spaces, forms and functions. We place enormous value on the role of the environment as a motivating and animating force in creating spaces for relations, options and emotional and cognitive situations that produce a sense of well being and security. (Malaguzzi, 1996: 40)

As well as its commitment to developing 'deep, deep insight of children by listening to them', Nutbrown and Abbott (2001: 4) identify two further significant features of the Reggio approach. These are *time* (to discuss children and their projects) and *cooperative working* (teachers always work in pairs, each pair being responsible in the pre-schools for a group of children).

The Reggio approach is also characterized by a variety of pedagogical tools for developing early years practice in a rigorous, open and dynamic way – for example, pedagogical documentation, where learning processes are documented in various ways so that they can be shared, discussed, reflected upon and interpreted. Hoyuelos (2004: 7) suggests that this documentation represents an extraordinary tool for dialogue, exchange and sharing. It supports the ideological concept of the transparent school. For Vecchi (1993: 96), the procedure of documentation is a 'democratic possibility to inform the public of the contents of the school' and Rinaldi and Moss (2004: 3) argue that it is 'a unique source of information – precious for teachers, children, the family and anyone who wants to get closer to the strategies in children's ways of thinking'. For a more detailed discussion of pedagogical documentation, see Dahlberg et al. (2007).

Reggio Emilia has become one of the best-known early education systems in the world. Every year, many early years specialists visit Reggio to study the approach and it has become so popular that since 1981 a Reggio exhibition – 'The Hundred Languages of Children' – has toured the world, and there are 'Reggio networks' in 13 countries around the world (see Sightlines for details of the UK network). Reggio has been particularly influential in the USA and Sweden (see Dahlberg et al., 1999). Johnson (1999), however, argues that the widespread acclaim of Reggio Emilia has led to a 'cargo cultism' in early childhood education. He suggests that the Reggio Emilia approach has been 'Disneyfied' and colonized by the US-dominated institutions and knowledge structures which have promoted it.

While there are clearly difficulties in attempting to replicate a system that developed in a particular (Italian) context and culture, the real significance of Reggio is that following visits to the region or the exhibition, many early years practitioners have been encouraged to critically reflect on and question their own practice (Moss, 2001b). As Curtis and O'Hagan (2003: 218) point out, 'adopting the approach means accepting and understanding the underlying principles and philosophy in the light of one's own culture'. Reggio has a lasting influence because, as Rinaldi and Moss (2004: 2) argue, 'Reggio is not a stable model producing predetermined and predictable outcomes, but a place where questions and uncertainty, change and innovation are welcome'. Moss (2001b: 125) reminds us that 'Reggio asks and expects us to ask many critical questions about ECEC. Reggio is so important because it reminds us that it is possible to think differently'. For Nutbrown and Abbott (2001), 'that capacity to provoke is perhaps one of the greatest and lasting legacies of any personal encounter with the Reggio Emilia experience'. As Gardner (2004: 3) asserts, early childhood centres in Reggio 'stand as a shining testament to human possibilities'.

SUMMARY

This chapter has discussed a range of findings from recent international studies of early childhood education and care. A number of significant trends have been identified. Over the last 20 years or so, demographic, political and economic changes have led to significant interest and investment in ECEC. Bertram and Pascal (2002) argue that this 'new ECEC policy

(Continued)

(Continued)

dynamic' is starting to make an impact throughout the world, which in some countries is 'revolutionary and unprecedented'. At the same time, there is a tension between market-driven policies and a new culture of professional inquiry (Penn, 2007). This is evident in approaches to the evaluation of ECEC and identification and measurement of 'quality'. The chapter discusses 'quality' as a problematic and culturally relative concept.

Two examples of internationally renowned approaches to early years provision (Reggio Emilia in Italy and Te Whāriki from New Zealand) are briefly summarized to introduce students to the critical insights that can be developed through comparison. As Bertram and Pascal (2002) and Moss et al. (2003) point out, there are several benefits to cross-national studies. First, by comparing provision in our own region or country with another, we may question previously taken for granted traditional assumptions and practices. This process helps to make domestic practice visible and reveals the particular understandings of childhood that influence policy. It promotes critical thinking. For example, as Moss et al. (2003) point out, why is it that children in the UK start school earlier than almost everywhere else in Europe, and with what consequences? Why is education organized differently in different parts of the UK? There are, of course, limitations to the use of cross-national data and evidence. As Bertram and Pascal (2002) argue, policy and practice in ECEC is deeply located in national understandings of the place of family and childhood in society. The local context therefore needs to be taken into account and cross-national work needs to be interpreted. Given cultural norms, what is appropriate for one nation may be totally unsuitable for another. Differences in language and meaning can be problematic. For example, in the UK, the term pre-school is taken to mean provision for children under five years, but in Sweden, it is often used to describe the year before the start of formal schooling at seven years of age. The use of international statistics can also be problematic and is open to interpretation (Bennett, 2003; Clark and Waller, 2007; Cohen et al., 2004).

Moss (2001b) makes several important points regarding provision for young children. He argues that in a consideration of provision, we should seek the views of the child. He argues that there are two possible constructions of early childhood institutions: as a place for the efficient production of predetermined outcomes, or as 'children's spaces' which provide opportunities for children and adults, the consequences of which may be unknown. The implication is that the term 'education and care' is too restricting – care is not just about arrangements for working parents. He also suggests that a broader view of childhood is needed to take into account the relationships between the early childhood system and the education system. Further, Moss and Petrie (2002: 40) develop the model of seeking the views of children. They see children 'as young citizens and equal stakeholders with adults'. Moss and Petrie challenge early years practitioners and policy makers to reconceive provision for young children. They argue that as children have equal status and ownership of their environment, the notion of 'children's services' should be replaced by 'children's spaces'. Interestingly, as Clark and Waller (2007: 185) note, Moss and Petrie's concept of children's spaces concurs with the OECD policy observations from 2006: 'The early childhood centre becomes a space where the intrinsic value of each person is recognized, where democratic participation is promoted, as well as respect for our shared environment' (OECD, 2006: 18).

Dahlberg and Moss (2005) continue the debate by providing a strong argument for 'a narrative of possibilities' where early years practitioners are encouraged to be open to new thought and possibilities for ECEC (as in Reggio) and not tied down by 'a narrative of outcomes' which restricts early years practice to that which is measurable and predetermined.

QUESTIONS FOR REFLECTION AND DISCUSSION

1. What is the benefit of cross-national study?
2. What critical insights have you gained about ECEC provision in the UK as a result?
3. Do you have to visit a country to gain an understanding of ECEC in that country?
4. Why is measuring the 'quality' of ECEC always subjective?
5. What are the implications of early years practice in Reggio and New Zealand for early years settings in the UK?

Recommended reading

Clark, M. M. and Waller, T. (eds) (2007) *Early Childhood Education and Care: Policy and Practice*. London: Sage.

Dahlberg, G., Moss, P. and Pence, A. (2007) *Beyond Quality in Early Childhood Education and Care: Postmodern Perspectives*, 2nd edition. Abingdon and New York: RoutledgeFalmer.

Einarsdottir, J. and Wagner, J. (eds) (2006) *Nordic Childhoods and Early Education*. Greenwich, CI: Information Age.

Moss, P. and Petrie, P. (2002) *From Children's Services to Children's Spaces*. Abingdon and New York: RoutledgeFalmer.

Recommended websites

OECD – Starting Strong: www.oecd.org/edu/earlychildhood; Childcare Canada: www.childcarein canada.org

SECTION 2

VALUES AND PRINCIPLES

6 CHILDREN'S RIGHTS TO PARTICIPATION

Gill Handley

Chapter objectives

- To discuss the difficulties of identifying what participation means in practice.
- To identify the conflicts between children's participation and protection rights.
- To consider the dilemmas and difficulties of judging children's competence in relation to participation.
- To introduce the dilemmas and conflicts in early years contexts.

This chapter begins by discussing the difficulties of defining children's rights. There is an analysis of the fundamental conflict between participation rights and protection rights, as advanced by the UNCRC (United Nations Convention on the Rights of the Child – United Nations, 1989), with specific reference to the lives of working children across the world, and the lives of young children involved in divorce proceedings in England. The role of competence in the exercise of children's participation rights and the problems of judging competence are discussed. A range of international participation initiatives is presented. Two case studies are included which address some of the complex issues involved in young children's active participation in decision making. Conclusions are drawn about the implications for early years work in relation to children's participation and how children's rights to participation might be advanced. Significant questions and suggested texts/websites for further study are given.

The main focus of this chapter will be on the participation rights of children and assessing how much legislation and practice uphold these rights, both in England and internationally. A major argument will be that the participation rights of children are among the most difficult and controversial children's rights to be implemented and upheld, and are the most likely to be inadequately addressed, because of the fundamental conflict between them and the competing rights to protection (Burr, 2004). It will be argued that the latter continue to take precedence as they fit with the predominant discourses of childhood, which see children as in need of guidance, protection and adult control, rather than as young citizens who are entitled to respect as agents in their own lives and able to actively participate (James and Prout, 1997). A major challenge for all those who work with children and young people is how to redress this balance.

WHAT ARE CHILDREN'S RIGHTS?

The language used in relation to children's rights, and rights in general, is confused and confusing. What is understood by the term 'rights' is not a given but reflects different and changing social and political ideologies and values (Roche, 2001). Take, for example, the current notions of individualistic human rights as defined in the European Convention on Human Rights (ECHRC, 1950) and the UNCRC (United Nations, 1989). These are rooted in Western philosophy and thought, rather than southern or eastern philosophies, as the latter tend to place greater emphasis on family and community responsibilities than on individual interests (Burr, 2002). The term 'rights' is also used to refer to both moral and legal rights, as well as notions of what ought to happen in everyday life (Eekelaar, 1992; Fortin, 2003; Freeman, 1983; Macormick, 1982). Although the notion of rights generally involves some idea of an entitlement to something, what the entitlement is to, and who is entitled, again vary and change with different historical, social and political contexts. For example, women in the UK were not seen as having a right to vote until the early twentieth century, and children were not seen as being a group of people eligible to have rights independently from adults until the latter part of the twentieth century; there is still debate as to whether or not children can be full holders of rights at all, if a precondition is seen as the capacity to be able to choose whether or not to exercise them (Fortin, 2003; Freeman, 1983).

There is also a continuing debate about the effectiveness of a rights-based focus per se, in empowering the disadvantaged and vulnerable, which includes children. It is argued that rights are abstract legal principles which cannot be exercised outside of human relationships and, as such, do not take into account the moral and caring relationships between people and the role that relationships have in empowerment (Blanchet-Cohen and Rainbow, 2006). It is further argued, by opponents of children's rights, that they are essentially 'ideological constructs of cultural imperialism serving the hegemonic agenda of the West … [and that] the language of rights is a cog in the machinery that restricts possibilities and draws actors into making certain choices' (Reynolds et al., 2006: 293). It can also be argued that a rights-based perspective is just another adult construction of childhood (Gabriel, 2004), which again neglects the child's own view and perspective on their lives, and further, that consultation with children may mean that children are open to being more observed and controlled by adults as the latter have greater knowledge of their interests and preferences (Clark et al., 2005). A further criticism of a rights-based perspective is that rights can be given a particular legal construction, which can be disempowering. As James et al. (2004: 201) point out, in discussing Dame Elizabeth Butler-Sloss's argument that 'the child [has] a right to a relationship with [his or her] father even if he [or she] did not want it': 'this particular construction of the concept of the child's right has the effect of transforming the child's right into a responsibility or even a duty to see his father, since such a conception of rights fails to endow the child with the equivalent right not to have such contact' (James et al., 2004: 201).

There is also the difficulty of defining what is meant by both childhood and its corollary, 'a child'. Examination of the understanding of the terms in different contexts has led to a social constructivist perspective of childhood which sees childhood itself as a social construct rather than as a biological given (Franklin, 2002; Jenks, 2004; Stainton

Rogers, 1992). What is seen as childhood, at what age it starts and at what age it ends, varies and changes (Aries, 1962; Fortin, 2003), and there may be different and competing constructions of childhood prevalent at the same time. For example, currently in England, children are seen either as innocent angels in need of protection or as 'villains' in need of control (Franklin, 2002; Goldson, 2001). Burr (2002) argues that street children in Vietnam are similarly seen as either victims or villains. Legislation also constructs childhood and 'the child' in different ways (James and James, 1999). For example, the age of criminal responsibility varies across European legislation from 8 in Scotland, 10 in England to 18 in Belgium. In English law, a child is sometimes seen as being a person under 16 and sometimes under 18. For example, a 16-year-old can work full time but cannot hold a tenancy. Critics of a 'social constructivist perspective' argue that it tends to see children and childhood as a 'series of adult constructions … forgetting real children' (Willan et al., 2004: 53) (see Chapter 5 for a more detailed discussion of childhood).

PROTECTION RIGHTS VERSUS PARTICIPATION RIGHTS

Notwithstanding these significant and important debates, over the last 30 years acceptance has grown, in social and political arenas, that children have their own individual rights separate from those of adults (Lansdown, 2001). Children are increasingly regarded as agents within their own lives. Rather than seeing children as passive recipients of adults' care and decision-making, children are increasingly being seen as competent to make a range of decisions about themselves (Alderson, 2005; James and James, 1999). It becomes increasingly important to acknowledge this competence when the damaging effect of adults' decisions in the past is recognized. For example, children suffered emotional trauma when adults decided that they should be separated from their parents by evacuation or when undergoing hospital treatment (Lansdown, 2001). Ideas of prescribed and incremental development, which medical and psychological theories have put forward, have been criticized for ignoring the complex and varied range of abilities children of similar ages may have, and for ignoring their individual capacities and competences (Alderson, 2005), and the different contexts in which they live (Walderkine, 2004). Kaltenborn (2001) found that, in relation to custody and residence disputes, even very young infants could be regarded as having enough emotional intelligence to be able to express reasonable opinions. This is not to say that the overall framework of children developing increasing abilities with age should be dismissed, or that children should be able to do whatever they choose, any more than adults can, but rather that a more complex pattern of competences and abilities should be acknowledged (see Chapter 7).

However, there has continued to be debate and controversy about the extent to which children's rights to protection from various forms of harm and exploitation should take precedence over their rights to self-determination, and, how far, and in what contexts, children can make decisions about their own lives. Child liberationists, such as Holt (1974) and Farson (1974), have argued that children of any age are in need of liberation from the domination and control of adults. This view has been challenged by those who consider that children need shielding from the responsibility and burden of making decisions (King, 1987). They see children as fundamentally vulnerable and dependent and, therefore, in need of protection from various forms of harm, exploitation and responsibility (James et al., 2004). The extremes of both positions can be challenged, but the fundamental differences in the images of childhood, and related perspectives on children's rights that they are then aligned with, do help in understanding the complexity of: 'how to identify children's rights, how to balance one set of rights against another, in the event of conflict between them, and how to mediate between children's rights and those of adults' (Fortin, 2003: 3).

These ongoing debates are reflected throughout legislation and practice in many spheres of children's lives such as health, planning, social work and education, within England, other UK countries and internationally. The next section will consider some examples of the complexities and conflicts in relation to the exercise of protection and participation rights of children in a number of different contexts.

THE UNITED NATIONS CONVENTION ON THE RIGHTS OF THE CHILD (UNCRC) 1989

The UNCRC was adopted by the United Nations in 1989. It was an attempt to improve the living conditions and experiences of children throughout the world. Its aims were to prevent the extreme suffering and exploitation of children, as well as to improve more everyday aspects of children's lives (Alderson, 2005). The 54 Articles of the Convention set out a wide range of rights, which, it argues, all children of the world should enjoy. These rights range from the right to life through to the right to play. Although not incorporated into the law of UK countries, the latter have ratified the UNCRC, as have all other countries in the world except Somalia and the USA. So, potentially, the UNCRC has a worldwide influence on the advancement of children's rights (Burr, 2004).

The UNCRC identifies three broad types of rights: protection rights, provision rights and participation rights (Alderson, 2005; Burr, 2004; Franklin, 2002). The participation rights include the right of children to participate in decisions affecting them (Article 12), the right to freedom of expression (Article 13), the right to freedom of thought, conscience and religion (Article 14) and the right for young disabled people to participate in their community (Article 23). Although the UNCRC raises the awareness of children's right to participate in various aspects of their lives, the effectiveness and practice of upholding these rights raise a number of ethical, process and practical issues which reflect the conflict between children's need for participation and protection, and the different ways childhood is constructed in different social and political contexts.

First, there is no clear definition of what participation means, and how it differs from consultation, involvement or citizenship (Willow et al., 2004). There have been various models and charts developed to help analyse the different extents to which children may be involved in decisions affecting them, and the processes which may be used (Crimmens and West, 2004; Hart, 1992). These range from Arnstein's (1969) original 'ladder of participation' which sees tokenism as the bottom rung and full control of decision-making process as the top rung, to less hierarchical, more circular models, such as that of Treseder (1997) which gives equal importance to the different degrees of participation, as each is seen to have relevance in different contexts. All tend to include practices which range from asking children to make a choice between a limited number of alternatives, to children identifying the problem and alternative solutions themselves (Crimmens and West, 2004). They can be seen to reflect, in various ways, the fundamental difference between children merely being asked for their views about something and children actually devising decision-making systems themselves (Alderson, 2005; Willow et al., 2004). The various processes involved can also be seen as reflecting the difference between seeing children as 'objects' of processes rather than as 'subjects' (Willow et al., 2004), and between seeing children as in need of protection rather than as being agents in their own lives. Although Treseder (1997) argues that all forms of participation can be empowering for young people, even when they have relatively little control and influence, provided the extent of their influence is clear and that adults and children work in partnership, where 'participants interact in ways that respect each other's dignity, with the intention of achieving a shared goal' (Blanchet-Cohen and Rainbow, 2006: 114). In reality, this may pose difficulties because the partnership working that effective children's participation requires is 'not something that comes naturally, as is often assumed … it calls for an attitude change that is difficult in an adult-led and increasingly result-based world' (Blanchet-Cohen and Rainbow, 2006: 125). The following example illustrates some of the complex issues and difficulties in effective participation and raises the question of how far children's participation in one-off events can be effective, if ongoing participation in decision making is not an everyday feature of child–adult relationships.

 Case Study

Blanchet-Cohen and Rainbow (2006) evaluated and analysed the experiences of adults and children, when 400 children, aged 10–12, were brought together from different countries, at the International Children's Conference on the Environment, in 2002. Although the evaluation is primarily concerned with effective participation, the experiences of participants were analysed in terms 'of the nature of the partnerships, rather than child participation [because the authors considered that] … partnership places the focus on the collective nature of change, which is inherent to meaningful child participation, for children are part of a society' (2006: 115).

The children identified the following challenges in working in partnership with adults: adults using acronyms and language that the children were not familiar with; adults not listening; adults not following things up; the frustration of financial constraints; the length of meetings not taking into account children's needs for breaks. Adults identified the following challenges: the additional workloads and time needed for consultation with the children; the need to constantly ensure the information was understandable to the children; 'finding the balance between the need to adjust the information to the developmental level of a child and still meaningfully involving children in the process' (2006: 121).

Discussion Points

The evaluation highlighted the need for children to be involved in the planning and wider context of decision-making processes so that they are more aware of the social, political, cultural and economic constraints to decision making. It also highlighted the need for both adults and children to develop skills and qualities essential for partnerships and participation, such as openness and good listening skills: adults could not be assumed to have these. It speculates that many of the difficulties in attempting participation as a one-off event such as this might be avoided if social systems were more child-friendly and encouraged participatory partnerships in everyday life.

Read the whole article: 'Partnership between children and adults? The experience of the International Children's Conference on the Environment' in *Childhood*, 2006, 13: 113–26.

Second, the exercise of participation rights under the UNCRC is not absolute. In relation to Article 12, it is dependent on the 'age and maturity of the child', and in relation to Article 14, it has to be consistent with the 'evolving capacities of the child' (United Nations, 1989). Thus, the level of competence of a child is one of the factors that have to be considered in relation to the exercise of his or her right to participation. How the level of competence is to be judged, and who is to judge it, is not clear, but, as later discussions suggest, in practice, it will be by various groups of adults, not children themselves.

Third, there is also evidence that the right to participation tends to be actively overruled when there is seen to be a competing right to protection, as understood under the UNCRC. The following is an example of children's right to protection being seen as taking precedence over their right to participation.

 Case Study

In relation to street children in Vietnam, aged between 6 and 16, Burr (2002 and 2004) found that the particular view of the rights to protection and education promoted by aid agencies, operating within the guidelines of the UNCRC, tended to conflict with what some children said they wanted, that is to work to earn money, and what they themselves defined as their needs. Some of the children identified the need to work as significant, as it enabled them to earn money, and thus not be forced to return to rural lives of poverty. By working from a young age, they were also able to give financial support to their families, who could not support them. Some aid agencies sought to protect the children from what was considered exploitation, by returning them to more adult-led environments, and by requiring them to receive formal day-time education. By doing so, the agencies failed to listen to the children, understand the contexts of their lives and give credence to the children's own decision to work and be part of the urban communities they saw as their families (Burr, 2002, 2004).

In Guatemala, similarly, the rights as set out under the UNCRC were found to have little relevance to the everyday lives of children working on the streets (Snodgrass-Godoy, 1999). Burr (2004) argues that the UNCRC rights are based on a Western view of childhood which sees childhood as idyllic. She argues that the assumption that southern and eastern children are seen as in need of rescuing by the more affluent Western countries fails to recognize the different needs of children in different social, political and economic contexts. Furthermore, where their needs, for example for income earned on the streets, conflict with the concept of rights to protection, education and family life as promoted by the UNCRC, the latter will predominate, even when children themselves express their own views to have the right to work. Ennew (1995, quoted in Snodgrass-Godoy, 1999: 437) points out that, in relation to Guatemalan street children, 'the UNCRC takes as its starting point western modern childhood, which has been globalised first through colonialism and then through the imperialism of aid'. This imperialism can affect both the effectiveness and the provision of services (UNESCO, 2006). Rather than the UNCRC upholding individual children's rights to participate in major decisions affecting them, these examples show that attempts to impose the UNCRC rights can negate children's participation rights. They also highlight some of the complexities of balancing competing rights for protection and participation in circumstances of extreme poverty. For example, it could be argued that the children do not have a real 'choice' when the alternatives are working or starvation. It could also be argued that respecting children's wish to work prolongs their exploitation and lack of real choice.

THE CHILDREN ACTS 1989 AND 2004

The UNCRC provided the context for the enactment of the Children Act 1989 in England, which saw a shift away from children being seen as passive recipients of adult care and control to them being seen as individuals to whom their parents had responsibilities. It recognized their right to be heard in relation to some significant decisions affecting them, by having their wishes and feelings taken into account (James and James, 1999).

However, it can be argued that the Children Act 1989 is limited in its support of children's participation rights, in terms of both its principles and its operation in practice (Fortin, 2003; Thomas, 2004). First, children's wishes and feelings are only likely to be considered once the courts become involved in decisions about their care (section 1 [3] [a]). Although there is some limited requirement on local authorities, outside of court proceedings, to consider children's wishes and feelings before making any decision affecting them (section 22), there is no general requirement for parents to 'have regard to a child's views when making any major decision affecting them' as there is in Scottish Law (Children [Scotland] Act 1996, section 6 [1]).

Second, although the child's welfare is paramount, welfare is seen in terms of protection and safeguarding, not in terms of rights or of promoting active participation (Lansdown, 2001). So, while a court has a duty under section 1 (3) (a) to 'have regard to ... the ascertainable wishes and feelings of the child concerned', the court only has to have regard to them, rather than actively consider or act upon them. In contact and residence decisions, they do not have to be considered at all if the parents agree on arrangements for the child (James et al., 2004; Monk, 2004), the assumption being that children's views are irrelevant if parents agree. Furthermore, any weight given to a child's wishes or feelings will depend on their age and understanding – in other words, their level of competence (Monk, 2004). Local authorities, similarly, under section 22, have a duty to ascertain a child's wishes and feelings but only in so far as it is 'reasonably practicable' to do so.

The Children Act 2004 is concerned primarily with the protection of children (Lumsden, this volume) and putting into place structures and procedures to help ensure that children are better safeguarded. Yet, despite this focus on improving the protection of children, section 58 of the Children Act 2004 failed to effectively 'ban smacking' for children in England and Wales. While it removed the defence of 'reasonable punishment' in cases where a parent, or those acting in loco parentis, were charged with assault occasioning actual bodily harm, inflicting grievous bodily harm, or causing cruelty to a child, the defence is still available, in effect, for those who smack or physically hurt their child in other ways, provided there are no visible injuries. In Scotland, section 51 of the Criminal Justice (Scotland) Act 2003 attempted to clarify the law, by allowing a defence of 'reasonable chastisement', while at the same time specifically prohibiting blows to the head, shaking and the use of an implement. This again, like the Children Act 2004, still allows smacking and other forms of physical punishment to be acceptable as they are seen as 'reasonable chastisement'. This is despite the views of children. In 2007, a review was undertaken to look at the effectiveness of section 58 in preventing the abuse of children. Children of the ages 4–16 were consulted and the report of their views (DCSF, 2007b: 15) concludes that 'overall, most children in this sample struggled to endorse smacking as an effective form of punishment'.

As well as continuing to uphold the rights of parents to smack their children, the Children Act 2004 does not appear to advance the participation rights of children, in so far as there continue to be limitations on the extent to which children's 'wishes and feelings' may influence decision making. For example, although the widening of the range of circumstances in which local authorities in England must include the wishes and feelings of children (section 53), could be seen as a positive step forward in relation to children's participation rights, any weight given to them will again depend on the child's age and understanding or competence (section 53 [1] [b] and [3] [b]). It could also be argued that the establishment of a Children's Commissioner in England (section 1), who has 'the function of promoting awareness of the views and interests of children' (section 2 [2]), can be seen as a step forward in the advancement of children's rights to participation. But, as Goldthorpe (2004) and Hunter (2004) point out, the abilities of the Commissioner to actively advance children's rights have been limited, as the role has been stripped of its powers to promote and safeguard individual children's rights and has a weaker role in promoting rights than its equivalent in Wales, Scotland, Northern Ireland and other European countries. As the Children's Rights Alliance in England's recent report (CRAE, 2008) into the implementation of the UNCRC in UK countries highlights, there is inconsistency in the current government approach to supporting children's rights generally. There is, for example, evidence of an increasing emphasis in policy and practice for consultation with children and young people in the development of services and policy, as shown by the recent consultation by the government in relation to the development of the Children's Plan for England and Wales (CRAE, 2008: 22). However, as the CRAE report points out, the government did not make use of the recent enactment of the Education and Inspections Act 2006, to make it mandatory for schools to have school councils as a forum for children's and young people's participation in their education.

THE EVERY CHILD MATTERS AGENDA

Following the publication of the Laming report (2003) into the death of Victoria Climbié, the Social Exclusion Unit's report (2003) on the outcomes for children in care, as well as consultation with children, families and professionals about important issues in childhood, the English government developed a broad policy agenda developed around five outcomes which, it advised, all services should work towards to improve the lives of children. These five outcomes are: being healthy, staying safe, enjoying and achieving, making a positive contribution and economic well-being (DfES, 2004e: 10). While the government acknowledges that, 'Real service improvement is only attainable through involving children and young people and listening to their views' (DfES, 2004e: 10), and while it might also be argued that including 'making a positive contribution' as one of the outcomes implies an emphasis on participation and requires various agencies and services to develop opportunities for children's participation in a range of decision making, much of the Every Child Matters documentation and associated guidance does not place significant emphasis on the continual and integrated participation of children across a range of services and decision making. As the Children's Rights Alliance for England (CRAE, 2008: 50) points out, the five outcomes are vague and 'open to variation, interpretation and misunderstanding', and they also do little to specifically draw attention to the participation of children in decision making in relation to services and practices relating to all five outcomes. They caution that there is a risk that participation has 'been ghettoized in the sense that it is perceived to relate to just one outcome – making a positive contribution – rather than being an integral element of achieving all five outcomes' (CRAE, 2008: 51).

COMPETENCE

There is much confusion within the law, both in UK countries and internationally, as to how the level of competence of a child is to be judged. In legal terms, competence is not necessarily linked to age. For example, in England, children aged between 16 and 18 are at present deemed to be sufficiently competent to make decisions in relation to sex and leaving school, but are not considered competent to vote or to marry without their parents' consent. Children aged 10 and over are held to be criminally responsible in

English law, and can be made the subject of antisocial behaviour orders under the Criminal Justice Act 1998, but are not deemed to be responsible enough to buy a pet until they are 12 (Fortin, 2003).

The case of Gillick *v* West Norfolk and Wisbech Area Health Authority [1985] was seen as a landmark case in terms of young people's rights and in establishing that competence is not necessarily linked to age. It established the principle that a young person under the age of 16 could consent to medical treatment without their parents' consent or knowledge, if they were deemed to be competent enough (BMA, 2001: 34). However, it did not clarify how to assess competence, and again the decision about competence lay in the hands of adults, this time in the hands of a medical practitioner. Moreover, a few years later, the Court of Appeal confused matters by deciding in two cases (Re: R and Re: W, cited in BMA, 2001: 35) that the courts could overrule a teenager's decision to refuse life-saving treatment even when they had been considered 'Gillick competent'. It seemed that the competence of a child could be overruled depending on the seriousness of the decision involved.

In July 2004, the government introduced new guidance for medical practitioners in relation to young people's right to confidentiality about sexual matters and for the first time enabled competent young people to consent to abortion without their parents' knowledge (DoH, 2004a). There was much media-reported criticism of the guidance, particularly in relation to abortion. Mrs Axon, a mother of two teenage girls, applied for judicial review of the guidance as she disagreed with parents not being routinely consulted in relation to abortion (Powell, 2004). However, the courts ruled against her and considered the guidance lawful. (The Queen on the Application of Sue Axon *v* The Secretary of state for Health (The Family Planning Association: intervening) [2006] EWCA 37 (Admin.)). In this situation, the Court again significantly upheld a young person's right to make their own decision about a major issue, abortion, and allowed doctors to support young people's right to make their own decisions. It will be interesting to see if young people's competence in other situations continues to be overruled depending on the seriousness of the decision, despite this recent ruling.

It is interesting to note the support of the government for children's right to make at least some decisions in relation to their health and bodies, in comparison to the lack of support for them to be more involved in decisions about their education. As Fortin (2003: 161) states: 'the principles of education law currently show little appreciation for the maturing child's capacity for taking responsibility for his or her school life or for reaching important decisions over his or her education'. For example, while the revised (non-statutory) exclusions guidance of 2007 encourages pupils under the age of 18 to attend the appeals hearing, the parent has to agree to the pupil's attendance and furthermore pupils under 18 have no right to appeal against exclusion from school themselves; it is only their parents who can do that. It is also parents who may be fined and imprisoned if children do not receive adequate education; children themselves cannot make a decision to leave formal education under the age of 16.

This confusion about required levels of competence for participation in decisions can also be seen in relation to contact or residence matters within the courts. In cases where contact is being considered with a parent about whom there have been allegations of domestic violence, the courts have sought the advice of two eminent psychiatrists about the age at which children's views should be taken into account. Sturge and Glaser's (2000: 620) advice is that:

> the older the child the more seriously [their views] should be viewed and the more insulting and discrediting to the child to have them ignored. As a rough rule we would see these as needing to be taken into account at any age; above ten we see these as carrying considerable weight with 6–10 as an intermediate stage and at under 6 as often indistinguishable in many ways from the wishes of the main carer (assuming normal development).

While this advice may not be entirely clear, it does emphasize the importance of taking into account children's views, whatever their age. Despite this, it appears from the following studies that children's views are not routinely sought by the courts or professionals involved, and that when they are sought, they may still not be actively heard by the courts.

May and Smart (2004) looked at three county courts' practices in relation to seeking children's views about contact and residence disputes. In half of the cases they looked at, a CAFCASS (Children and Family Court Advisory and Support Service) officer or a social worker had been asked to prepare a welfare report, which is expected to include the wishes and feelings of the child as well as advice about the effects of various decisions on the welfare of the child. May and Smart (2004) found that in only half of these cases – thus only a quarter of their total sample – had the children actually been consulted. They found that, of those consulted, children over seven tended to have their views taken seriously, particularly if they could 'vote with their feet' and where there was conflict between the parents. May and Smart were left particularly concerned about the young children involved in disputes, as they appeared to have clear views which were more often overlooked, particularly if they did not accord with the recommendations of the CAFCASS officer, and thus were effectively denied a voice in the proceedings.

James et al. (2004) considered how child welfare professionals from CAFCASS represent a child's views to the courts in family proceedings. They included both private law cases, such as contact and residence matters, and public law cases where local authorities had sought court orders to protect children from harm. They found that the professional's own understanding and construction of childhood influenced how they balanced the tensions inherent in wishing to protect the children from the responsibility of making a choice about their future care, while also ensuring their wishes were made known to the court. Generally, a more protectionist and welfare perspective dominated and children's voices were filtered out and effectively silenced if they did not fit in with the perspective of the professional involved (James et al., 2004).

It appears from the above studies, that family proceedings under the Children Act 1989 are 'more likely to remain a site for upholding contingent and highly romanticized ideas of family life rather than a space for listening and responding to the voices of real children' (Monk, 2004: 166).

Participation of Young Children

While the above issues are relevant to the participation of children of all ages in decision making, 'much of the practice-based literature on children's participation and specific guidance about children's involvement in decision making tends to relate to children older than eight, particularly teenagers. Young children are almost invisible and babies appear not to exist at all' (Kirby and Marchant, 2004: 93). Where they are consulted, this can sometimes be at worst damaging, and at best ineffective, if the media used are designed for older children, or if they are one-off events unconnected with children's lives, and where 'adult" consultation" has dangerously come to mean an expert adult intervention done to children, with or without their genuine consent, often by adults who do not know them and have no other involvement in their lives' (Kirby and Marchant, 2004: 93).

As discussed above, Blanchet-Cohen and Rainbow (2006) argue that many of the difficulties in achieving meaningful and effective participation could be avoided by systems and processes involving children as active participants in everyday life. If social and educational systems encouraged children to participate in such decision making from an early age, active 'citizenship' would be more a reality for them and, further

> such a shift would reduce the need for one-off, distant consultations because genuinely participative cultures would provide contexts in which young children could easily be consulted about a range of issues. For example, in community regeneration initiatives, local parent and toddler groups in the area would already be routinely ascertaining young children's views. In the development of health services, children who are spending time in hospital would be used to 'having a real say' in how things are for them. Curriculum development would be a regular focus for young children in school (Kirby and Marchant, 2004: 95).

This philosophy and practice of active participation from an early age is advocated by the OECD's *Starting Strong II* report (2006: 219) which reviews the OECD countries' policies in relation to early childhood care and education. This report recommends that governments recognize the important and influential voice of young children. It gives section 3 of Norway's Kindergarten Act 2004 as an example of legislation that explicitly supports the UNCRC participation rights of very young children in all aspects of life in the kindergarten, as it states that:

- Children in kindergartens shall have the right to express their views on the day-to-day activities of the kindergarten.
- Children shall regularly be given the opportunity to take an active part in planning and assessing the activities of the kindergarten.
- The children's views shall be given due weight according to their age and maturity.

(OECD, 2006: 219)

While highlighting the importance of individual children's voices being heard, *Starting Strong II* also points out that encouraging young children's participation in early years settings should not mean that 'individual choice is put forward as a supreme value' (OECD, 2006: 219), but that awareness of the democratic values of social and community responsibilities are also encouraged. It argues that 'children should be encouraged to participate and share with others, and … learning [should be] seen as primarily inter-active, experiential and social. *Learning to be, learning to do, learning to learn and learning to live together* are each important goals for young children' (ibid.).

However, balancing children's individual rights and those of the group within a child-care setting is a complex task. How, for example, should an early years professional man-age a situation where an individual child wishes to pursue a task they are engaged in when a group activity is planned, if both individual agency and sharing experiences are important values? Furthermore, as Cameron (2007) argues, how do practitioners man-age to balance children's agency 'in an advanced liberal state such as England [where] there is a paradox between valorizing independence as an expression of individual autonomy and the highly governed practice, through regulation, of early childhood ser-vices' (Cameron, 2007: 467–8). Dictates of curriculum or the pressure to demonstrate out-comes may make the encouragement of participation and agency far less of a priority.

SUMMARY

The notion of children having participation rights, what these are and how they can, or should, be exercised is of current and continuing significance for all those who work with children and are concerned about their well-being. In practice, balancing a child's right to protection with their right to participate is difficult for all involved with children. Promoting children's rights to participate does not mean advocating that children should make all decisions themselves, whatever their age or level of competence. However, it is clear that children are not able to participate effectively in many decisions affecting their lives. The influence of dominant constructions of childhood, as well as of prevalent incremental the-ories of development, can prevent a child's individual needs and levels of competence being recognized, and can lead to him or her being seen as one of a uniform group of peo-ple rather than a separate and unique person. As discussed above, this can be seen within the courts making contact and residence decisions in England and within the work of aid agencies working under the auspices of the UNCRC.

It is a difficult challenge for all of us, as adults used to having various amounts of power and control over children, to acknowledge and promote the participation rights of children (Lansdown, 2001). Those working in early years contexts face particular difficulties, as the younger the child, the more incompetent he or she tends to be viewed and the less likely he or she is to have their right to participation addressed. However, various methods of facilitating young children's participation are being used in settings as diverse as nurseries and local council planning departments with encouraging results and significant implica-tions for future practice (see Willow et al., 2004 for a helpful review of various initiatives).

It is incumbent on all of us to recognize the importance of children's active participation in all areas of their lives, not only because it is their right, but also because it can lead to bet-ter decisions as well as improving a child's self-esteem and confidence (Thomas, 2001). Children's effective participation will not become a reality unless we are able to actively challenge our own values and beliefs about children, as well as those of the many institu-tions, agencies and organizations which influence children's lives.

QUESTIONS FOR REFLECTION AND DISCUSSION

1. Why is it difficult to define children's rights?
2. Are children's rights, as set out under the UNCRC, universally applicable?
3. Is a rights-based approach helpful in improving the lives of children?
4. How can competence in young children be assessed?
5. How can young children be actively involved in research?

Recommended reading

Children's Rights Alliance for England (2007) *The State of Children's Rights in England*. London: CRAE.

James, A. and James, A. (2004) *Constructing Childhood: Theory, Policy and Social Practice*. Basingstoke: Palgrave.

OECD (2006) *Starting Strong II: Early Childhood Education and Care*. Paris: OECD.

Willow, C., Marchant, M., Kirby, P. and Neale, B. (2004) *Young Children's Citizenship: Ideas into Practice*. York: Joseph Rowntree Foundation.

Recommended websites

Children's Rights Alliance for England: www.crae.org.uk
Participation Works: www.participationworks.com

7 PROTECTING AND SAFEGUARDING CHILDREN

Celia Doyle

Chapter objectives

- To help the reader understand the nature of safeguarding and protection.
- To enhance the reader's awareness of the contexts in which abuse can occur.
- To help the reader recognize key features of the different forms of abuse including the targeting and grooming of young children by sex offenders.
- To help the reader appreciate how child victims might respond to abuse, and why they do so.
- To assist the reader to acknowledge and understand the obstacles to recognition.

You should be aware that you may find some of the material in this chapter emotionally demanding.

This chapter provides an introduction to some of the key concepts that will help early years workers protect children who might be subjected to abuse and neglect. The main emphasis of this chapter is on abuse by people who are responsible for the care of children, particularly parents. The aim of the chapter is to help those studying early childhood and early years practitioners gain sufficient understanding of key areas of child protection to enable them to recognize abuse in all its forms. Additionally, an appreciation of the obstacles to recognition is an essential aspect of the chapter. The focus is on recognition rather than on policy and procedures. It is important that all people working with children acquire information about what they are required to do in the event of their suspecting or finding that a child is being abused (Calder and Hackett, 2003). They need to be aware of the procedures specific to their profession, position and locality, such as the All Wales Child Protection Procedures (Welsh Assembly Government, 2007). However, procedures cannot be implemented if a practitioner fails to recognize that maltreatment is occurring.

In more recent years, the case of Victoria Climbié (Laming, 2003) has clearly demonstrated this. Victoria suffered beatings from her aunt who was her main carer and the aunt's boyfriend. They hit her with shoes, football boots, a bicycle chain, a hammer, a coat hanger and a wooden spoon. She was also left naked for long periods, except for a black plastic bag, lying in her own urine and faeces in a bath. She was eventually killed by her aunt and her aunt's boyfriend. The post-mortem revealed severe burns on her body and 128 injuries. This abuse did not occur overnight. Her suffering was over an extended period, during which she was seen by a number of officials including hospital staff and social workers. All of them failed to recognize the signs of abuse.

Innumerable public inquiries into the deaths of children have shown that recognizing abuse is by no means straightforward (Reder et al., 1993). However, some knowledge of the underlying dynamics in abuse cases will assist accurate recognition and the appropriate implementation of procedures.

PROTECTING AND SAFEGUARDING

One of the responses of the UK government to the Laming Report was the publication of *Every Child Matters* (DfES, 2003). This recommended changes to children's services to ensure every child has the support he or she needs to:

- be healthy
- stay safe
- enjoy and achieve
- make a positive contribution
- achieve economic well-being.

Subsequently, the Children Act 2004 gave effect to these proposals. There are five main parts. Part 1 provided for the establishment of Children's Commissioners to promote the views and interests of children throughout the UK. Other parts related to the better integration of the planning and delivery of children's services throughout England and Wales.

In Northern Ireland, the Children (Northern Ireland) Order 1995 has been supplemented by amendments and the Protection of Children and Vulnerable Adults (Northern Ireland) Order 2003. Similarly, Scotland has seen a number of policy developments, such as 'It's Everyone's Job to Make Sure I'm Alright' (Scottish Executive, 2002) and the Protection of Children Act (Scotland) 2003, as a result of the Laming (2003), Bichard (2004) and other child death inquiries (e.g. Dumfries and Galloway Child Protection Committee, 2000).

The remainder of the chapter focuses on 'abuse', that is behaviour by children's carers or other powerful people who prevent children from enjoying and achieving by threatening their physical and mental health and their safety. The next section looks at the definition of abuse in more detail.

WHAT IS ABUSE?

One of the complexities faced by those trying to intervene in abuse cases is that many concepts are 'socially constructed' (Hallet, 1995). This means that different cultures and societies view behaviours very differently. For example, in relation to slavery, many past civilizations viewed it as perfectly natural and 'normal', whereas in a large number of modern societies, slavery is unacceptable. Similarly, certain types of behaviour towards children, such as denigrating and beating them, is seen as abusive in some cultures, whereas in others, tenets such as 'spare the rod and spoil the child' and 'children should be seen and not heard' form the bedrock of child-rearing practices. It is therefore difficult to give precise definitions of 'abuse'. However, a key defining feature of child abuse is that there is at least one other person, usually a parent figure, who is misusing the power they have over the child. Hence:

- Physical abuse is the *misuse of physical power* in such a way that it causes physical and emotional harm to the child.
- Neglect is the *failure to use, or misuse of physical and resource power* in such a way that it causes a variety of damage to the child including physical, social, developmental and emotional harm.
- Sexual abuse is the *misuse of sometimes physical but more often superior expert power* (greater knowledge) to coerce and sexually exploit children.
- Emotional abuse is the *misuse of a range of powers* to undermine and damage a child's sense of self-worth.

RECOGNIZING DIVERSITY

Maltreated children will come from a variety of backgrounds, representing a range of ethnic groups, religions and cultures. Their families will have varied structures including households with several generations living together or ones with just one adult. Children and their parents will also have a range of abilities and disabilities.

There are some factors which create additional risks for children with disabilities. While the conditions of some disabled children might mean they are less isolated and see many more helpers and professionals than others, the conditions of others may result in an isolated child totally dependent on very stressed and relatively unsupported parents. Polnay et al. (2007) also point out that disabled children may have limited mobility so cannot readily escape abuse and also might have communication problems that result in an inability to disclose maltreatment. Treatment might also be more difficult and Kennedy (2002) provides eloquent testimony to the issues facing abused children who are also deaf.

Doyle (1998) found that children in families in which a member had a disability were more at risk of emotional abuse. However, it was not always the disabled child who was abused. Some adult survivors explained that while their brother or sister with the disability was cared for with great tenderness and consideration, they were the target of all their parents' anger and frustration. Alternatively, they were simply ignored while family life revolved around the needs of their disabled sibling.

In terms of children from different ethnic groups, there is no clear evidence that children from any particular cultural background are more at risk. Chand (2008) notes that 'mixed heritage, black and Black British children are over-represented on child protection registers' but advanced the view that families in these groups might be being unjustifiably pathologized. However, if children from particular sectors are under-represented, then there is equal concern that abuse in these groups is being ignored because professionals are worried about being seen to be discriminatory.

In conclusion, diversity needs to be acknowledged but it can add to the complexity of intervention because workers have to avoid condemning childcare practices that are different but not worse than the mainstream, while not leaving children to be harmed by parenting that is both different and abusive.

WHERE DOES ABUSE OCCUR?

Abuse can occur everywhere, in both private and public arenas, although the more private the arena, the greater the risk of abuse. This means that mistreatment is often located in relatively isolated, private families and institutions. There is no one type of family or home in which abuse either always or never occurs. Nonetheless, four groupings of factors point towards increased risks to children. These groupings or contexts – which are not always mutually exclusive – are the unexceptional, chaotic, rigid and deviant ones. These are described briefly below.

Unexceptional context

This is a setting in which children's needs are normally met. Unfortunately, a number of crises and stresses mean that the carer/parent can no longer cope. Sometimes, other children in the family continue to be well cared for but, rather like Cinderella, one child is singled out for mistreatment. In other instances, all the children are affected.

Example: A mother with several very young children suffered from severe postnatal depression after the birth of her new baby. Other adults such as her partner and health professionals did not notice that there was a problem. The children became neglected.

Chaotic context

Here, there is a general lack of boundaries. The physical and emotional care of the children is erratic. Similarly, discipline is inconsistent with the same behaviours sometimes tolerated and at other times harshly punished depending on the parents' moods. Children are often forced to take on adult roles including parenting the parents or acting as sexual partners. Lack of appropriate boundaries and vigilance means that the children are also exposed to sex offenders' predatory behaviour.

Example: Jane was six years old and lived with her mother, her sister aged three and baby brother of 18 months. No fathers were in evidence although the mother had a constant stream of casual boyfriends. Jane was regularly left to parent the other children while the mother went out socializing. Jane was beaten for offences such as making the gravy too lumpy when she made the family meal, being too tired to manage a large pile of ironing and losing her key when she was meant to let herself in after school.

Rigid context

The care of the children is negative, rigid and punitive. The parent figures have to be in control at all times and worry about losing 'a grip' on the situation if they do not retain all the power. There is an undercurrent of fear, with the parents terrified of anarchy among their children if they 'give an inch', while the children are scared of their parents' extreme wrath if they make the slightest error. Babies are often subject to strict routines but most difficulties arise once they are toddling. Their parents are intolerant of the mess, defiance and tantrums, which are an inevitable part of toddlers' natural curiosity and increasing independence.

Example: Mandy aged 7 and her brother aged 4 had, since infancy, been subjected to a very harsh regime by their father. When taken out, they would sit for hours without daring to move, speak, eat, drink or go to the toilet. Most people failed to recognize the abuse but instead congratulated the parents on having such remarkably well-behaved children.

Deviant context

Sometimes mimicking any one of the above contexts, here the family system contains one or two people who are seriously damaged and who abuse their power and yet are skilled at exploitation and manipulation. Often, these people pose considerable dangers to children. They appear to derive satisfaction from inflicting physical injury and emotional distress, lack empathy and have little remorse. This grouping also includes people who are 'addicted' to hospitals and medical care but present their children rather than themselves for treatment. Their fabrication of illness in their children can be emotionally and physically damaging and in some circumstances fatal.

Example: Many of the most extreme examples have made headline news, including the cases of Fred and Rose West (Gloucestershire Area Child Protection Committee, 1995) and Victoria Climbié (Laming, 2003). The case of nurse Beverly Allit (Clothier, 1994) who injured and killed several children on a hospital paediatric ward is frequently cited as an example of fabricated, induced illness.

UNDERSTANDING AND RECOGNIZING PHYSICAL ABUSE AND NEGLECT

This is not the place to detail all the diagnostic signs of abuse. Even experienced paediatricians and other medical specialists find it difficult to determine the exact cause of many injuries, even with the help of sophisticated X-ray and other equipment. However, there are some physical signs of abuse and neglect that can raise a query.

The most obvious are bruises and lesions on the skin of small children. Babies not yet able to roll over or move very far rarely sustain bruising. If they have, then the carers should be able to give a clear explanation that is consistent with the injury. Finger-tip bruising on tiny babies may indicate a carer who is losing control and gripping the child too hard.

When injuries are observed in young children, it is worth asking how they were sustained and whether or not they have been seen by medical staff. To the untrained eye, cigarette burns could be mistaken for a skin condition such as impetigo but whether the cause is impetigo or burns, the child needs to be examined by a doctor. Conversely, what sometimes looks like bruising on the back or bottom is really 'Mongolian blue spot', a harmless birthmark frequently seen on children with a black, Asian or Mediterranean heritage.

Although there are medical or genetic conditions that delay growth, children who are emotionally or physically neglected may also show growth retardation. Non-organic failure to thrive is a diagnosis made when all medical conditions are excluded. It can be confirmed when, in the absence of medical treatment, growth charts show children gaining weight whenever in hospital or care and losing it again after returning home.

UNDERSTANDING AND RECOGNIZING SEXUAL ABUSE

According to Finkelhor (1984), in order for an incident of sexual abuse to occur, there has to be:

- someone who wants to sexually abuse a young child
- someone who finds a way of overcoming internal inhibitors (their conscience)
- someone who finds a way of overcoming external inhibitors (for example, protective parents, friends)
- someone who finds a way of overcoming the child victim's resistance (which may be to abuse a child too young to resist effectively).

People who molest young children have a sexual predilection for children independent of their gender orientation (i.e. homosexuality or heterosexuality). If an adult male or female is only sexually attracted to other adults, male or female, then there is very little risk of child sexual abuse. However, some people can only relate sexually to children. Here, there is a high risk of abuse and the offenders often fit the typical image of a 'paedophile'. Finally, there are some adults who do not discriminate sexually between adults and children. They pose a considerable risk but may not be so readily recognized as sex offenders, especially if they have adult partners.

Children may also engage in sexual activities with other children. When one child is more powerful than the other, either because of age, more knowledge, physical strength or other features, then the activities can become abusive.

The ensuing profile of offenders is based primarily on research into adult male sex offenders. The sexual and offending behaviour of both women and adolescents differs from that of adult males. Despite this, there is reason to believe that female and teenage sex offenders share many of the characteristics described below.

Sex offenders are preoccupied with their own needs and can only see the situation from their own point of view. However, they can sometimes learn to say the 'right' thing. They may appear to be surrounded by family and friends but these relationships are superficial and often exploitative, and frequently offenders use them to reassure or attract others. Many have excellent social skills and appear charming and plausible. They frequently collect labels of respectability in order to disarm carers. Nevertheless, there are some offenders who are 'loners' and clearly have difficulties forming relationships with non-vulnerable adults but, conversely, they are very good with children. They know what will attract and disarm a child and can play engagingly with young children.

Sex offenders do not offend as a sudden whim or as a 'one-off '. Their assaults are planned. Collecting child pornography is not a harmless diversion; it is often part of the planning process. They will target a child or group of children (Doyle, 1987). Many will have a preference for a child of a particular gender or type but children outside their target group will still be at risk. Having chosen a victim, they will then 'groom' the child. Some offenders use force and threats but most use patience, gently persuading the child to trust them so that the child inadvertently becomes a 'willing' victim. During the assault, they will treat the child as an object for their own gratification, sometimes covering the child's face so that they cannot be reminded of their victim's personality. After the assault, they will again 'groom' the child, using either threats or persuasion to stop the child telling anyone about the abuse.

Sex offenders have distorted attitudes to children. They believe that even very young children enjoy sexual activities and are ever ready to seduce adults. They will, for example, interpret a small child showing underwear or in tight clothing as 'being provocative' and wanting sex. They also view children as objects designed for adults' sexual pleasure. Often, society supports these attitudes – for example, we objectify children and often refer to the child as 'it'.

When confronted with their offending behaviour, sex abusers say nothing, make excuses ('I was drunk m'lud') or try to elicit sympathy ('feel sorry for poor me'). Some become threatening, constantly make formal complaints to thwart investigations or denigrate workers by using sexist and racist innuendos. Finally, sex offending against children is not a behaviour that can be 'cured'. It can only be controlled, and only controlled with difficulty (Doyle, 1994).

UNDERSTANDING AND RECOGNIZING EMOTIONAL ABUSE

It is often difficult to define emotional abuse but there are two important aspects. First, emotional abuse consists of both acts of commission – for example, verbal abuse – and acts of omission – for example, the refusal to praise or encourage a child. Second, there is a misuse of power – parents and other carers exploit their power over the child to actively abuse them or fail to use their power so as to neglect the child's emotional needs. This is illustrated by the following catalogue of emotionally abusive behaviour:

- *Fear inducing*: this includes holding a child hostage with a knife to his or her throat, or creating insecurity by constantly leaving the child with lots of different 'strange' carers.
- *Tormenting*: this includes pretending to break a child's favourite toy or threatening to kill a child's pet.
- *Degrading*: this can be deliberate humiliation, embarrassing a child in front of other people, or denigration and verbal abuse.
- *Corrupting*: this can consist of using children to carry drugs or taking them on burglaries to climb through small windows. It also includes destructive modelling such as the violent father who encourages his young son to treat all women with derision and hit his sister and mother.
- *Rejecting*: rejection can be active, such as telling a child she is unwanted, or passive through the avoidance of emotional warmth, praise or cuddles. Closely allied to this is ignoring behaviour, refusing to give the child any attention.
- *Isolating*: this may be through locking the child away in a room or cupboard for very long periods. It can also include preventing a child from socializing or having any friends.
- *Applying of inappropriate roles*: this can include being made the scapegoat for all the family's ills, being used as a weapon against the other parent or 'the authorities'. It can also mean being overprotected or infantilized or, alternatively, forced to shoulder too much responsibility.

Emotional abuse can occur outside the family in the form of school bullying or racist taunts by neighbours. It can also be found in every type of family, regardless of race, size, social class or structure. However, children in those families in which there are already a number of stressors are more likely to be emotionally abused (Doyle, 1997).

UNDERSTANDING AND RECOGNIZING CHILDREN'S REACTIONS TO ABUSE

One of the paradoxes encountered in child protection work is that rather than try to escape from the abuse, even very young children will hide the signs of mistreatment, refuse to disclose and show a high level of attachment to their abusers. This can be explained partly by the natural feelings of love and attachment that small children develop for their carers in order to ensure survival (Bowlby, 1965). However, this does not fully explain why this attachment is maintained in the face of abuse. It can, nonetheless, be understood if account is taken of the impact of trauma and maltreatment and the psychological process that helps people cope with trauma.

The Stockholm syndrome is a recognized range of protective processes with relevance to abused children. The syndrome was first identified when bank employees were held hostage in Stockholm, and it has been observed in hostage, kidnap, concentration camp, domestic violence and other abuse situations. There are a number of stages that victims experience. However, as with grief processes, these stages are not experienced by everyone nor in a clearly defined order.

- *Frozen fright*: when confronted by a situation of terror from which there is no flight or fight possible, people 'freeze'. This results in compliance where all the victim's energy is focused on the abuser and is useful because it conserves energy for a time when flight or fight may become possible and compliance is less likely to antagonize the aggressor.
- *Denial*: the initial frozen fright gives way to a sense of unreality – 'this isn't happening to me'. This is a useful temporary state which guards against people being overwhelmed by the terror of the situation. But for some victims of abuse, this can become an entrenched denial of the severity and pain of the abuse or of the events ever having occurred.
- *Fear and anger*: once reality has sunk in, victims feel fear and anger but it is too dangerous to express these emotions against abusers so victims often project it onto 'outsiders'. Victims believe that they are more likely to survive if their abusers are basically good and care for them – they therefore look for signs of goodness in their abusers and are grateful for any indication of kindness.
- *Depression*: victims also turn their anger against themselves, leading to depression and self-deprecation. They feel useless, worthless and powerless. Having convinced themselves that the abuser is good, they begin to believe that they are being justifiably mistreated because they are bad.
- *Psychological contrast*: the process towards despair or acceptance may be accelerated by psychological contrast, which substantially weakens victims, making them more compliant. It is a well known form of interrogation and torture. One person acts as the 'good guy' while the other is the 'bad guy'. Alternatively, one person behaves in a kindly manner and then suddenly becomes threatening and aggressive. In abusive homes, one parent may be cruel while the other tries to compensate by being kind. Or, one parent is abusive and then feels guilt, so is very kind to the victim – until the next time.
- *Acceptance*: finally, victims of maltreatment reach a state of acceptance. They no longer question the rights or wrongs of what is happening to them. Children may appear 'well-adjusted' and their behaviour may seem calm and compliant. They may well have an unquestioning acceptance of the values, justification and behaviour of their abusers.

RECOGNIZING ABUSE AND THE OBSTACLES TO RECOGNITION

There are aspects of a child's appearance, behaviour, development and statements that might be suggestive of abuse. However, recognition is not straightforward and the final section summarizes the obstacles to recognizing abuse.

Appearance

This includes injuries where there are inconsistent explanations or ones that do not fit with the injury. Neglect might be present if a child is smaller, more poorly clothed or dirtier than most of the children in the family or area. Over-dressed or very loose, swamping clothes may be masking emaciation or injuries. Emotional abuse might be present in a child who appears too clean and smart, especially if he or she is very frightened of making a mess. Finally, there should be concerns when a child shows frozen awareness or appears over-anxious.

Behaviour

A child who abuses other children, draws or plays out violent or sexual scenes with peers or toys might be mimicking behaviour they have experienced. Marked changes in behaviour, an inability to concentrate and anxiety about going home are always worth exploring, as is rummaging in bins or stealing food and comfort items.

Development

Any developmental delay can be an indicator of abuse, but equally significant is a sudden regression, such as the child whose language acquisition suddenly declines or the previously continent child who becomes incontinent.

Statements

Children may disclose abuse directly, clearly and frankly but some may start to try to disclose indirectly by asking what appears to be a strange or rather personal question. Disclosure sometimes comes through children writing poems or stories; if the child has been sexually abused, these may be sexually explicit. Evidently, very young children will have difficulty articulating their experiences but children as young as two or three years old have been able to convey aspects of the abuse they have suffered.

Workers' attitudes

One of the biggest obstacles to recognition is the professional worker him or herself. Many professionals cannot accept abuse; it is too painful, so they ignore the signs or go out of their way to advance more comfortable explanations. They may also convince themselves that parents would never harm their children and that the whole discourse of child protection is exaggerated. Other professionals are so emotionally exhausted and burnt out that they no longer feel any concern for the child and ignore any potential signs because of the difficulties and challenges it will pose for them.

Problems recognizing the signs

The points below summarize why recognizing child abuse is not always easy. Sometimes the signs are indistinct, ambiguous or misleading. However, there are other instances where the signs are comparatively clear but professionals fail to acknowledge them due to their own emotional barriers such as a reluctance to face a child's suffering. Early years workers need to be aware of the following obstacles to recognition so that they do not make assumptions about the presence or absence of maltreatment:

- Appearance, behaviour and developmental problems can be equally indicative of some other distress or worry.
- Many injuries or skin discolouration can also be indicative of an accident, disease process or birthmark.
- Children with certain disabilities, those for whom English is not their first language and pre-verbal children may not have the vocabulary or communication skills to disclose clearly in English.
- A 'nice' family can contain an abuser. Some professionals use checklists, which mislead them because although abuse often occurs in identifiable 'risk' situations, it can also occur anytime, anywhere and in any type of family.
- In some cases, the abuse is 'victim specific', so that carers/parents who seem to be exemplary in relation to their other children can still abuse one particular victim.
- In sexual abuse cases in particular, the skill of the perpetrator in grooming the victim and their potential protectors into silence is considerable.
- There is the phenomenon of the Stockholm syndrome. Children may appear deeply attached to their parents even when being abused by them.
- Professionals may ignore obvious signs because it is too emotionally painful to think about a child's suffering or they are too emotionally exhausted to contemplate the anguish the child has experienced.
- More insidious reasons for professionals denying probable signs of abuse can be because they are overly concerned that they may be 'making a mistake', they are reluctant to 'rock the boat', they do not want to take any responsibility for initiating an investigation or they are worried about damaging their relationships with the parents. They have lost sight of the fact that the child's welfare is paramount.

 Case Study   Brook

Brook aged 5 has a sister, Sky aged 8 and a brother, Dale aged 2. All three children have the same white mother, Ruby. Sky's father was African Caribbean but was killed in a car accident when Sky was 18 months old. All that is known of Brook's father is that he was a white man and never lived with Ruby. Dale's father is white and is Ruby's current husband.

Since Brook started school a year ago, he has been a cause for concern. He is much smaller than the other children in his class. Ruby, her husband, Sky and Dale are all well built. Brook's speech is indistinct, his development is generally delayed and he has difficulty concentrating in class. His clothes are always old and worn and he never brings toys from home. Ruby explained that he always breaks his toys and spoils his clothes so that it is not worth buying him new things.

He has frequent bruising to his legs, back and face. His mother says that he is clumsy and often fights with the other children. The staff have noticed his clumsiness in school but he is withdrawn rather than aggressive with both staff and other children. He often appears to be afraid of trying anything new in case he makes a mess or a mistake.

When he is asked to draw pictures or talk about home, he always says how much he loves his mother and shows no fear of her.

Discussion Points

1. Is this a clear-cut case of abuse or could there be alternative explanations for all the various points of concern?
2. What other information – if any – would you need to make firmer or alternative judgements?

 Reflection

There are many indicators of abuse. Brook could be failing to grow, developmentally delayed, fearful of trying anything new and withdrawn because of emotionally abusive behaviour and neglect. The cause of his bruising and general fearfulness could be physical abuse.

The fact that he does not complain about any maltreatment or seem fearful of Ruby and is attached to her is not an indication that he is not abused. Children may become attached to their abusers, directing their fear onto other people or situations.

Nonetheless, his small stature, clumsiness, developmental delay and quiet anxiousness could simply be innate characteristics. We know little about his genetic inheritance such as the physical size of his father. He may be small because his father was. It would be useful to obtain information about his father if possible.

Although the bruising is suspicious, it could be caused by a combination of falls and bullying by other children. We need to obtain information about the other children and adults in contact with Brook to find out if people other than his parents could be harming him. It is also necessary to exclude any medical condition that might be the cause of his small stature, his clumsiness or a susceptibility to bruising.

Information about his brother and sister could help, although if they are well cared for, it could be that this is a case where one child is singled out for abuse. Perhaps the mother had an extreme dislike of Brook's father and is projecting this onto his child. Alternatively, Dale's father may be irritated by the presence of another man's son. It is essential to check that neither parent is known to the police for acts of violence or offences against children.

INTERVENTION

Children who have been abused can be offered help on an individual, family and group basis (Doyle, 2006). Much of this therapeutic work is undertaken by specialist therapists. Nevertheless, there is much that non-specialist early years workers can do to assist the healing process.

First, it is important to work with all the other professionals involved in safeguarding children. This is advocated by government policy (Her Majesty's

Government, 2006a). This means preparing well for multidisciplinary forums such as case conferences, core groups and even courtrooms, being clear about the information that needs to be shared with other professionals, and being confident enough to contribute in these forums. In child protection cases, each individual has part of a jigsaw puzzle – only by putting all the various pieces of information together is a picture of the situation revealed.

One significant factor for early years workers to bear in mind is that they are the experts in the day-to-day understanding of young children. Not only may they have had academic training in child development but they will be spending many hours in the company of a diverse range of younger children. They will consciously or unconsciously be absorbing information about the range of 'normal' baby, toddler or young child behaviours. Because of the problems of recognition, they may miss some cases of child abuse. Nevertheless, any feelings they have that all is not well with a particular child are likely to have some foundation. But the majority of early years workers are female and many are young – they therefore do not represent the more powerful sectors of society. Unfortunately, in some multidisciplinary forums, they may feel some inadequacy and find their views are disregarded, while the more powerful professions – health, law enforcement, social work, for example – dominate proceedings. It is important that early years workers give voice to their concerns and have the confidence to do so, knowing that they are the expert in the field. A key aspect of multidisciplinary work is to respect and understand the perspective of all the other professions. Valuing the unique contribution of everyone in contact with the child is indispensable to the welfare of abused children.

Secondly, some early years workers will also be in a position to advise parents on how to provide caring discipline and boundaries for young children without resorting to aggression and assault. Smacking children only teaches them that bigger people can hit smaller ones and that violence is legitimate. Furthermore, if parents have failed to bond with their child or are dis-inhibited by drink or drugs, there is the risk that what started as a smack ends up as a prolonged and life-threatening assault.

Thirdly, research (Doyle, 2001, for example) has shown that it is possible for a range of people to increase children's resilience and provide the positive, valuing messages that counter the negative messages inevitably communicated to children by abuse. This is illustrated in the example of Yasmin below.

 Case Study   Yasmin

Yasmin is the second of four children. She has a sister, Meena, who is two years older and twin brothers, Kiran and Harish, who are three years younger. Yasmin is now in her twenties. She recalled how she was physically and emotionally abused by her parents and neglected. Starved of love, she was offered affection by a male neighbour who regularly sexually abused her.

She found out that, while Meena, Kiran and Harish were the offspring of her mother and the person she viewed as her father, she had been the product of a rape by a distant relative. Initially, her mother had been too humiliated and ashamed to tell anyone or seek an abortion. Just before Yasmin's birth, her mother told her husband what had happened. He had been supportive and agreed to keep the rape secret and let others assume that Yasmin was his own daughter. However, neither parent could accept Yasmin nor bond with her; they were both too aware of the circumstances of her conception. Despite their best intentions, they neglected and abused her.

Yasmin's grandmother also lived in the household and knew nothing of her conception through rape. She provided Yasmin with physical care and showed her affection. This positive relationship enabled Yasmin to thrive and develop a sense of self-worth. When she started in a reception class, her teacher realized that she had a very musical ear. Throughout her school career, Yasmin was made to feel special by her teachers who valued her musical ability and her very lovely singing voice. All the messages from her school were positive as was the attitude of her grandmother. Yasmin began to form the view that she was being abused by her parents because they did not understand her talents and resented her special abilities. Although in her teenage years she became depressed, self-loathing and engaged in some self-harm by cutting herself, she had a deep-seated belief that she was valued and worthy. She therefore sought counselling and now feels that her self-esteem is buoyant and her future bright.

 Discussion Points

Yasmin had a particular talent that enabled her teachers to value her. However, all children have some personality features and aptitudes that can be valued. Early years workers can help safeguard children by adopting positive outlooks, valuing all children.

They can also help indirectly by contesting any attitudes that objectify children. For example, if they write or talk about children, they can avoid referring to 'the child' (where there is no indication of gender) as 'it'; just as when referring to adults, they can pluralize, i.e. use 'they' or 'he or she'. They can also avoid and even challenge phrases that demonize children (Goldson, 2001), e.g. referring to them as 'little devils' or 'little monsters'.

SUMMARY

As this chapter has indicated, it is important for practitioners to understand the underlying dynamics of abuse because the laws, policies and procedures are worth nothing if practitioners do not know when to implement them. All people working with young children, including students, as well as those developing safeguarding policies, need to appreciate the nature of abuse, the different contexts in which abuse occurs and the various ways in which it can be manifested. They need however to be sensitive to the diverse forms of family

(Continued)

(Continued)

life and not assume that childcare practices that are not mainstream are harmful. However, they will benefit from an understanding of the power that abusers hold over their victims, whether or not those abusers have any power in wider society. They also need to be aware that abused children might, like hostages displaying the Stockholm syndrome, protect those who harm them and deny any mistreatment. Practitioners and students on placement need to reflect on their practice. In doing so, they can usefully question whether they resist the idea that abuse can occur in their particular practice setting because to do otherwise would cause them too much effort or discomfort.

Usually, there will be signs that children are being abused. However, it is important not to underestimate how difficult it can be to identify these signs. Early years practitioners have to maintain a fine balance between underreacting by failing to recognize signs, and overreacting by making assumptions of abuse when there are alternative explanations. The more knowledge and understanding acquired, the easier it is to achieve that balance.

QUESTIONS FOR REFLECTION AND DISCUSSION

1. How are concepts of child protection socially constructed?
2. What are the major obstacles to the recognition of child abuse and neglect?
3. Why is the 'Stockholm syndrome' significant?
4. What are the implications of Laming for all early years practitioners (2003)?
5. How does child protection practice benefit from a multidisciplinary approach?

Recommended reading

Corby, B. (2000) *Child Abuse: Towards a Knowledge Base*, 2nd edition. Buckingham: Open University Press.

Doyle, C. (2006) *Working with Abused Children*, 3rd edition. Basingstoke: Palgrave Macmillan.

Lindon, J. (2008) *Safeguarding Children and Young People: Child Protection 0–18 Years*. London: Hodder Education.

Wilson, K. and James, A. (eds) (2007) *The Child Protection Handbook*, 3rd edition. Edinburgh: Baillière Tindall, Harcourt Publishers.

Recommended websites

National Society for the Protection of Children (NSPCC): www.nspcc.org.uk;
The Children's Web Mag, an online journal about child welfare: www.childrenwebmag.com

8 UNDERSTANDING DIVERSITY

Prospera Tedam

Chapter objectives

- To explore the concept of 'diversity' within the context of early years care and education.
- To identify the role of professionals, parents and the wider community in supporting young children to gain an understanding of difference.
- To highlight relevant national and international legislative and policy frameworks which underpin diversity.
- To develop students' understanding of the barriers to equal opportunities and to explore strategies for removing the barriers.

The purpose of this new chapter is to provide students with an understanding of contemporary research concerning diversity and inclusive practice in the early years. This chapter will explore the concept of diversity and the idea of valuing individuals and their differences as a means to further enriching society and achieving social justice. The chapter will also argue that understanding diversity will add value to the professionals' approach to working with young children, who all have individual characteristics that make them unique and form part of their identity. The role that professionals, parents and the wider community have in encouraging and supporting young children in understanding issues of diversity in contemporary society will be explored in detail. An overview of current national and international legislation and policy frameworks which underpin diversity will be given and the implications for early years practice will be outlined. The chapter will also consider the barriers to equal opportunities for children, families and early years practitioners, and explore ways of removing barriers to offer equality of service, regardless of individual differences such as special needs, abilities, 'race', gender or socio-economic status. Two case studies will be used to enhance the reader's understanding of the value of diversity and the nature and meaning of inclusion within society.

Nelson Mandela, in 1994, during his inauguration as Prime Minister for South Africa, stated 'no one is born hating another person because of the colour of his skin, or his background or his religion. People must learn to hate, and if they can learn to hate, they can be taught to love, for love comes more naturally to the human heart than its opposite' (Mandela, 1994; cited in Brown, 2001: xii). It is argued here that this statement forms the foundation on which issues of diversity should be developed and understood, especially in relation to children who should be taught, at an early age, to appreciate and respect difference and to value their uniqueness as human beings.

This view is supported by the Department of Health (2007a: 9), where it is suggested that in terms of early years provision, 'providers have a responsibility to ensure positive attitudes to diversity and difference – not only so that every child is included and not disadvantaged, but also so that they learn from the earliest age to value diversity in others and grow up making a positive contribution to society'.

People who work with children will be striving to support the development of children into adulthoods which are positive, productive and respectful. Our values would be in question if, during the early years, children were not taught to love and respect each other and were instead taught to hate, disrespect and discriminate against other children who are different from themselves.

DIVERSITY LANGUAGE AND TERMINOLOGY

According to Thompson (2006), societies are characterized by differentiation. This means that societies are made up of a diverse range of people whose social divisions such as gender, socio-economic status, age, race, etc. play a central role in determining the opportunities available and the power distribution and status of individuals, groups and communities. We cannot ignore the fact that contemporary British society is becoming more and more diverse, due primarily to immigration and the resettlement of people from around the globe. According to Haynes (cited in Coombe and Little, 1986), the end of the Second World War saw Britain turning to her colonies for semi-skilled and unskilled labour – this resulted in the migration of people from the Caribbean and South Asia to work in the UK. The end of the economic boom in the final quarter of the twentieth century saw a rise in poverty and disadvantage for many black people in the UK, which was characterized by low income, poor housing and social exclusion (Cohen et al., 2001). More recently, the free movement of members of the European Union has further contributed to the diversity in Britain.

In 1996, NCH Action for Children conducted a study which revealed that about 3.2 million people, or 6 per cent of the population, were from minority ethnic groups with around 36 per cent of this figure being children under 16 (NCH Action for Children, 1996: 24–5). This challenges professionals in the early years education and childcare sector to not only become aware of the benefits which this diversity brings to our society, but also consider the tensions that may arise due to insensitivity, misunderstanding or intolerance to difference. Diversity enriches society through the different ideas, knowledge and experiences that people hold.

There are many aspects of difference between and among people including: gender, age, religion and faith, ethnicity, race, economic status, health, sexuality, family structure and disabilities, yet this list is not exhaustive. There also exist additional characteristics which further differentiate people. For example, a child of Somali origin may also be

Muslim, female, disabled, born in Britain or may be a refugee or 'asylum seeker'. For the purposes of this chapter, the focus will be on age, gender and sexuality, race and economic status. While the author understands the importance of all forms of difference, there is little opportunity to explore these areas in detail. Where this is the case, the reader will be signposted to additional relevant texts that discuss these themes in greater depth.

RACE AND ETHNICITY

This section will begin with conceptualizing 'race' and 'ethnicity' in relation to how these concepts are used within this chapter. The concept of 'race' can be understood as a social construct as: 'a vast group of people loosely bound together by a historically contingent, socially significant element of their ancestry' (Delgado and Stefanic, 1999: 165).

Ethnicity, according to Storkey (1991: 109–10, cited in Thompson, 2006: 72), can be defined as: 'All the characteristics which go to make up cultural identity: origins, physical appearance, language, family structure, religious beliefs, politics, food, art, music, literature, attitudes towards the body, gender roles, clothing, education'.

From a very early age, children will notice difference in skin colour but are unlikely to make sense of this until they are a little older. The views of their family, friends and the media all contribute towards their understanding of race and will also influence their views of people who are different from them. Very young children do not have the capacity to be racist, however, once they begin to question the difference within their school or provision, it is the role of professionals to help them make sense of race and to understand the need to treat all people in a fair manner. The role of the media is a powerful vehicle for fuelling racialized and discriminatory behaviour and attitudes. Siraj-Blatchford (1994) suggests that the media portrayal of black people as inferior or problematic, and the stereotyping of minority ethnic communities, misinform people and can negatively shape the opinions and conceptions of young children.

Early years professionals will need to be aware of racism and its longer-term effects on children's self-esteem and identity. Incidents of racism which are not properly dealt with will send the message that practitioners or early years provisions condone racist and discriminatory behaviour and attitudes. Victims of racism, no matter how young, have to be supported and reassured that the incidents will be dealt with in an appropriate manner. Perpetrators of racial abuse should be cautioned in an age-appropriate manner and the parents or carers duly informed and advised on how to ensure that such behaviour is unacceptable. The Swann Report (Swann, 1985) highlighted that a small majority of teachers were consciously racist and a good number were 'unintentionally racist', and as a result made children from Black and minority ethnic groups feel inferior by the use of certain books and other educational material.

A child's early years are important because it is the period during which children develop self-awareness and begin to form their racial and personal identity, and practitioners should be skilled enough to support children through this period.

Early years professionals should understand the implication of discrimination legislation in general and the Race Relations (Amendment) Act 2000 in particular for their work:

- Early years professionals should examine teaching resources such as books, toys and artefacts to see if they positively represent all sectors of society.
- Practitioners should receive training on race equality issues and be required to attend refresher courses on similar topics (Qualifications and Curriculum Authority, 2007, online).

 Case Study

Suzie is a five-year-old Chinese girl who has recently started the Foundation Stage at her local school. Prior to this, Suzie attended a local authority-run day nursery. Suzie had been at the new school for nearly five weeks and seemed to be enjoying school until one day when she returned from school sullen and upset. She told her parents about her day at school. Suzie started off by saying that she no longer liked her hair and wanted to have blonde hair. When asked by her parents why she felt this way, Suzie explained that she was upset because during the school break, she had made a 'den' with her friends but then was not allowed into the 'den' because the criteria for going into the den was that one had to have 'blonde hair'. Suzie's parents explained that Suzie had nice hair and that her hair is and would remain as it is. Suzie's parents decided to talk to her about difference, explaining that everyone is different and special, adding that her different hair colour and texture should be a source of pride. Suzie appeared to understand the discussion; however, getting her to school the following day was difficult as she was concerned that she would still not be allowed to play in the 'den' because her hair was not blonde. Suzie's parents arrange a meeting with the class teacher to discuss their concerns.

 Discussion Points

1. What issues are raised for you in this case study?
2. How could the class teacher support Suzie to feel accepted and not excluded?
3. Is there a need to speak to the children concerned?
4. What could happen if this issue is not addressed?

INCLUSION

For the purposes of this chapter, this section will focus on inclusion in the wider context of early years, as the next chapter will explore inclusion in terms of Special Educational Needs (SEN).

Inclusion is a term which often generates debate and discussion, and there is no fixed definition for inclusion. There is a school of thought which defines inclusion as 'a process of identifying, understanding and breaking down the barriers to participation and belonging' (Early Childhood Forum, 2003 online). There is another school of thought which suggests that 'inclusion' is a universal human right with the aim of embracing all people, irrespective of race, disability, gender, sexuality, and medical or other need.

Inclusion has been described as a process and not a static state and it cannot be said to be universal in its application. The process of inclusion creates a supportive and nurturing environment for young children and early years practitioners should strive towards making their settings inclusive and nurturing. For this author, talking about 'inclusion' means that invariably, some people or groups will be 'excluded' and so it is important to identify the meaning of inclusion within specific contexts. Young children need to be included and need to feel that they are not different. Ensuring the inclusion of all children in early years will stem from the provision of equal opportunities for children to participate in and learn with their peers, irrespective of their gender, socio-economic background and race.

 Case Study

The following discussion took place between a six-year-old child with additional needs and a member of staff at the local after-school provision.

Staff: 'Children, would you all please line up behind the table?'
*Ben: (stands in the line but keeps moving about)
Staff: 'Ben, the instruction was to line up and stand still.'
*Ben: (still talking to a friend and moving about)
Staff: 'Ben, do you understand English?'
*Ben: 'Yes, I do.'
Staff: 'Then, what part of "line up behind the table" was said in Greek?'

 Discussion Points

1. What questions are raised for you by the above?
2. How could the member of staff express themselves more appropriately?
3. Are there grounds for a complaint against this member of staff?
4. What future training needs (if any) would you recommend for this member of staff?

Children today need a range of educational opportunities to assist them in achieving their full potential. Children need to develop the skills, attitudes and knowledge which will enable them to interact positively with people from diverse backgrounds and groups.

According to Bondy et al. (1995), the concept of inclusion is not restricted to children with disabilities but also children living in poverty, children for whom English is an additional language, homeless children and so on.

The role of parents, professionals and the wider community is central in ensuring that children have an understanding of and respect for diversity. Children and young people are influenced by the society in which they live and belong, therefore professionals will need to begin from the point of building good working relationships with parents by understanding the difficulties they face, their strengths, skills and expertise (Brown, 2001).

It is useful to note the reasons why it is important for children to understand difference and diversity. According to Brown (1998), there are three main reasons why these issues are important for children:

- **Legal issues** – understanding diversity on the part of early years practitioners will assist in challenging any personal prejudices or stereotypes they might have and will enable them to work in compliance with the law.
- **Ethical issues** – to some people, it may seem moral and ethical to provide fair treatment and equality of opportunities to all people, regardless of individual differences. There is also the recognition of social justice and its centrality in discussions of diversity and equal opportunities.
- **Social issues** – children will learn from what they have observed of inclusive and non-discriminatory practices and are likely to grow into adults who will respect diversity and who can make positive contributions to their communities and the nation as a whole. In this respect, Graham (2007: 65) asserts that as a strategy for equality, 'diversity recognizes that everyone has a contribution to make' and children, as much as adults, are central to the understanding and respect of diversity.

GENDER EQUITY

Gender debates in relation to biological and social differences between the genders are important in early years professional training and work and have been seen by some as being socially constructed, and children tend to be socialized into either the male or female role (Woodhead and Montgomery, 2003). It is further suggested by Woodhead and Montgomery (2003: 181) that it may be difficult to understand the nature of childhood without taking into account the differences in 'girls' worlds and boys' worlds' and that children learn gender-appropriate behaviour by observation.

The area of play is an important one in early years settings as children begin to identify with aspects of play that are likely to reflect their gender. The type of play children engage in, for example dolls for girls, as suggested by Haralambos and Holborn (2004) serves to reinforce the stereotype of women as carers, while boys are often given toys which are designed to develop their scientific and constructional skills.

Professionals are encouraged to support children's play and experiment with toys, games and activities that transcend gender.

It is difficult to imagine how young children will perceive gender equity if in practice there are far more females than males in the early years profession.

This chapter does not seek to explain why the early years profession is as gendered as it is, as this is an extensive area worthy of a much fuller debate. Instead, this section aims to highlight the need for a balanced gender mix in practitioners, in order that children learn from and understand diversity from a gender perspective.

Owen (2003) asserts that in 1991, of a total of 57,000 nursery nurses, there were only 600 men, which is a little over one per cent. The report continues to state that by 2001/2002, this picture had not changed significantly. There is therefore the need for children to see both females and males in the caring profession as this is likely to challenge their stereotypes about gender and gender-related roles in early years provision. Cameron (2006) confirms that this trend is similar in other European countries with Denmark having the highest employment rates for males in the early childhood workforce, primarily due to the effective marketing and recruitment strategies adopted.

SOCIO-ECONOMIC STATUS

Vast differences exist between children in the early years in terms of their parents' or families' socio-economic status. With parental unemployment, low-income families and widespread childhood poverty, early years settings are certain to have children whose socio-economic background means that they are 'different' and possibly excluded by other children. The media plays a significant role in making young children aware of the 'must-have' toys, games and gadgets and, in some settings, children are allowed to take these into school to 'show and tell' at various points in the term, thereby placing pressure on the other children to own such toys and games (see Chapters 1 and 2).

Poverty in the 21st century is widespread and is usually understood in terms of material, social and emotional shortages. There are currently around 3.8 million children living in poverty in the UK – this equates to 1 in 3 children, which is a significant increase from the 1970s when the figure was 1 in 10 (Wyse, 2004).

The impact of poverty on children is devastating and as recent research by the End Child Poverty Campaign indicates, poverty shapes children's development and can shorten lives (End Child Poverty, 2008, online). It is useful, therefore, for early years professionals to understand the nature and impact of poverty on children's learning, achievement and social presentation and to ensure that children in their care are treated equally and fairly, irrespective of their family's socio-economic background.

In order to ensure equity when working with young children; it is essential that professionals do not encourage the excessive display of wealth by some children, as this greatly disadvantages and disempowers children from other socio-economic backgrounds. Professionals will also need to ensure that their requests of parents and carers to provide, for example, costumes for various activities are reasonable and do not in any way undermine the position of parents and carers. Children from lower socio-economic backgrounds may also be black, disabled and/or asylum seeking, which places them in a situation of multiple disadvantage. This needs to be carefully considered by practitioners to promote equality of opportunity for children they work with.

SOCIAL JUSTICE

Social justice and equality are closely linked, and, as Kobayashi and Ray (2000) assert, educational institutions contribute to the defining of which social inequality issues will be tolerated by the public. Vincent (2003: 18) argues that social justice can be understood within a framework and has a number of facets. These are associational, distributive, and cultural justice. Associational justice is the absence of the 'patterns of association amongst individuals and amongst groups which prevent people from participating fully in decisions which affect the conditions within which they live and act' (Gewirtz, 2001: 41, cited in Vincent, 2003). This understanding of associational justice is one which has the closest links to the theme of this chapter. One could argue that the inability of children to participate fully in matters which affect them and any treatment meted out to children as a result of their age, gender, race and socio-economic status is one which infringes on social justice. Vincent (2003) goes on to perceive distributive justice as the process through which goods and services are shared in society. This form of social justice relates to the socio-economic status of children, groups and communities. The final framework for understanding social justice is the cultural perspective, which implies disrespect and non-recognition of cultures that are different from our own. Social justice and anti-discriminatory practice go together and can be used as a vehicle of empowerment and celebration of diversity and difference. Early years professionals will need to understand the value of advancing the notion of social justice, in order to effectively challenge discrimination and promote equality of opportunity for all children.

A PROFESSIONAL APPROACH TO WORKING WITH DIVERSITY AND DIFFERENCE

Early years professionals provide the preparation of children for the future, support the elimination of the disadvantages faced by some groups of children and also strive to provide an environment free from discrimination (Willan et al., 2004). In order to achieve this effectively, they are required to first and foremost understand difference and diversity, the impact on various groups of children and the exclusion faced by some of such children. Robinson (2005) suggests that early years professionals should feel able to take risks in challenging inequality and discrimination and that practitioners should make this a priority area. All early years settings have to ensure that their staff (permanent and temporary) understand the legislative and policy framework governing their service area and are aware of the implications of non-adherence to the law.

A professional approach for practitioners involved in early years settings takes account of practitioners' understanding of the importance of respecting difference and acknowledging the benefits of difference. It is also important to mention that within staff teams, there will be diversity in personality, attitudes, backgrounds, gender, faith and religious beliefs, culture, language and abilities. The starting point, therefore, for professionals will be to acknowledge the differences which exist among colleagues and to treat everyone with respect. It is only by working in this inclusive way as practitioners that young children will be able to learn inclusive and non-discriminatory behaviour and attitudes.

POLICY FRAMEWORKS

A range of legislation exists, both nationally and internationally, that provides a framework for anti-discriminatory practice generally and more specific legislation affecting children. The success or failure of these pieces of legislation will rest on practitioners' ability to translate them into practice within their early years provision for children. In addition to specific pieces of legislation, government guidance on various topics has been written and should be read and applied alongside relevant legislation. For example, the most recent publication by the Department for Children and Families (DCSF) in 2008, entitled 'The Inclusion of Gypsy, Roma and Traveller Children and Young People', highlighted children in this category as being the group which is most 'at risk' in education, due primarily to low achievement exacerbated by factors such as racism, discrimination and stereotyping. Lord Adonis, the Parliamentary Under Secretary of State for Schools, stated in his foreword that 'we need to create an inclusive learning environment for all children' and that raising the achievement of Gypsy and Roma children is 'the responsibility of everyone within the education system' (DCSF, 2008c: 5).

THE NATIONAL PICTURE

The rights of children in Britain are enshrined in a number of specific legislation. In England and Wales, the Children Act 1989 and the Education Act 1944 emphasize children's right to be protected from unfair discrimination. The Race Relations (Amendment) Act 2000 was introduced following an enquiry into the murder of a black teenager, Stephen Lawrence, in 1993 and placed statutory duties on local authorities, including local education authorities to promote race equality and equal opportunities and to ensure positive relationships among people of different races (Maynard and Thomas, 2004). The MacPherson Report in 1999 found that institutional racism was the reason for the flawed and poorly handled investigation into the black teenager's death. The Report defined institutional racism as:

> The collective failure of an organisation to provide an appropriate and professional service to people because of their colour, culture, or ethnic origin. It can be seen or detected in processes, attitudes and behaviour which amount to discrimination through unwitting prejudice, ignorance, thoughtlessness and racist stereotyping which disadvantage minority ethnic people. (MacPherson, 1999: paragraph 6.34)

What this means for schools and early years provision is that policies, procedures, rules, practice and guidelines should seek to include all children. A report by the DfES in 2006, a concerning pattern of high numbers of exclusions of African-Carribean boys in comparison with the white peers was highlighted and echoed previous studies which suggested that schools' policies were discriminatory towards African-Carribean boys (DfES, 2006b: 10).

More recently, the Children Act 2004, which came into force as a direct result of the death of Victoria Climbié, and the subsequent enquiry by Lord Laming into the eight-year-old girl's death highlighted the government's vision for all children in England and Wales to: stay safe, be healthy, enjoy and achieve, make a positive contribution and achieve economic well-being. These targets, known as the five outcomes, demonstrate a commitment on the part of the government and public authorities to ensure that all children in England and Wales achieve a good standard of life and maximize their potential.

In addition to the above, in the Childcare Act of 2006, which has been described as a pioneering piece of legislation due to its focus on early years and childcare provision in England and Wales (DfES, 2004e), sections 1–5 emphasize the need for local authorities and NHS trusts to work together towards the reduction of inequalities between and among children and to support the achievement of the five outcomes as stated above. The Act further places a duty on local authorities to assess childcare provision in their areas and to ensure that children with disabilities and children from low-income families are provided with services to meet their needs (Childcare Act 2006). The Disability Discrimination Act 1995 (DDA) sets out two main duties towards children with disabilities. The first duty is not to treat a child 'less favorably' and the second is to make 'reasonable adjustments' for disabled children. These duties apply to all areas of early years provision. Also, the Education and Inspections Act 2006 (DfES, 2006c) introduced a duty on all maintained schools in England to promote community cohesion. This duty came into effect on 1 September 2007. Ofsted is also required to report on the contributions made in this area. This commenced in September 2008 (Multiverse, 2008, online). Further, the Department for Children, Schools and Families has published *Guidance on the Duty to Promote Community Cohesion*, which defines community cohesion as:

> ... working towards a society in which there is a common vision and sense of belonging by all communities; a society in which the diversity of people's backgrounds and circumstances is appreciated and valued; a society in which similar life opportunities are available to all; and a society in which strong and positive relationships exist and continue to be developed in the workplace, in schools and in the wider community. (DCSF, 2007d: 3)

THE INTERNATIONAL PICTURE

From an international perspective, the 1989 United Nations Convention on the Rights of the Child (UNCRC) highlights a number of Articles that are relevant to the discussion on valuing diversity and the provision of equality of opportunity for children. In particular, Article 2 of the Convention states that 'each child should enjoy the rights set out in the convention without discrimination of any kind, irrespective of the child's parent's or guardian's race, colour, gender, language, religion, political or other opinion, national or social origin, property, disability, birth or status'.

The Human Rights Act 1998 which has been incorporated into UK law stipulates a number of rights that every human being is entitled to. A human rights perspective suggests that all people are treated fairly, without discrimination and with equality of opportunity. Public bodies or persons carrying out a public function can be in breach of various articles under the Human Rights Act 1998. In particular, Article 14 prohibits all forms of discrimination and it is imperative that education and early years settings promote anti-discriminatory practice by adhering to the obligations of the Human Rights Act. The European Commission (EC), in a *Handbook on Equality Data* (Makkonen, 2006: 11), affirmed its commitment to tackling discrimination and ensuring equality for all, in a strategy document entitled 'Non-discrimination and equal opportunities for all – A framework strategy'. This strategy affects all countries in the European Union, including the UK. The Handbook makes interesting reading and provides a powerful statement about equal opportunities:

> Denial of equal opportunities comes at a high price for those concerned and the society at large, as discrimination prejudices the rights and opportunities of individuals, leads to the wasting of human resources, and causes social disintegration. Furthermore, given Europe's current demographic tendencies — low birth rate, ageing population and thus a shrinking workforce — equal treatment is no longer only a question of social justice but also of economic necessity. (Makkonen, 2006: 11)

The international movement of people across national and international borders due to economic, political and social reasons has created an increase in immigrants coming into the UK. The Refugee Council defines an asylum seeker as one who 'has left their country of origin and formally applied for asylum in another country but whose application has not yet been decided' (Refugee Council, 2008, online).

A refugee, according to the same source, is a person whose 'application for asylum has been successful and who is allowed to stay in another country having proved that they would face persecution back home' (Refugee Council, 2008, online). Asylum and refugee children in the UK alone, according to Rutter (2003), number about 120,000 and yet research suggests that refugee children are less likely to access early years provision and that these children are currently underrepresented in early years provision. There is also further evidence by Rutter and Hyder (1998), suggesting that refugee populations have more children under five years of age than the general population.

IMPLICATIONS FOR EARLY YEARS PROFESSIONALS (EYP)

The range of legal and policy frameworks on the subject of anti-discrimination and inclusion is vast and covers a range of specific issues. EYP will, as part of their training, be expected to learn and understand these concepts and the implications for professional practice. Additionally, EYP can be held accountable for any behaviours and attitudes which are not aligned with legislation and which are likely to bring the profession into disrepute. Anti-discriminatory legislation and policy will set boundaries and parameters for professionals during their work with children and will also serve as guidelines for best practice.

Parents, families and carers of children will be able to use relevant legislation as a kind of 'quality assurance' tool in determining the extent to which their provider is working to promote the inclusion of children within their settings. EYP should promote a culture of openness and trust, in which children can share their fears and hopes for the present and the future. In talking about difference, professionals need to be aware of the language they use to describe children who are different, as children in their care will pick up such language.

Professionals will need to be aware of certain groups of children – for example, asylum-seeking and refugee children who access their provision may require additional support in understanding the culture, expectations, procedures and regulations in the UK. EYP are required to promote equality of opportunity for the children and families they work with and can do this by:

- ensuring equal access by children, carers and families to resources and available learning opportunities
- receiving training to enable them to challenge discrimination firmly and with confidence
- being aware of their duties towards disabled children and the implications of the Disability Discrimination Act 1995 on their work with children
- being aware of and changing practices, policies and procedures that might unintentionally discriminate against children with disabilities
- liaising with health visitors and other health professionals about the health needs of the refugee and asylum-seeking children in their care.

BARRIERS TO EQUAL OPPORTUNITIES

Despite being grounded in policy and legislation, it can be difficult to practise in an inclusive way and, whether by intent or sheer misjudgement, practitioners can find themselves in difficult situations which are likely to create unhealthy working environments. This section will briefly outline some of the barriers to achieving equal opportunities for children in the early years sector. According to Brown (2001), the main barriers to achieving equal opportunities for children include the following:

- Being uninformed – being unaware of equal opportunities and how it affects children can be a significant barrier to achieving equity within the early years setting. Professionals are required to engage in ongoing development which continues to challenge their thinking and their practice.
- Being insensitive – as unique individuals, our attitudes and behaviours are shaped by our values, beliefs and life experiences, some of which may result in professionals being insensitive to the needs and emotional well-being of the children they work with. Being sensitive to a particular issue will convey the message to a child that professionals are interested in and concerned about their well-being and development, whereas insensitivity is likely to result in children feeling unimportant and helpless.
- Individual stereotypes – we are all social beings who learn from our environment and experiences and these shape our thought processes and the way in which we view the world. EYP are not value-free and will invariably hold stereotypes about certain groups of people and individuals and take

these with them into practice (Siraj-Blatchford, 1994). For example, assumptions about certain groups in society will create barriers to the provision of equal opportunities for children in these groups.

Overcoming the barriers

Lynch (1987) argues that it is possible to educate teachers and staff in schools on prejudice reduction by way of acquiring the relevant principles of social justice and respect for all people. By so doing, the barriers to achieving equal opportunities for children will be minimized and overcome. Some of these are:

Encourage open debate and discussion
Open debate and discussion should be encouraged within the workplace, and practitioners should feel able to share their anxieties around issues of diversity to enable a learning environment which is open to a sharing of experiences and skills in the area of difference within the early years setting.

Promote regular interaction/collaboration between parents and professionals
Following on from the previous point, early years professionals should engage in regular interaction and collaboration with parents and carers of the children in their care in order to dispel some of the stereotypical views they might hold about certain people and groups of people.

Maintain a reflexive approach
Being reflexive when working with children and their families, according to Robinson and Diaz (2006: 169), involves the deconstruction of 'tolerance' to one of 'respect'.

Staff composition
Early years staff teams should as closely as possible reflect the diversity of the wider community and societies in which we live. This will not only send a strong message to children and their families and carers, but will also provide role models for many of the children who access the provision.

Creative use of resources
Another means of overcoming barriers to equal opportunities in early years settings is to provide resources that will suit a wide range of children. For example, provide toys that can be used by able-bodied as well as disabled children, games that can be used by children of either gender and books, videos and music that reflect different cultural and ethnic communities.

Also, involve families and carers in activities within the provision to reinforce a commitment to equal opportunities and the diversity of skills, expertise and knowledge provided by families and carers of children. For example, an early years provision which encourages parents and carers, of either gender and any ethnicity, to support group activities or volunteer within the school or provision will send a strong message about their commitment to equality of opportunity for the benefit of the children.

Ouseley and Lane (2006) identify further ways through which EYP can overcome the barriers to providing equality of opportunity to children. A summary of these is given below:

1. Professionals will need to ensure that all children are given the equal opportunity to learn and develop in an environment which is free from discrimination, stereotyping and labelling.
2. Professionals should be conversant with and able to apply the legal framework which governs diversity, including the Race Relations Amendment Act 2000, the Human Rights Act 1998, Disability Discrimination Act 1995, the United Nations Convention on the Rights of the Child, the Equality Act 2006, the Children Act 1989 and 2004, and the Childcare Act 2006.
3. Every child should be encouraged to develop the full range of cognitive, behavioural and critical awareness skills.

It is imperative that all professionals working with children are aware of the legal framework and policies which underpin diversity and equality of opportunity for children. Aspects of the relevant legislation and policy have been explored in this chapter. An understanding of and commitment to promoting inclusion and social justice is crucial, if it is to be achieved. Children in early years require guidance and positive experiences of human values that accept and embrace diversity among people. There is a clear role for parents and carers, early years professionals and the wider community to ensure that children grow and develop tolerance, understanding and appreciation of diversity in contemporary society.

SUMMARY

This chapter has sought to provide a basis for critical reflection on the part of early years practitioners about inclusion and equal opportunities for children. The government has shown a strong commitment to issues of inclusion and requires professionals in this field of work to adhere to and promote inclusion in their places of work. This can be achieved through an examination of professionals' own values, views, experiences and attitudes to difference and through 'unlearning' some of the potentially divisive and unhelpful attitudes and views that they may hold about certain groups in our society (Siraj-Blatchford, cited in Pugh and Duffy, 2006). It is a welcome development that in recent times the Commission on Racial Equality (CRE), the Disability Rights Commission (DRC) and the Equal Opportunities Commission (EOC) have merged into the Equality and Human Rights Commission from 2007, and seeks to promote equality and human rights for all, reduce inequality, build positive relations, eliminate discrimination and ensure the fair participation of all people in society (Equality and Human Rights Commission, 2007).

Diversity should be promoted in all early years settings, regardless of the nature and scope of difference in a given area. It is not acceptable to deny the promotion of diversity with the excuse that particular early years settings have little or no enrolment from minority communities. The aim of promoting diversity should be to enable children to appreciate difference as they grow and develop into citizens of a diverse country and world.

The following quote sends a strong message to all about difference and diversity:

> As individual practitioners we cannot make the world free of inequalities and a safe place to be, but we can do our very best to ensure that our early years settings are small models of what we would like the world to be. (Lane, 2007: 1)

 QUESTIONS FOR REFLECTION AND DISCUSSION

1. Consider your personal values, beliefs and attitudes about diversity and social justice and explore where these came from and how they have shaped your identity.
2. How easy is it to challenge discriminatory attitudes and behaviours by colleagues?
3. Why is it important for early years practitioners to have a social justice perspective?

Recommended reading

Brown, B. (1999) *Unlearning Discrimination in the Early Years*. Stoke-on-Trent: Trentham Books.

Coombe, V. and Little, A. (1986) *Race and Social Work: A Guide to Training*. London: Tavistock Publications.

Robinson, K. H. and Diaz, C. J. (2006) *Diversity and Difference in Early Childhood Education*. Maidenhead: Open University Press.

Thompson, N. (2006) *Anti-discriminatory Practice*, 4th edition. London: Macmillan

Recommended websites

The Equality and Human Rights Commission: www.equalityhumanrights.com;
The Refugee Council: www.refugeecouncil.org.uk

INCLUSIVE PRACTICE FOR CHILDREN WITH SPECIAL EDUCATIONAL NEEDS (SEN)

Christine Hickman and Kyffin Jones

Chapter objectives

- To discuss the concept of inclusion in relation to young children with special educational needs (SEN).
- To consider the historical and legislative profile of SEN provision.
- To discuss how the individual needs of pupils with SEN may be met.
- To acknowledge the importance of a multi-agency approach.
- To consider the Every Disabled Child Matters campaign.

This chapter will discuss the issues surrounding the inclusion of children with special educational needs in the early years. Inclusion as a term and philosophy will be defined and discussed within a historical and legislative context in relation to special educational needs. Case studies will be used to demonstrate a range of provision for a range of need. While the importance of a multi-agency approach is commented upon, the main focus is an educational perspective.

'I had a really great time. Nobody talked to me all night!' (Michael, aged 7) Michael illustrates one of the underlying principles of the education of children with special educational needs (SEN) – the notion that how they see the world and what is important to them are individual and might differ from adults' reality. Michael has Asperger's syndrome which is characterized by impairment in social interaction (Blakemore Brown, 2001), and for him an enjoyable night at his local youth club entailed being completely ignored by his peers. This gave him the space to read his favourite science textbooks uninterrupted. What is clear, however, is that without a firm understanding of Michael's identity, both our assumptions and our interventions will not be accurate and might even be detrimental. This chapter will introduce a range of themes relating to the field of SEN while emphasizing the need to adopt a highly individual and sensitive response, one which pays heed to the child's own identity and perspective. While this chapter will recognize that specific disorders and conditions can be linked to general strategies and good practice, it will also urge the reader to look more widely than simple labels and categories in order to optimize interventions.

It is true that an understanding of the principles of conditions such as Asperger's syndrome might in some way aid the practitioner, but they are worth nothing without a clear understanding of the individual's perspective. If Michael is to be a fully functioning and included member of society, his inclusion is in some way dependent on our skills to understand him as much as his skills to fit in with us.

Inclusion, therefore, is not simply the debate about pupils with SEN being educated in mainstream schools, it is about the role society has in including all children equally.

THE LEGISLATIVE FRAMEWORK

It is clear from the wealth of literature on the subject that the movement towards inclusive education has been part of the educational scene in Britain for many years (Booth and Ainscow, 1998; Ainscow et al., 2006; Drifte, 2001; Dyson and Millward, 2000; Jones, 2004; Norwich, 1997; O'Brien, 2001; Wilson, 1998; Wolfendale, 2000 Roffey, 2001; Tassoni, 2003). Some maintain that it can be mapped back to the Education Act 1944 which extended the right to education to most (but not all) of Britain's children, as Stakes and Hornby (1997: 24) highlight:

> Children with SEN were to be placed in one of eleven categories of handicap: blind, partially sighted, deaf, partially deaf, epileptic, educationally subnormal, maladjusted, physically handicapped, speech defective, delicate and diabetic. The 1944 Act required that LEAs had to ascertain the needs of children in their area for special educational treatment. It indicated that this should be undertaken in mainstream schools wherever possible.

It is important to note that, at this time, disability was firmly categorized into medical subgroups and that the remit of education was to treat rather than educate. Subsequent reports such as that by the Warnock Committee (DES, 1978) highlighted the principle of integrating children with disabilities and developed the process of obtaining a statement of special educational need – in effect, a contract between pupil and educational provider based on careful assessment. The findings of Baroness Warnock and her team helped inform the subsequent 1981 Education Act. A greater emphasis was given to the education of children with special needs during the 1980s and early 1990s and this culminated in the implementation of the Code of Practice for Special Educational Needs in 1994, updated in 2001. At the time, this was the most prescriptive guidance on special needs to have been issued by the UK government. It aimed to expand the roles and responsibilities of schools and local education authorities (LEAs) highlighted in the 1981 Education Act. This trend of redefining SEN provision has continued and during the past decade has gained momentum and evolved considerably.

The Code of Practice (DfES, 2001a) stresses that 'provider' means all settings which early years children may attend, therefore adherence to such guidelines impacts upon a wide range of professional practice. The early years have specified strands in the Code: *Early Years Action* and *Early Years Action Plus*. According to Drifte (2001: 4), 'both stages involve individualised ways of working with the child, including the implementation of IEPs (Individual Education Plans), on a gradually increasing level of involvement'.

Early years provision has always crossed over fields, i.e. health and education, therefore previous legislation such as the 1981, 1993 and 1996 Education Acts may not have enabled a more cohesive approach to SEN in the early years (Wolfendale, 2000: 147). However, more recent legislation appears to be addressing this (Roffey, 2001: 14). *Curriculum 2000* contains an inclusive statement concerning the provision of effective learning opportunities for all pupils. It sets out three principles that are essential to developing a more inclusive curriculum:

1. Setting suitable learning challenges.
2. Responding to pupils' diverse learning needs.
3. Overcoming potential barriers to learning and assessment for individuals and groups of pupils (QCA, 2000).

Every Child Matters (DfES, 2004e) outlined five outcomes for all children of all ages: be healthy, stay safe, enjoy and achieve, make a positive contribution and achieve economic well-being. This agenda illustrates the government's aim to work with practitioners within a 'conceptual–philosophical framework' (Wolfendale and Robinson, 2006) and to create a more resolute coordinated package of support. The intention of bringing together services into single settings is one which most parents with children with disabilities welcome. For example, a child with a combination of difficulties could find themselves with as many as 315 different service-based appointments over a period of nine months (DfES, 2007b). The importance of early intervention and assessment, coordinated service provision and working with families for children with special needs and disabilities was underlined in the DfES and DoH (2003) guidance *Together from the Start*. The inception of Every Disabled Child Matters (EDCM), a campaign set up to advocate for the rights of disabled children and their families has underlined the strength of feeling by this group of stakeholders. Such campaign objectives as every family being entitled to a key worker on diagnosis, and every extended school and children's centre to deliver a full range of services to disabled children, are on the EDCM agenda (EDCM, 2006).

Removing Barriers to Achievement (DfES, 2004b) links the notion of the five outcomes for children with the needs of children with SEN. It echoes the intentions of collective responsibility for the child with SEN. The Early Years Foundation Stage (EYFS) documentation has provided practitioners with guidance and advice on supporting children's learning, development and welfare (DfES, 2007a). The fact that children learn and develop in different ways and at different rates is stressed, which has great relevance for the inclusion debate. Linking in to the outcomes of *Every Child Matters*, one of the aims of the EYFS is 'providing for equality of opportunity and anti-discriminatory practice and ensuring that every child is included and not disadvantaged because of ethnicity, culture or religion, home language, family background, learning difficulties or disabilities, gender or ability' (DfES, 2007a: 7).

Aiming High for Disabled Children: Better Support for families (DfES, 2007d) sets out the government's aim for all children to have the best start in life and ongoing support for them and their families so that they may reach their full potential. The three areas of (i) access and empowerment, (ii) responsive services and timely support and (iii) improving quality and capacity are considered to be the priority areas to improve outcomes for disabled children (DfES, 2007b). The thrust for joined-up care and support, involving a range of professionals, will necessitate action concerning staff training as awareness levels and more specific training are prioritized (DfES, 2007b). A common thread throughout this documentation and policy is the need for meaningful parental involvement. Wolfendale and Robinson (2006) underline the essential role that parents and families play. EDCM (2006) has the right of parents and families to shape service delivery at its heart. The government's intention to have long-term change in children's services is set out in the Children's Workforce Strategy (DfES, 2005) and the Multi Agency Toolkit (DfES, 2005). The overarching aim of such documentation is the consolidation of good practice in training and working procedure, with the emphasis on support for multi-agency working. While this has gone on for many years, many would admit it was organized and implemented on an ad hoc basis.

THE GLOBAL AND NATIONAL PERSPECTIVE

Inclusive policies have been found increasingly higher up the agenda of the UK government, local education authorities and individual schools. This is due in some part to the United Nations Educational, Scientific and Cultural Organization (UNESCO) Salamanca statement on principles, policy and practice in special needs education published in 1994. This statement urged national governments to pursue inclusive educational practices for all children.

It is the consensus of many educationalists (for example, Booth and Ainscow, 1998) that the goal of inclusive education is a worthy one but it leads us to ask two questions. First, what do we mean by inclusive education or 'inclusion', and second why do we need it? Finding a concrete definition of inclusion can be difficult and it is clear that confusion abounds, affecting providers, parents and the pupils themselves.

The Centre for Studies on Inclusive Education (CSIE) is an independent educational charity set up in 1982. In their literature, they define inclusion as, 'disabled and non-disabled children and young people learning together in ordinary pre-school provision, schools, colleges and universities, with appropriate networks of support' (CSIE, 2000: 1).

Such a short definition belies the incredibly far-reaching, controversial and challenging task of the inclusion movement. Essentially, the CSIE is advocating the end of segregated education and with it the traditional model of special education in this country. It follows that there must be a compelling argument behind this radical approach if one is to answer the second of the above questions. Why do we need inclusion? Again, the CSIE (2000) answers this in a succinct and direct way – 'because children – whatever their disability or learning difficulty – have a part to play in society after school; an early start in mainstream playgroups or nursery schools, followed by education in ordinary schools and colleges is the best preparation for an integrated life' (CSIE, 2000: 2).

Early intervention is an essential component to any debate on early years and inclusion (Mortimer, 2002). This is typified by the example of Ashlyn (see case study on p. 133–4). Both Ashlyn and her parents benefited from the intervention of a Portage worker. Due to the introduction and implementation of strategies, as well as awareness raising in respect of the diagnosed condition, this family was able both to address the child's immediate needs and develop a positive ethos towards the notion of having a child with a disability. As DfES (2007b: 35) observe, 'Early support for disabled children and their families is essential to prevent problems such as deteriorating health, family stress and breakdown, children potentially being placed in care, and deteriorating emotional and social development for disabled children and their siblings'.

In this respect, the English government's agenda includes healthy living, community support, multi-agency working and a focus on families. Initiatives such as Education and Health Action Zones and Sure Start are examples of these ideals (Wolfendale, 2000: 149). The flexibility of the Foundation Stage curriculum in England has been cited as a reason for the success of inclusion in the early years (Wolfendale and Robinson, 2006).

INCLUSION: A HUMAN RIGHT?

It is clear therefore that issues of equality and human rights are central to such a rationale, and as the above DFES quote highlights, education is only one part of the picture. The drive towards inclusive education has to be seen in a wider societal context if it is to be meaningful and successful. In other words, inclusion should be less about teachers and pupils and more about the responsibilities of all citizens. As Huskins (1998: 10) makes clear, 'communities have responsibility for providing the social, health and educational services necessary to complement the role of families in promoting the development of the "whole" child and for addressing social inequalities'.

As mentioned previously, there has been a need to bring together the differing areas in the field of early years. Inclusion is promoted by careful, joint planning, utilizing a broad range of expertise from a range of professionals in a cohesive manner. The experiences of John (see case study on p. 134) illustrate the need for the concept of inclusive practice to be taken beyond the realms of the mainstream versus special school debate.

Soon after gaining power in May 1997, the Labour government published the White Paper *Excellence in Schools* in June of that year. This was followed by the Green Paper, *Excellence for all Children*, published in September of the same year. These documents highlighted a clear shift in traditional policy towards children with disabilities. The educational landscape has changed considerably since the Education Act of 1944. Merely providing a school place for children with special needs is no longer acceptable; the quality of that education has to be second to none. The right for disabled children to access coordinated and accessible services is now at the heart of the inclusion agenda. The 1995 Disability Discrimination Act, for example, makes specific reference to steps being taken to prevent children with disabilities from being treated less favourably than other pupils, and to the provision of access for all children (DDA 1995).

MODELS OF DISABILITY AND THE ROLE OF SPECIAL SCHOOLS

If large numbers of children with SEN are in specialist provision, we need to ask why. This has resonance for the very young child with a disability, whose future may seem to be firmly placed in a specialist setting. The answer to this question might lie in the dominant position of the medical model. In this model, the child's needs are defined in medical terms and the idea that these children have different and exclusive needs is perpetuated. Also implicit in the medical model are the notion of impairment and the idea that problems are predominantly found within the child. Inclusion is aided by the use of educational terminology, such as 'learning difficulty', rather than reliance on categories ('autistic child') or medical labels. However, there is often a strong desire for a diagnosis and its subsequent 'label', as that is seen to be the route to support and funding for the child. It is here we see the areas of health and education both involved with a child, and where we would aim to see multi-agency working and partnership. The Early Years Development and Childcare Partnerships (EYDCP) bring new opportunities for a coming together and joining up of different settings, services, agencies and disciplines (Mortimer, 2002: 47). Hall (1997: 74) describes the causal link between the medical model and segregated specialist education thus:

> The medical model is only able to see the child and his impairments as the problem, with the solution being to adapt the child and his circumstances to the requirements of the world as it is. All of the adjustments must be made to the lifestyle and functionality of the child. Hence a range of prosthetic devices will be offered, along with a separate educational environment and transport to facilitate attendance. The notion that the world might need to change hardly arises because the child *has* and *is* the problem.

The final sentence of the above quote is important and outlines the argument of the Disability Movement, which has gained momentum in both the global and national arena. This argument advocates the use of the social model of disablement. Such a model is concerned with environmental barriers, and the notion that it is these barriers that disable people, therefore disability is seen as a socially created problem (Gelder, 2004). The Disability Movement makes it clear that the effective removal of impairments is rare, but a great deal more can be achieved by removing those barriers, which include not only the physical environment, but also associated policies and attitudes.

This sentiment was made law within the provisions of the Special Educational Needs and Disability Act (2001) and this has wide implications for the inclusion of children who were excluded from mainstream institutions for reasons of accessibility. Accessibility mirrors our interpretation of inclusion as a varied and individual concept. What is required is a broadening of the concept of access to include whatever barriers to learning impact on the individual child.

Sainsbury (2000), an adult with autism, is aware of the debates regarding identity, inclusion and disability rights and advocates a wide interpretation of these factors to meet the particular needs of those on the autistic spectrum. This is demonstrated by her definition of access and what constitutes an optimum learning environment for pupils with Asperger's syndrome: 'we don't need ramps or expensive equipment to make a difference for us; all we need is understanding' (Sainsbury, 2000: 9). This is illustrated very well by the staff training in John's school (see case study on p. 134).

Although the social model is now favoured above that of the medical model by many disabled people and their advocates, it is also true that for a great number of educationalists, parents and children, the segregated model has a lot of defenders. Jenkinson (1997: 10) categorizes the perceived advantages, which are broken down into practical and economic factors, together with specific effects on disabled and non-disabled children. She highlights the efficiency of necessary aids and equipment, specialist teachers and ancillary services to be located in one place. This complements the perceived benefits to the students found in smaller classes with more one-to-one attention and a curriculum pitched at an appropriate level. With the introduction and development of a more flexible early years curriculum in the Foundation Stage in England, it is thought by some that even when segregated provision may be the long-term option, the child will be successfully included in the early years (Wolfendale and Robinson, 2006). If, as cited earlier, the EYFS is providing for equality of opportunity as a core intention, then we might hope that children in the early years will be able to experience an inclusive start to their education. The principle of the unique child (DfES, 2007a: 8) and the notion of personalized learning (DCSF, 2008a) are key features of a system which is guided by individualized learning.

It is worth noting that, according to Wyn Siencyn and Thomas (2007), the last few years have seen changes which have led to some dramatic differences between Wales and England. However, SENDA 2001 makes provision for both Wales and England, and Wales has an SEN Code of Practice. It is interesting to note that the term Additional Learning Needs (ALN) is gradually replacing SEN as the preferred term (Wyn Siencyn and Thomas, 2007). Parents whose language is not English felt there were barriers to support for early identification and inclusion (WAG, 2003, cited in Wyn Siencyn and Thomas, 2007). In Scotland, the Education (Scotland) Act 1980 was still guiding provision for children with SEN until the Additional Support for Learning (Scotland) Act 2004 came into place (Carmichael and Hancock, 2007). The overall aim is for full integration and inclusion of all children, although specialized care and education is recognized as being necessary for some children (Carmichael and Hancock, 2007). From this, we can see that while there are some similarities between practice throughout the UK, there are also some significant differences and we should not assume that English provision is generalized.

It is fair to say that the majority of professionals in specialist provision feel they are working in the best interests of the children they teach. In many respects, 'special education' is seen as a worthy profession with established models of good practice and pedagogy. Any suggestion that they are helping to deny disabled children basic human rights or perpetuating institutional discrimination would be denied by many. A more cynical observation would be that it is in the interests of the two branches of education to remain distinctive, preserve the status quo and consolidate their expertise and influence. As Gelder notes, 'An inclusive approach may meet resistance from specialists in special schools because they feel their expertise is being overlooked. There may be resistance from teachers and practitioners from mainstream services, because they feel ill equipped to implement inclusive practice' (DfES, 2004b, cited in Gelder, 2004: 105).

HINDRANCES TO INCLUSION

Current government policy in England seems to be increasing its scrutiny of student attainment and performance-related indicators with the publication of school league tables (Gabriel, 2004). To some teachers, inclusion is perceived as a hindrance to these factors as it is often felt that inclusion is merely the opposite of exclusion. As a result, many teachers see the acceptance of children with emotional and behavioural problems into their class as synonymous with inclusion and to the detriment of their mainstream peers.

Social inclusion can therefore cause a great deal of anxiety in schools, as staff might be reluctant to consider issues of behaviour within the context of special needs: 'Teachers in normal schools may be willing to accommodate the "ideal" child with special needs in their classroom – the bright, brave child in a wheelchair – they will still want to be rid of the actual "average" child with special needs – the dull, disruptive child' (Tomlinson, 1982: 80).

It could be argued that we have a long way to go before the Audit Commission's Report of 2002 findings that too many children wait for too long to have their needs met and children who should be able to be taught in mainstream settings are turned away, are remediated entirely (DfES, 2004b). The aim of special schools sharing specialist skills and knowledge to support inclusion has a patchy national profile, and many parents still have concerns that their child's needs will be met at their local mainstream school. However, Ofsted (2006) found that pupils with even the most severe and complex needs are able to make outstanding progress in all types of settings (DfES, 2007b: 12). Fortunately, the concept of education for *all* is a right that is enshrined in law at local, national and international levels. Issues regarding the inclusion of children with SEN are ongoing and often controversial, highlighting the evolutionary nature of this debate. However, we must not lose sight of the fact that in the recent past, many of the children at the centre of this agenda were deemed ineducable. Scholars must recognize the nature of these advances and place the current arguments into this wider historical perspective.

The following case studies demonstrate the experiences of two children in the early years and the varied nature of SEN and support. They show the difficulties facing practitioners involved in setting up appropriate interventions together, with an indication of the areas that require targeting.

 Case Study

Ashlyn was born prematurely and has a diagnosis of cerebral palsy. She is 18 months old. Her parents were devastated when they were given the diagnosis by their GP, and had no idea what the future may hold for them and their daughter.

A referral was made to the local Portage service. This was funded by the LA. Fortnightly visits were set up by the Portage home visitor, whose background was in physiotherapy. In the first visit, Ashlyn was observed and the Portage worker played with her. The Portage checklist was introduced to her parents and they were encouraged to set aside a regular time each day to work with Ashlyn. Written weekly teaching activities were agreed with

(Continued)

(Continued)

Ashlyn's parents, based on her priority areas of need. In Ashlyn's case, these were gross motor skills, fine motor skills, self-help and communication/socialization. The parents then did daily activities with their daughter. This made them feel totally involved in her progress, and they said they felt their knowledge about Ashlyn's condition was greatly enhanced.

New teaching targets were developed over time; each stage was evaluated, taking into account the views of the parents. Ashlyn has made considerable progress. Ashlyn's mother has joined a parent support group which has a toy library. Both parents feel more positive about the years ahead.

 Case Study

John is 7 years and 10 months old. He has recently been given a diagnosis of autistic spectrum disorder. John attends a large inner-city, mainstream primary school.

John has odd and idiosyncratic speech, which is a feature of Asperger's syndrome. This often has a maturity beyond his years, e.g. 'I find this work tedious in the extreme', or will feature alliteration, which amuses John but annoys or confuses his peers – 'Today is torturous Tuesday, telemetry is tenaciously taught'. Both peers and staff find it difficult to understand what he is saying as he often mumbles or whispers his words and makes little use of eye contact or gesture. He seems to 'switch off' if adults address him directly, or if they talk at length.

John is an avid reader of books, particularly dictionaries and non-fiction books relating to football statistics. As a consequence of his communication difficulties, John is ostracized and bullied by his peers who find him odd.

John has begun to go up to groups of boys at lunch time and forcefully push them, causing them to chase and physically abuse him. Staff have repeatedly told him not to, but this has no effect and John gives the impression he enjoys the chase and insists that he is *playing* with the boys. When they call him names, he turns them into alliterations, which makes this spiral of bullying continue.

Following a meeting with the autism outreach service, a volunteer has come in at playtime and has introduced some playground games, based upon a football theme. He wrote a simple set of rules to accompany each game for the children to refer to. John was excited to read the rules and became animated when the games were played. He tried to direct his peers, and it was noticeable that they were far more accepting of him in this context.

Staff have followed on from this approach in the classroom and have started to write down information for John to refer to. John also has a small selection of prompt symbols to help him remember such social rules as using a person's name to indicate that he is addressing them. He has responded well to this and staff have noticed that he is far more willing to communicate with them. They have also made attempts to use his knowledge of football-related statistics and his knowledge of unusual words to lift his profile within the class. His peers are very impressed with his knowledge, and while they still regard him as odd, they respect his abilities and tolerate his differences.

SUMMARY

These case studies serve to illustrate the notion that there are aspects of good practice that are generic with regard to the support of these children and work across the board. These include:

- the use of structure and routine
- practitioner language
- visual systems
- individualized motivators
- practitioner awareness and knowledge
- the appropriate and creative use of support staff
- knowledge of the individual child's perspective and sensibilities
- a recognition of the role of other children and peer relationships
- a recognition of the role of parents
- a commitment to an inclusive philosophy.

It is equally important, however, that strategies are optimized to take account of those individual factors particular to the child. These include the sensitive use of John's football interests and his highly visual learning style.

It is not the purpose of this chapter to provide a 'one size fits all' definition of inclusion, but rather to promote the notion that it is a process which is highly individualized and wider than the issue regarding specialist versus mainstream provision. As Ainscow et al. (2006: 3) observe:

> Even if we know a considerable amount about the implications of inclusive values for any particular context, we still do not know how best to put them into action, since making sustained principled changes within schools is notoriously difficult. Therefore effective early years practitioners will be those professionals who are able to look beyond labels, diagnoses and particular settings and look to individual factors to ensure the child with SEN is both prepared for, and accepted within, society.

QUESTIONS FOR REFLECTION AND DISCUSSION

1. What are the benefits of early intervention?
2. Consider the current debate regarding the inclusion of pupils whose behaviour presents challenges in mainstream settings. What is your opinion on this aspect of inclusion?
3. How does the legislative framework regarding access issues affect children you know or have worked with?
4. What issues are there in respect of promoting self-advocacy with children who have special educational needs?
5. How should the rights of parents and guardians be taken into account?

Recommended reading

Drifte, C. (2001) *Special Needs in Early Years Settings: A Guide for Practitioners*. London: David Fulton.

Jones, C. (2004) *Supporting Inclusion in the Early Years*. Maidenhead: Open University Press.

Pugh, G. and Duffy, B. (2006) *Contemporary Issues in the Early Years*, 3rd edition. London: Sage.

Roffey, S. (2001) *Special Needs in the Early Years: Collaboration, Communication and Coordination*. London: David Fulton.

Recommended websites

Every Disabled Child Matters: Getting rights and justice for every disabled child – www.edcm.org.uk;

Portage: home-visiting educational service for pre-school children with additional support needs – www.portage.org.uk

SECTION 3

PRACTICE

10 STUDYING THE WORLDS OF YOUNG CHILDREN: KNOWING AND UNDERSTANDING

Jane Murray

Chapter objectives

- To examine the contexts and rationales of the study of children's spaces and actions in Western society.
- To discuss children in the contexts of childhood.
- To consider why early years practitioners need to know and understand about the spaces and actions of young children.
- To reflect on learning about knowing and understanding children.
- To explore the domains in which knowledge and understanding about children are developed.

'To understand a child we have to watch him at play, study him in his different moods' (Krishnamurti, 1981: 47). Western views of the child may not consistently align with views from other parts of the world, but, in common with many of them, there exists recognition across the countries of the UK that knowledge and understanding of young children come from observing and studying children (DfES, 2007a, 2007b; DfES/QCA, 2003; DoH et al., 2004; LTS, 2008; Scottish Executive, 1999; Sproule et al., 2005; YAAD-GOS, 2006). The study of children informed by observation emerges, in part, from a rich tradition and wealth of literature (Aylott, 2006; Froebel, 1826; Isaacs, 1954; McMahon and Farnfield, 1994; Montessori, 1912/1964; Nightingale, 1859; Nutbrown, 2006; Owen, 1813; Pestalozzi, 1894; Piaget and Inhelder, 1969). This historical context persists as an underpinning to policy in many Western countries and it is where much of the practice in early years settings has its roots. Observation of young children's actions can inform practitioners' knowledge and understanding of children and consequently often directs much of the provision in early years settings.

At the turn of the twenty-first century, greater awareness emerged of the necessity to acknowledge the child as an agent in matters affecting him or her (HMG, 2004; UNESCO, 1989). Consequently, questions have arisen about the best ways to respect children by identifying and promoting their rights (Alderson, 1995, 2001; Alderson and Morrow, 2004; Christensen and James, 2008; Rose, 2003; Thomson and Gunter, 2006).

This chapter explores ways in which we come to our understandings of children in the context of 'childhood' and it considers why knowledge and understanding of children may be important. It also explores a range of models for gaining knowledge and understanding of children which may be adopted by early years workers and of how that knowledge can be used within a collaborative framework to support children and their families.

CHILDREN IN THE CONTEXT OF CHILDHOOD: CONSTRUCTION, DESTRUCTION OR CO-CONSTRUCTION?

Childhood is a social construction (Brooker, 2002; James and Prout, 1997), but there are many childhoods (Jenks, 2004), and many of the images of 'childhood' that saturate our lives are not positive. These are the images that effect a *destruction* of 'childhood'. This destruction seems to occur when children are *overpowered*, rather than *empowered* by adults, caused by 'the huge imbalance of power between adults and children' (Holland, 2004: 69). This may be counteracted to some extent by altruism. One expression of this is in the United Nations Convention on the Rights of the Child (UNESCO, 1989). A paradox within contemporary society emerges: children are widely observed as part of their exploitation; thus, any notion of a childhood with guaranteed protection becomes damaged to the point of destruction. As this is happening, international organizations such as the UN and OECD monitor and advocate the safeguarding of children. This is discussed further in Chapter 6.

In England, the government focuses on constructing one version of childhood through policy (DfES, 2004c). Millions of taxpayers' pounds have been spent to expand children's services, particularly in areas of socio-economic deprivation, and centralized frameworks underpin children's daily experiences (DfEE, 1999a; DfES, 2007a), constructing a mono-model of childhood. This is regulated by statutory assessment and public reporting of English children's output in league tables, which, whilst the mainstay of English educational policy since 1988, have been viewed internationally as detrimental to individual children and social cohesion (Pont et al., 2008). The English inspection body (Ofsted) is now also responsible for inspecting standards for all government-funded childcare (HMG, 2006a), where even the 'productivity' of the youngest children is judged. This is observed by practitioners, inspectors, parents, the government, the public and, increasingly, the children themselves, as the move towards self-advocacy appears to gather pace (Carr, 2001; Clark and Moss, 2001; Claxton, 1990; Cousins, 1999; Nutbrown, 1996), supported by research (Schweinhart, 2001; Schweinhart et al., 1993 and Sylva et al., 2004).

This simplistic mono-model of childhood is easy and cheap to measure and widely published. However, as Pont et al. (2008) identify, a simplistic model of childhood may not be what is needed. Within its Curriculum for Excellence (SECRG, 2004), the Scottish government appears to recognize that an alternative may be preferable, by acknowledging that people, including children, are complex (Ryder and Wilson, 1997). In fact, despite the growing rhetoric regarding children's self-advocacy, children can hardly be said to be co-constructors of their own development in a centrally dictated culture. The English government has made some concession to this with the Primary National Strategy, which purports to recognize the individual (Leadbeater, 2004), but focus on publicized league tables steers a straight course towards homogeny.

Fielding refers to the prevailing culture in England as 'offensive' and 'dishonest' (2001). Alternatively, childhoods – as individual as the children to whom they each belong – can be co-constructed with children to acknowledge the value of children's explorative interactions with the world. To co-construct childhoods requires spaces for children to develop in ways appropriate to their individual needs, capturing:

> joy, spontaneity, complexity, desires, richness, wonder, curiosity, care, vibrant play, fulfilling, thinking for yourself, love, hospitality, welcome, alterity, emotion, ethics, relationships, responsibility. (Moss and Petrie, 2002: 79)

In early childhood services, it may be helpful to consider how we can co-construct children's lives *with* them (Carr, 2001; Claxton and Carr, 2004; James and Prout, 1997; Makin, 2006; Singer, 1993). When practitioners are genuinely reflexive to children's *own* interests and understandings of the world and *their* place in its constant metamorphosis, children's meaning-making has the space it needs to flourish. In this environment, each step of each child's learning about their place in the world has the potential to reach deep, satisfying levels (Laevers, 2000), creating the foundation upon which new understandings can be co-constructed as time goes on.

Respectful co-construction is at the core of early years pedagogy (Anning et al., 2003) and it demands of the practitioner complex interactions which identify, interpret and scaffold children's learning, sometimes within very short spaces of time. Siraj-Blatchford et al. refer to these interactions as 'sustained, shared thinking' and this social constructivist model in the Socratic tradition is well-rehearsed (Alexander, 2008; Bruner, 1996; Rogoff, 1990; Schaffer, 1992; Vygotsky, 1978). The genuinely reflexive approach creates many challenges for the practitioner, not least of which is development of a facilitative environment. This requires sensitive, skilful and knowledgeable provision of spaces, time and interactions in order to fully nurture individual children's development, care, health and learning. The ability to provide at least some of the spaces within which the development of humanity is co-nurtured with children, their primary carers and the community is a key pedagogic tool. Like the carpenter's tools, it must always be in a state of readiness and this requires the practitioner to engage constantly in critical reflection and refinement.

WHY DO EARLY YEARS WORKERS AND OTHERS NEED TO KNOW AND UNDERSTAND ABOUT THE SPACES AND ACTIONS OF YOUNG CHILDREN?

In twenty-first century Western society, it is difficult not to gain some knowledge of children, since we are compelled to observe images of childhood that invade our lives through a range of media. Advertisers use and abuse the fascination with children to make money. More recently, use of the World Wide Web in the portrayal of children has become prevalent (Holland, 2004), presenting a clear and present danger for children and childhood, where adults' views and uses for images of children are prioritized over children's needs. Where this happens, there is likely to be little or no dialogue between the observer and the observed, and little or no agency on the part of the observed child.

Another type of child study is emerging from the statistical data held by different local and national government departments. In England, this derives from assessments of children's performance, health and welfare and, although much is used to detect trends, thereby enabling government departments to plan strategically, much is attributable to individual children, through, for example, each child's 'unique pupil number' (UPN), despite the existence of the Data Protection Act (HMG, 1998) in England. As new data emerge, so another view of childhood is constructed, although that view is always tempered by the nature of the data commissioned. It may be argued that there is an underlying altruism in this type of child study, since it is a tool used by government to hold public services accountable for their actions, flagging up any ineffectiveness in service delivery; indeed, the Freedom of Information Act (Department for Constitutional Affairs, 2004) in England ensures that much of this type of data is available on demand. However, while observation and judgement are well-used components of this type of child study, its large scale requires simplistic measurement, which significantly diminishes the likelihood of the human-scale elements of effective dialogue between the observer and the observed and any agency of either.

In addition to these purposes for the study of children, there exists an altruistic rationale for child study, evident in good early years practice across children's services. High quality observations enable practitioners, parents and the children themselves to gain a deep knowledge and understanding of individuals' development and learning. This is the type of study that incorporates observation by professionals who make time and space to know the child (Carr, 2001; Scott, 2001), who judge with an expert and nurturing eye (Athey, 2007; Bruce, 2005; Edgington, 2004; Nutbrown, 2006), who work in partnership with primary carers (Draper and Duffy, 2001; Willey, 2000) and who involve children in developing their own futures (Carr, 2001; Clark and Moss, 2001; Ofsted, 2004a). For early years workers, the study of children should be regarded as a tool to support the *co-constructions* of individual childhoods.

If one accepts central accountability as a fact of life in contemporary Western society's culture (Shuttleworth, 2003), but equally that a decentralized approach may be more appropriate to the learning needs of very young children (Moss and Petrie, 2002), the role of the practitioner is key in both answering to the paymaster, also in preserving time and space for individual children to develop at a pace and in appropriate ways. Traditionally, early years workers have often compromised, perhaps because they have found it difficult to stand their ground in the face of hegemonic opposition by school leaders who do not fully understand the requirements of young children (Aubrey et al., 2002). Staggs (2004: 14) acknowledges: 'Many practitioners are intuitive … they aren't very good at arguing their case.' However, professional judgements based upon a multiple-perspective evidence base of high quality observation, dialogue and child agency are likely to give practitioners a stronger voice in asserting their intuition in a professionally coherent manner. Athey recognizes that there is a need for those working with young children: 'to advance their own theory and to become their own experts … to assist the process of accountability that requires an articulate rather than an intuitive professional knowledge' (1990: 19).

The study of children provides a window on their learning and development, but also an indicator for the next stage: the zone of proximal development (Vygotsky, 1978). This is vital to effective provision for children and is a strong rationale for all early years workers to have a deep knowledge and understanding of child development.

Carr (2001) uses the word 'surveillance' to describe the onus on early years practitioners as assessors, aligning this function with external accountability. However, in proposing her *Learning Stories* model, she empowers the practitioner who knows the individual children well: 'We have a responsibility to ensure that the new communities we are constructing for children … are ethical and safe environments' (2001: 20). Early years workers need to work in close partnership with children and their primary carers to translate their requirements into reality. This partnership provides the backdrop for dialogue and children's agency but it is observation by the practitioner that joins these elements with professional judgement to create a fuller picture of the child's interests to provide a direction for supporting development.

LEARNING ABOUT KNOWING AND UNDERSTANDING CHILDREN

Nutbrown (1999: 127) suggests three purposes for the assessment of children:

- teaching and learning
- management and accountability
- research.

This rubric demonstrates that children's actions may be scrutinized for a range of reasons. However, each of these purposes has the potential to place children as objects and, in England, this seems to be the case, as teaching and learning and research become increasingly bound up in management and accountability.

This is a relatively recent phenomenon, though. Teaching and learning, for example, was, through past generations, an activity born from altruism for young English children (CACE, 1967; GBBECC, 1933): a route to enhancing the individual lives of children. Despite a few studies (for example, Galton et al.'s ORACLE project, 1980), Qvortrup identified as late as 1990 that children were exempt from statistics and other social reports. However, the neo-conservative policies which have prevailed in England in recent years see a robust economy as the prime reason for education (DfEE, 1998a; DfES, 2004c), and the government appears willing to speculate to accumulate. Statistics emerge from teaching and learning and research focused on every aspect of childhood, and are used to inform management and accountability at every level.

Of concern is that children are rarely consulted in these matters. It is often people set in more powerful positions than the child or their carers who judge the child and make decisions based on those judgements which may seriously affect children's lives. Statistics are used as the lever to direct funding to and from children's services in health, education and social care, when those standing in judgement often do not know the child or their carers. Influential opinions are often based on flimsy evidence such as secondary report and snapshot observations.

As part of her *Learning Stories* model, Carr (2001), on the other hand, suggests a more complex approach to the study *of* children *for* children, aligned with the New Zealand early childhood curriculum *Te Whāriki* (Ministry of Education, 1996) which focuses on the child as part of the community (see Chapter 5). Carr identifies four audiences as recipients of assessment documentation:

- community agencies
- families
- practitioners
- children.

This view acknowledges the challenges and benefits of retaining complexity in gaining understanding of children and in how that understanding might be put to good use for supporting their development. Within such a model, components such as observation, emancipatory practice and professional judgement merge to achieve a whole picture of the child, through the eyes of all those involved in the child's life. Each is explored below:

Observation

Observational assessment has a rich tradition for those working with children. Owen (1813), Montessori (1912/1964) and Isaacs (1954) were keen proponents and Florence Nightingale described observation as 'an essential element in good practice' in nursing (1859). Contemporary literature and policy (Aylott, 2006; Bruce, 2005; DfES, 2007a, 2007b; McMahon and Farnfield, 1994; Nutbrown and Abbott, 2001) build on the work of those early pioneers. However, observing children to gain a deep understanding of their development, health, welfare and learning in order to make provision for their needs can be less straightforward than it might initially appear.

One example of this might be the technique used. While a universal schedule might appear to provide a framework for a 'fair test', it is important to consider the elements within that framework that may be open to deviation, for example:

- environment (time, place, antecedents)
- the mood, interactions and interests of the observed child
- the experience, background and personality of the observer.

Clearly, elements of each of these affect processes and outcomes of any observation, which must mean that it would be very difficult indeed to ensure that one observation is as fair a test as any other. For this reason, it is most important to ensure that any observer acknowledges the likely variants surrounding any observation.

Emancipatory Practice: Dialogue and empowerment

When I began my teaching career with a class of 30 six-year-olds in 1983, I had received no training in how to develop and maintain a dialogue with primary carers or, indeed, my colleagues. In fact, this barely mattered, since we had one very short annual meeting with parents and all the classrooms were completely separate from each other. Curricular freedom abounded in those days – there was no National Curriculum – and teachers usually worked unilaterally. In those days, there were very few adults other than teachers (AOTTs) working in classrooms; dialogue was reserved for the staff room! At the time, in England, there was one major exception to this and that was the 1981 Education Act, which promoted a multi-agency approach to supporting children with special educational needs. This proved to be a template for much that was to come later.

Current policy and practice encourage early years practitioners to discuss planning and implementation with a range of colleagues and from a range of agencies. Integrated children's services have clearly been identified by international bodies such as the World Health Organization (1999), the United Nations Children's Fund (2003) and the United Nations Educational, Scientific and Cultural Organization (2004) as highly desirable and, in England, multi-disciplinary approaches have become legislation through the Children Act (HMG, 1989, 2004) and the Childcare Act (HMG, 2006a), with research such as that of Sylva et al. (2004) to support them.

Effective dialogue with parents has also been identified as a key indicator for children's effective learning and development, and early years practitioners work hard to develop these relationships through effective, equal and long-lasting dialogue: 'Wise practitioners look to learn from the parents of the children they are trying to help' (Draper and Duffy, 2001: 149).

Dialogue between young children and practitioners that is equitable and respectful is a key learning tool for both children and practitioners and links to other areas of the study of children, as Cousins (1999: 28) observes: 'Listening to children and observing them go side by side' and, indeed, Clark and Moss (2001: 2) identified methods of doing precisely this in order to 'find practical ways to contribute to the development of services that are responsive to the "voice of the child" and which recognise children's competencies'. Jordan (2004: 31) additionally emphasizes this approach sited in early childhood centres in discussing 'dialogues with children in support of teaching and learning'.

Key to effective dialogue is that it leads to and emerges from the development and nurture of effective relationships: 'Relationships have been emphasised as central to the trajectory from early childhood experience into later learning' (Carr, 2001: 16), and the works of Catherwood (1999) and Gerhardt (2004) demonstrate the pivotal role of early emotional development for later cognitive development.

As part of their work in supporting children to contribute to dialogue about issues affecting them directly, Clark and Moss (2001) identify six domains in England where children's participation is becoming far more prevalent:

- the law courts
- research
- the arts
- therapy and counselling
- environment and community development
- charities.

As discussed further in Chapter 6, international policy (UNCRC, 1989) has affected national legislation in relation to children's agency (HMG, 1989; 2004; 2006a) and this in turn is affecting practice. Schweinhart et al. (1993) offer an excellent rationale for children's agency in early years education and care, and Scott describes children's agency as 'finding out what they think and feel and responding honestly to their ideas and emotions' (1996: 43).

As a result of the policy focus, the empowerment of children in matters affecting them has an increased focus in rhetoric and, to some extent, in practice. Many schools have set up councils for children to be involved in decision making, and inspection regimes across the UK recognize a limited role for children's participation in matters affecting them. However, settings may not find it straightforward to relinquish control to children, which is necessary to rise to the top rung of Hart's ladder of children's participation (1992).

Table 10.1   Hart's ladder of children's participation

8	Child-initiated, shared decisions with adults		Degrees of Participation
7	Child-initiated and directed		
6	Adult-initiated, shared decisions with children		
5	Consulted and informed		
4	Assigned but informed		
3	Tokenism	Non-participation	
2	Decoration		
1	Manipulation		

source: Hart, R. A., 'Children's Participation: From tokenism to citizenship', *Innocenti Essays No. 4,* UNUICEF International Child Development Centre, Florence, 1992.

Making professional judgements

The definition of effective professional judgement is not easy to make because early years workers bring so much of themselves to their work. As Anning et al. observe, 'Though it was possible to characterise the 20 professionals as coming from a specific tradition or work culture – welfare, education, health – their personal lives and work histories gave each practitioner a unique set of values and beliefs' (2004: 61). Karstadt et al. assert that: 'professionalism can be difficult to define' (2000: 26) – it must be difficult to know whether or not judgements based on that professionalism are 'right'. In looking at Rubin's famous optical illusion, one observer may say, 'it is a vase', whereas another may say, 'it is two faces gazing at one another'.

Answers are open to individual interpretation. Interpretations will depend upon the experiences that the observers bring to the observation. Equally, the children whom practitioners judge may well interpret situations differently, dependent upon their experiences or personalities. Practitioners bring the sum of their personal and professional experiences to the judgements they make and, although this adds significant richness (Gammage, 2006), it means that those judgements can never be wholly objective. However, though inherent in subjectivity, or that which Eraut (1999, cited in Anning et al., 2004: 64) terms 'P' (personal) knowledge, can, as Eraut asserts, be diminished by combining it with that which he defines as 'C' (codified) knowledge, derived from reading the wealth of accumulated knowledge available from libraries and databases. For early years workers, this often means combining knowledge of child development with that of individual children, and within that there may exist an underlying tension between models of planning that precede children's actions and those which are responsive to those actions, by default following on from those actions. The practitioner must ask: 'In taking full account of the needs of young children, which should come first?' Centralized models tend to focus on planning as the first step, but in localized approaches, individual children's actions are accounted for as the precursor to the planning. This is because the more human scale of the localized approach can account for individual requirements as they differ and change. However, the latter approach is more complex and difficult to administer in comparison to the first and demands far more practitioner expertise and professional judgement.

In making judgements about young children's development, it is crucial that practitioners recognize that every family has a different home culture. When practitioners study children, an evidence base is important (DoH et al., 2004). However, a limit to this exists and, at that limit, the mark of a truly professional practitioner is that he or she acknowledges the inevitable bias in making judgements; bias can never be completely extinguished, since each of us is the sum of our parts. An explicit and considered reflection of this bias, used together with an element of 'instrumentality (thinking, rationality and logic)' (Manning-Morton and Thorp, 2003: 155), may be the factors that turn judgements into professional judgements. However, in all this, Nutbrown reminds us that young children are not mere objects to be examined like inanimate laboratory specimens, and urges practitioners to see them as people who deserve rights and respect:

Adults with expertise who respectfully watch children engaged in their process of living, learning, loving and being are in a better position to understand what it is these youngest citizens are trying to say and find ways of helping them to say it. (1996: 55)

It is also important to consider those adults who are usually the prime advocates of their children: parents (Clarke and Fletcher, 2004; Whalley, 2007). Practitioners and parents learning from each other will provide a fuller picture for each and place the child as the central focus in servicing their needs (Bronfenbrenner, 1979), but this can only happen when practitioners regard 'parents as equal and active partners' (Whalley, 2000: 322) and early years workers set up a free flow of information with parents, as well as other agencies.

DOMAINS IN WHICH KNOWLEDGE AND UNDERSTANDING ABOUT CHILDREN ARE DEVELOPED

While the study of children by those in children's services to inform practice and procedure has been recognized practice for many years, there is a belief that a shift has occurred in recent years that places children in a more autonomous position within that study. Changes include recognition that childhood is not just a preparation for adulthood, but a time and space in its own right and an acknowledgement that children should be accorded respect as bona fide actors in their current lives. This is discussed in further detail in Chapter 6. Within this context, this section considers the roles of early years workers in developing their knowledge and understanding of young children and how that may benefit the children both in their present and future.

Ways in which early years workers promote respect for young children within their worlds are dependent on a variety of factors, for example:

- who initiates the study
- who agrees to the study
- what the study explores and reports
- the respect afforded to children and others
- the role(s) of children in the study (actors, subjects, objects or other)
- who has access to the findings
- how the findings are used
- who uses the findings
- how the findings are stored.

Observing children might be considered an element of research, which is defined by Stenhouse as 'systematic enquiry made public' (1975), and developed further by Saunders (2006):

'systematic'	= logical, methodical, theory-informed ...
'enquiry'	= hypothesis-testing or 'experimenting', not proving, or simply reflecting ...
'public'	= accessible to others and for 'peer review'...

Early childhood researchers must conduct their work ethically (BERA, 2004; DoH, 2005; ESRC, 2005) and early years workers need to consider ethical issues in their observations of children. When observing children, it is important to ask:

- Are the reasons why we are studying children and their contexts in the best interests of the child?
- How are the children's rights respected?
- Are children given all the opportunities possible to take ownership of the study?
- Do the children have a chance to give voluntary informed consent prior to the study? (Do children know and understand what is happening and why? Can they give informed permission for it to take place? Do they understand that they can withdraw consent and can this be done at any time?)
- Is the study of children conducted in an open manner, without deception?
- Have the most appropriate methods for working with children been explored and selected?
- Are all elements of the study legally compliant?
- Are distress and discomfort avoided and is intrusion on children's lives minimized?

(Alderson, 1995; BERA, 2004; Christensen and James, 2008)

Separate groups within children's services might study children for different reasons but early years workers must liaise across services to share information about children and their families (DfES, 2004b). It is also important that early years workers consider how children and parents might be involved: does the study of children in order to know and understand them empower or disempower them in matters affecting them (UNCRC, 1989)? Practical ways of achieving these demands in hard-pressed sectors are a constant challenge. However, we must pursue this, since we know that when this does not happen, tragedies can occur, such as the death of Victoria Climbié (Laming, 2003). Speaking in ways that others can hear and listening to what others have to say, but above all, entering partnerships with a willingness to make them work are key to successful multi-agency collaboration. Knowledge and understanding of a child can only be useful if it is used to the benefit of the child by all those concerned with supporting the child.

Three case studies are presented below. Each is located in a different sector: health, social care and education. Read each, then consider the questions which follow.

Health context

 Case Study

In her role as midwife, Sukinah was caring for Anna and her new baby Sam on the maternity ward. Three days after Sam's birth, when Anna was being visited by her partner and their older child, three-year-old Maisie, Sukinah observed that he had a significant yellow tinge to his skin. Sukinah was aware that in many neonates this is common because of physiological jaundice, caused by a build-up of bilirubin. This can cause serious neurological disorder. In Baby Sam's case, Sukinah was particularly concerned because he was born at 37 weeks and she had observed that his weight had dropped by about 10 per cent since birth, despite the fact that he was feeding well. These factors can indicate a type of brain damage that causes cerebral palsy and hearing loss. Sukinah discussed the case with the doctor and a blood test and a phototherapy light to cover Sam's crib were arranged. The blood test indicated that there was no cause for concern and within two days, Sam's skin had lost its yellow hue, he had begun to gain weight and Sam and Anna were able to go home. Sukinah's careful observation, combined with her knowledge of physiological norms and possible outcomes of anomalies, enabled her to take a course of action that protected Sam from possible permanent neurological damage.

Social care context

 Case Study

Michael, a social worker, visited siblings Rita (aged 8) and Adel (aged 7) at their foster family's home, with the intention of establishing their care experience and where they would like to live in the future. When working with the family in their own home, Michael had established that their mother was in a violent relationship and that the children had been neglected. Michael witnessed this neglect in the children's dirty clothes, untreated lice in their hair and empty cupboards in the kitchen. On one occasion, neighbours had reported finding Adel and Rita sobbing on their doorstep at three o'clock one morning, while their mother was out with her boyfriend. Michael has spent time with the children's mother during the past few weeks and knows that she is desperate for the children to return. Michael has also visited the children's school and has spoken to the children, who say that, despite being happy at their foster home, they would like to return to live with their mother. He ensures that they are aware of the reasons why they had been placed in the foster home and makes a report that advocates that the children may return, once it has been established that they will be safe and nurtured by their mother who must demonstrate that she no longer has any contact with the violent boyfriend. Michael's careful direct and indirect observation establishes an holistic view of the children's situation that will enable their safety, care and happiness to be of prime consideration.

Education and care context

 Case Study

One September morning in the nursery, Sue, an early years professional, observes Devan (aged 3 years 1 month) for 30 minutes, noting every one of his actions and interactions. Among other activities, Devan stands near the sand tray, watching other children playing in the sand, moves to stand near another practitioner who is telling stories to a group of children and plays alone with a small red car, making it roll along a window sill for several minutes. Sue does not interact with Devan during the time she is observing him, but after the children have gone home, Sue reflects on what she observed because she wants to plan for ways to support his future learning.

Discussion Points

1. In each of the cases above, how might the early years worker link with other agencies to support the child?
2. In each of the cases above, how might it be beneficial or otherwise for each early years worker to share information with other services about the child and family they have been working with?
3. What might be the practical barriers to the early years workers sharing information about children across different services?
4. What ethical issues might each early years worker need to consider in sharing information with colleagues about the children in the case studies above?

SUMMARY

Gaining knowledge and understanding about young children is a process interwoven with actions, cultures, contexts, legislative frameworks, ethical considerations, relationships and experiences. Highly skilled early years workers promote children's agency to ensure a respectful and empowering environment for the children with whom they work. They select and use methods and techniques judiciously and interweave their judgements with child and primary carer dialogues to inform provision for children's development, health, care and learning.

A greater holistic picture of the child and childhood appears to be perceived and constructed now more than ever before, through the combination of perspectives from different disciplines within integrated services, parent partnership and an emerging picture of children's self-advocacy. The data – intended to be used to support the child to fulfil his or her potential – contribute to the construction and perception of society now and in the future and attempt to ensure that public money is spent in line with policy and legislation. These intentions have been devised by a democratically elected government, but practitioners must consider the effects on children and their families of the inappropriate gathering and use of data.

If we accept that views and realities of childhood are a social construction, then we must accept that some views and realities of childhood can also become a social destruction. The early years worker can have a powerful role in protecting, promoting and *co-constructing* children's development, happiness and meaning-making. To achieve this, the early years worker needs to work continually, sensitively and skilfully to know and understand each child.

 QUESTIONS FOR REFLECTION AND DISCUSSION

1. How does what we see affect what we think?
2. How does what we think affect what we see?
3 How can early years workers ensure that young children's views are heard and accommodated?

Recommended reading

Alderson, P. and Morrow, G. (2004) *Ethics, Social Research and Consulting with Children.* London: Barnardo's.

Carr, M. (2001) *Assessment in Early Childhood Settings: Learning Stories.* London: Sage.

Green, S. and Hogan, D. (eds) (2005) *Researching Children's Experience.* London: Sage.

Sharman, C., Cross, W. and Vennis, W. (2007) *Observing Children and Young People.* London: Continuum.

Recommended websites

Barnardo's: www.barnardos.org.uk/

National Children's Bureau: www.ncb.org.uk/Page.asp

JOINED-UP THINKING IN PRACTICE: AN EXPLORATION OF PROFESSIONAL COLLABORATION

Eunice Lumsden

Chapter objectives

- To explore the development of interagency collaboration.
- To examine the language of collaboration.
- To discuss policy drivers for integrated practice in children's services.
- To consider the characteristics of effective communication.
- To discuss the place of training and the inclusion of service users.

The Children Act 2004 received royal assent on 15 November 2004 and purported to herald a new era of services for children and families in England and Wales. High on the political agenda and enshrined in legislation is the importance of integrated services and, by implication, the need for improved collaboration between professionals (DfES, 2004d). Since the first edition of this chapter, the 'new era' has seen a plethora of policy initiatives aimed at embedding multiprofessional working and the integrated provision of universal services for children and families. The *Every Child Matters* agenda (DfES, 2004e) has provided the policy framework for the development of, for example, the *Common Core of Skills and Knowledge for the Children's Workforce* aimed at all people working with children and families (DfES, 2005) and workforce reform has become central to the facilitation of change. The Integrated Qualifications Framework (Children's Workforce Development Council, 2008) aims to ensure mobility for all those working in the children, young people and families sector. In addition ContactPoint (Children Act 2004), which should be in place by 2009, heralds a radical change to the storing and sharing of information between different professionals by providing a central point for information on all children and young people to be held. In addition, the government have also taken the spirit of the *Every Child Matters* agenda forward and set out the vision for the next ten years in the Children's Plan (DCSF, 2007a).

In order to support the reader in developing insight into this complex area, this chapter intends to provide a greater understanding of professional collaboration by examining the development of interagency collaboration, clarifying the language of working together, and considering who is and should be involved in collaboration, the ingredients of effective communication and the reasons why working outside professional boundaries still remains problematic. It also considers the role of initial training for early years practitioners in developing the key skills required by professionals working under the current policy of *Every Child Matters: Change for Children* (DfES, 2004e).

THE DEVELOPMENT OF INTERAGENCY COLLABORATION

It is important to understand that while integrated approaches to professional engagement with children and families are currently at the fore, the practice of agencies working together is not a new concept. It has been observed in practice ever since the protection of children has been the subject of state intervention, with professionals historically working together to provide services and share information (Children Act 1989; DoH, 1991; Fitzgerald and Kay, 2007; Loxley, 1997). Despite this, one of the common factors identified in child death Inquires is the difficulty that professionals have in working together to safeguard children (Laming, 2003). Indeed, it is the death of Victoria Climbié on 25 February 2000 that has fuelled the political agenda that is legally requiring effective integrated working (see Chapter 2), though the foundations of the agenda can be found before her death in the Children Act 1989 and in Working Together Under the Children Act (DoH, 1991). This legal and policy initiative underpinned 'the increased emphasis that recent governments have put on joint working' (Harrison et al., 2003: 8). They quote Tony Blair (the then Prime Minister of the UK) who argued that: 'whether in education, health, social work, crime prevention or the care of children, "enabling" government strengthens civil society rather than weakening it, and helps families and their communities improve their performance ... New Labour's task is to strengthen the range and quality of such partnerships'.

Indeed, as Butcher (2002: 189) states: 'the collaborative imperative is "at the heart" of the framework for change' and the Assessment Framework of Children in Need and their Families (DoH, 2000) hoped to enhance the multi-professional approach. There are also many examples of effective interagency initiatives and multidisciplinary teams working in health, education and social care settings – for example, the Child and Adolescent Mental Health Services, the Sure Start initiative and centres of early excellence, such as Pen Green in Northamptonshire (Carnwell and Buchanan, 2005; Housley, 2003; Leiba, 2003; Lloyd et al., 2001; Pinkerton, 2001; Thompson, 2003; Whalley, 2001).

The legacy of Victoria Climbié (as discussed in Chapter 7) is that her death provided both the government and professionals with the permission to refocus on the importance of working together, thus integrated services are at the heart of the government initiative *Every Child Matters*, and the Children Act 2004 provides the legal framework to facilitate the programme of change. In order to meet the challenge, the government produced the following agenda of change to overhaul and improve the provision for children and their families:

- the improvement and integration of universal services in early years settings, schools and the health service
- more specialized help to promote opportunity, prevent problems and act early and effectively if and when problems arise

- the reconfiguration of services around the child and family in one place – for example, children's centres, extended schools and the bringing together of professions in multidisciplinary teams
- dedicated and enterprising leadership at all levels of the service, and the development of a shared sense of responsibility across agencies for safeguarding children and protecting them from harm
- listening to children, young people and their families when assessing and planning service provision, as well as in face-to-face delivery. (DfES, 2004e: 4)

The strong focus on raising standards in the early years means that, as early years practitioners, you will be instrumental in developing the workforce which will not only develop current practice but also put the evolving policy into practice, especially in relation to the outcomes below that children have identified as being important:

- being healthy
- staying safe
- enjoying and achieving
- making a positive contribution
- achieving economic well-being. (DfES, 2004e: 9)

The need to have more 'joined-up' working and services was taken a step further by the Childcare Act 2006 (DfES, 2006c). This saw the removal of any distinction between education and care for the youngest children, and it also saw the introduction of the Early Years Professional Status which has both collaboration and contributing to multi-professional teams included in the standards (Children's Workforce Development Council, 2006). Therefore, for students and practitioners in the early years, this could be seen as an exciting and challenging time, as the importance of government policy that involves 'joined-up thinking' and collaborative working becomes integral for improved outcomes for all children. Organizations working with children have a duty to work in partnership and there is an integrated framework for inspection to ensure that policy becomes reality (DfES, 2004e).

One way in which the agenda of integrated services for children and families in England is being translated into practice is through the rapid development of children's centres. This development of provision is unprecedented, and the way in which each centre is visualized varies across the country, with different counties having a variety of models. For example, some centres are attached to schools, others to private, voluntary and independent (PVI) settings, some are being purpose-built and others, often in rural areas, bring together different settings under the umbrella of a 'virtual' children's centre. While there is evaluative research being undertaken into Sure Start children's centres (Melhuish et al., 2007; Weinberger et al., 2005), research into how the new wave of children's centres is impacting on practice remains at an embryonic stage, especially in relation to the impact on the staff. The study of one setting in the Midlands (Lumsden and Murray, 2007) specifically focuses on capturing staff perspectives at the transition from a nursery to a children's centre and one year later (see case study below).

 Case Study

The changing face of services for children and families and the need for integrated provision and multiprofessional working is captured by one setting in the Midlands in England. It has a long history of providing nursery provision and has responded to political changes in order to maintain sustainability. The recent transition into a children's centre was a strategic move to ensure that the provision remained viable in the complex and competitive landscape of early years provision. However, the setting had originally been a war-time nursery and, rather than closing down when the war ended, became a Local Education Authority nursery providing term-time care. In order to remain viable, the setting has had to be mindful of wider changes, and April 2004 saw the setting combine local authority education provision of free nursery education (two and a half hours) with neighbourhood nursery provision to more effectively meet the needs of working parents. The *Every Child Matters* agenda presented the opportunity to review the nature of the setting further and September 2006 saw the transition into being a children's centre. It is now open all year and provides 8am to 6pm provision. Ironically, an historical investigation of the nursery log found that on 11 March 1947, the setting was allowed to have the same school holidays as schools and reported that the 'mothers [were] greatly concerned as they needed nursery provision 8am – 6pm'. Thus, 60 years later, the setting reverted back to the all-day provision, the main difference being the nature of the services being offered. The newly formed children's centre has to provide a range of services that are responsive to the needs of the local community. While, historically, the school log provides evidence of multiprofessional working, highlighting visits from the school nurse, public health services, representatives from the former children's department and other education colleagues to observe practice, the future direction for the setting is to develop integrated services and multiprofessional working to meet the demands of the current step change in service delivery.

While the setting could be applauded for its willingness to embrace this change, the challenges cannot be underestimated. The integrating of new workers with different professional qualifications, roles and salary structures brings with it concerns, fears and different professional cultures. For this setting, at the point of transition, staff concerns highlighted a mixture of looking forward with trepidation. There were concerns over new contracts, pay, staffing and what it would mean to no longer be a 'nursery' – what would their identity be as they had always been a nursery? There were also concerns about being financially viable and pressures on staff of managing change.

The second phase of the research a year later found that staff were embracing the changes, were still worried about staffing levels, finance and the pressures of 'change', and had a new concern about the integration of different professionals and roles. However, they were really embracing the challenge and beginning to see the benefits. Some staff clearly indicated that they wanted to cross over from working in the nursery to find out more about the roles of the new professionals and the provision being developed in the rest of the centre.

 **Reflection**

So what does this case study tell us about the challenges of the new agenda for integrated services and collaborative practice? The main challenge appears to be managing change effectively when the playing field of pay and conditions varies depending on professional background. Therefore, while applauding the vision and the developments that have so far taken place, if practitioners are to consistently work effectively together, there needs to be a greater understanding of why this area is problematic and what can be done to develop a greater shared understanding of how we will navigate through the emerging issues.

THE LANGUAGE OF COLLABORATION

Regardless of experience, you will find that the language of collaboration is varied, and there is not necessarily a common understanding of what the different terms encompass and who is included in the collaboration process. In practice, the terms partnership, collaboration, interagency work and working together are often used interchangeably and different professionals can have different interpretations of what they mean. Therefore, for the purposes of this chapter, collaboration will be used as an umbrella term embracing the different terminology in common usage.

Over the last 30 years, these terms have evolved to become integral to discussions about how professionals can develop working patterns that meet the complex needs of adults and children, and 1973 saw the government specifically addressing collaboration (DHSS, 1973). Since then, there have been a series of government publications and legislation embracing issues of partnership between professionals and the involvement of service users (Children Act 2004; DCSF, 2007a; DoH, 1991, 2000; Loxley, 1997; Sanders, 2004). Initially, the focus was on health and social care with child protection procedures being pivotal in the development of collaborative working in relation to children and their families (Calder and Hackett, 2003; DoH, 1991; Sanders, 2004). Education has also increasingly become an active player and the importance of collaboration between health, social care and education is central to the government initiative *Every Child Matters* that underpins the Children Act 2004. The message is very clear that professionals and those using the services provided need to be working together more effectively.

While this is the current situation, there is a lack of clarity over what is meant by the terms. Lloyd et al. (2001) provide some useful definitions to assist practitioners in their understanding of the language of working together (see Table 11.1). One term missing from their list is partnership, though this term is in frequent use in health, social care and educational settings. Harrison et al. (2003: 4) reviewed the literature on partnership and highlighted 'that there is no single, agreed definition and that sometimes the term is used interchangeably with the term collaboration'. They suggest that a more helpful approach is to consider the characteristics of partnerships that are successful:

- involve more than two agencies or groups, sometimes from more than one sector (private, public, voluntary) and include the key stakeholders – that is, those who are primarily affected by the problem and/or have a responsibility for developing solutions
- have common aims, acknowledge the existence of a common problem and have a shared vision of what the outcome should be
- have an agreed plan of action or strategy to address the problem concerned
- acknowledge and respect the contribution that each of the agencies can bring to the partnership
- are flexible in that they seek to accommodate the different values and culture of participating organization
- consult with other relevant parties that are not in the partnership
- exchange information and have agreed communication systems
- have agreed decision-making structures
- share resources and skills
- involve the taking of risks
- establish agreed roles and responsibilities
- establish systems of communication between partners and other relevant agencies. (Harrison et al., 2003: 4)

Table 11.1   Terminology

Interagency working	More than one agency working together in a *planned and informal way*
Joined-up	Deliberate and coordinated planning and working which takes account of different policies and varying agency practices and values. This can refer to thinking or to practice or policy development
Joint working	Professionals from more than one agency working directly together on a project – for example, teachers and social work staff offering joint group work. School-based interagency meetings may involve joint planning which reflects *joined-up* thinking
Multi-agency working	More than one agency working with a young person, with a family or on a project (but not necessarily jointly). It may be concurrent, sometimes as a result of joint planning or it may be sequential
Single-agency working	Where only one agency is involved, may still be the consequence of interagency decision making and therefore may be part of a joined-up plan
Multiprofessional workings	The working together of staff with different professional backgrounds and training
Interagency communication	Information sharing between agencies – formal or informal, written or oral

Source: Lloyd et al. (2001)

Sanders (2004) also contributes to the debate about language by considering the impact of whether inter, multi or trans are used. He states: 'These word parts have different meanings. "Inter" means between, implying the link between the two entities; "multi" means many, and "trans" means across' (Sanders, 2004: 180). He goes on to argue that while multi and inter are most frequently used, multi is preferred because it implies more than two in relation to collaboration. Loxley (1997) draws attention to the fact that the only explicit attempt at identifying what is meant by the term was by the Joint Working Group on collaboration between Family Practitioners committees and District Health Authorities (DHSS, 1984). She discusses their view of collaboration as 'mutual understanding and respect for each other's role and responsibility; identification of areas of common interest and concern; the establishment of common goals, policies and programmes' (Loxley, 1997: 20). Banks (2004) and Whittington (2003) provide useful discussion about this area and discuss a continuum of working together. Banks (2004) introduces the different levels of working together: strategic and team/operational. Whittington (2003: 24) adds a further level of intermediate partnership and collaboration. For him, the continuum ranges from less to more integrated services. At one end, there are separate services which 'collaborate on an ad hoc basis' and, at the other, care trusts which exemplify organized integrated services.

Banks (2004) also cites the work of Carrier and Kendall (1995) in relation to the useful distinction between multiprofessional and interprofessional working. She states: '*multiprofessional* working, where the traditional forms and divisions of professional knowledge and authority are retained … *interprofessional*, where there is a willingness to share and give up exclusive claims to specialist knowledge if the needs of service users can be better met by members of other professional groups' (Banks, 2004: 127).

As she goes on to argue, many teams are somewhere between these two and the main aim of this approach is a belief in the idea that the service user will receive a better service. While this may be the case, this approach to the delivery of services is not without difficulties, as professionals with different values, cultures, ideologies and professional identities come together (Banks, 2004; Calder and Hackett, 2003; Loxley, 1997). Indeed, research into this area (Banks, 2004: 134) has highlighted that some of the difficulties in professional working together 'are around the incompatibility of the managerial structures, procedures and systems operating in the parent agencies employing the practitioners'. Calder and Hackett (2003: 10) add to this debate and include factors such as different 'background and training'; 'varied attitudes to family life'; 'stereotypes and prejudices'; and 'communication'. The debate becomes more complex when we consider the balance of power between the professionals involved in the collaboration and how this impacts on services being provided. For example, how can different professionals come together and work effectively on the same case when there is a lack of parity in pay scales, work conditions and context? However, there is another layer and one which is arguably the most important in service delivery – that is the diverse needs of the community for whom the services are provided (Leiba and Weinstein, 2003; Loxley, 1997).

Working together therefore is a complex area, bringing together not only the needs, experience and professional identities of those involved but also the complex needs of those requiring services. As Loxley (1997: 49) states: 'If collaboration is to be a reality and not a myth, these differences need to be identified and acknowledged at all levels, so that they may be honestly faced and taken into account when assessing whether collaboration is feasible, and/or the most effective or efficient response'.

Accepting that there is not a definition that encapsulates all the complexities of collaboration indicates that there may be a case to simplify language associated with working together in order to provide a shared foundation on which to build our knowledge and working practice. Those working with children and their families and those engaging in early childhood studies not only need to have a shared understanding about the different terminology in use (see Table 11.1), but also an understanding of the ingredients of effective collaboration, the range and depth of working collaboratively and the impact of the power imbalances between professional groups and professionals and their clients.

COLLABORATION IN PRACTICE

Another area to consider is who is involved in the collaboration. Is it just the professionals, in other words, those who perform the services, or does it include the recipients of their services, namely children and their families? The needs of those who use the services of health, education and social care are so varied that it is essential that they are active participants in the process so that professionals do not make assumptions about what they think their needs are (Leiba and Weinstein, 2003).

Indeed, working in collaboration with service users is recognized by policy makers and is enshrined in legislation such as the Children Act 1989 and 2004; and UNCRC 1989. The Children's Plan (DCSF, 2007a) clearly places the needs of families at its heart. Therefore, working together should be for the benefit of both the service providers and those using the services. However, despite the area of service-user participation growing in importance, there is little research into the impact of service-user involvement:

> The few studies summarized ... indicate that genuine user involvement is patchy and very much dependent on individual champions of local circumstances. Progress is being made and most agencies have started policies and procedures for user involvement, although these vary in the comprehensiveness of their aims and the extent of implementation in practice. (Leiba and Weinstein, 2003: 67)

Further, Leiba and Weinstein (2003: 69) argue that there is a 'continuing concern about the quality of involvement, tokenism and lack of resources'. This situation must raise questions about how we can ensure a meaningful partnership between providers and 'consumers'. In relation to children and their families, if they are to be seen as active participants in the process with rights to receive services and input in their development, professionals need to recognize and actively value their involvement. Shaw (2000: 29) also raised the issue that researching into the value of service-user involvement is 'still fairly novel'. However, if their views, opinions and experiences are to be valued, then this position needs to be challenged. The question needs to be asked: how can we involve the service user in a meaningful way?

One way might be to assume that service users, clients or patients are active participants. Loxley uses cooperational theory which assumes that people want to work together for their own benefit. She states:

> At an individual level the power of the client or patient to participate depends on the degree of choice available to him/her, that is the person's power to reciprocate or withdraw. In a market-place such power is exercised as a consumer. In the public sector services, the pseudo-market creates purchasers who are agents for the users. (Loxley, 1997: 39)

Therefore, how can the 'consumers' of care services have the same power they have when they are consumers of services in the market place? This is a challenging question and one which demands careful reflection. Valuing the service users' understanding and perception of their own needs has been the subject of much debate (Dominelli, 2002; Leiba and Weinstein, 2003).

For Leiba and Weinstein, 'service users are the most important participants in the collaborative process' (2003: 63). They view them as the 'experts' on their individual situations who have an opinion to give. They argue that 'one way of preventing carers from feeling marginalized and to make good use of the special understanding they have of the situation is to engage them fully' (2003: 66). However, they highlight that some professionals can feel 'threatened' by this process and some service users 'uncomfortable'. They state that 'these anxieties must be recognized and opportunities provided to talk them through, if they are not to become barriers to change' (2003: 66). The concerns about involving service users is also echoed by Thorpe (2004: 22) who discusses the fact that while service-user involvement is seen as positive, there are concerns 'that many policymakers and practitioners are only paying lip-service to the idea of user-driven services'. However, as Leiba and Weinstein (2003: 69) state: 'If we listen carefully to service users and carers … one of the things they tell us is that professionals should collaborate more effectively with each other. Absence of interprofessional collaboration causes breakdown in communication, delays in service delivery and general confusion and frustration for service users.'

While children's and their families' involvement in the collaborative process is to be valued, the power balance between them and the professionals also needs to be recognized, especially when issues of care and control are at the forefront of working together. As Pinkerton (2001: 251) points out, 'child Protection work brings into particular sharp relief the difficulties there can be for partnership'. However, this power imbalance is not just evident in social work but in education and health as well. One way that the power imbalance is also highlighted is in relation to the name given to the people with whom professionals work. Indeed, in this chapter, the terms client and service user are interchanged, however, they can also be patients or even consumers of our services. An additional complication is the age of the person who is this 'consumer'. If it is a child, at what age can they be involved in the partnership process for the dialogue to be meaningful? This leads on to the debate about whether it is the professional with all their knowledge, understanding and training that knows best or the child and/or family being worked with. It is this area of knowledge that adds another area of complication to the collaborative process for both professionals and clients. Different members of the process may not value the role they have to play because they do not have the same qualifications or, indeed, social standing as other members of the partnership.

It is also important to recognize that collaboration needs effective communication. For Thompson (2003: 67), 'effective communication is not simply a matter of personal skills and individual efforts. Rather, it also depends on such important things as organizational systems, cultures and structures'. The specific nature of professional language adds a further complicating factor – different professions have their own language and set of abbreviations which can act as a barrier to communication; the same terminology can mean different things. For example, working in partnership in a school setting may refer to the agenda of working effectively with parents and, in a social care setting, working with other agencies and/or clients (Braye, 2000). Therefore, if professionals struggle with communication, how can service users hope to begin to engage in the process of collaboration?

There are, however, examples of positive strategies being developed to facilitate overcoming the language barriers. For example, the Sheffield Care Trust has developed a glossary of jargon for service users participating in council meetings (Thorpe, 2004). Another example is provided from the National Forum of People with Learning Difficulties, where a 'traffic light' card system is used. Everyone at the meeting has three cards: one used to stop people talking over them, one when they do not understand what is being discussed and another when they agree with what is being said (Leeson and Griffiths, 2004). While this method relates to people with learning difficulties, it is a method that could be used with children and adults alike. Indeed, there are many occasions when this system would have benefited my understanding of a multiprofessional meeting.

If we are to move forward in relation to participation and actively involving children in the collaborative process, professionals need to reflect on their language and think about different strategies that can be employed to break down the barriers (Thomas, 2000). Indeed, actively including children in this process of simplifying language can bring clarity to the fog in which adults sometimes find themselves. Mission statements are an example here, as many organizations invest a considerable amount of time in trying to find a way to summarize their existence. As a recent observer of a child participation council, it was fascinating to see how one of the young participants reduced a two-paragraph mission statement to four words that encapsulated the meaning of the message succinctly. He went on to say that he could not understand why adults had to use so many words.

Thus, it is not surprising that the language of collaboration and how this collaboration translates into practice are challenging and complex. The growing literature in this area (Draper and Duffy, 2001; Harrison et al., 2003; Leeson and Griffiths, 2004; Loxley, 1997; Weinstein et al., 2003) raise issues around definition, interpretation and the interchangeable nature of the language used and who should be involved in the process. Despite the complexities in this area, it is clear that collaboration has been integral to different governments' policies for several decades. As Leeson and Griffiths (2004) highlight, the work of Plowden (see CACE, 1967) drew attention to home–school links, and Loxley (1997) provides a useful time line of documentation and legislation from 1971 onwards, where collaboration is included.

EFFECTIVE COLLABORATION

If the agenda of change for children is to move forward positively and children are to be supported in meeting the outcomes of the *Every Child Matters* agenda, effective collaboration at all levels must be the goal to strive for. As previously indicated, while working together is not new, the challenge is to explore what the ingredients are that have worked well and use these as the basis for moving forward. There also needs to be acceptance that working in partnership with children and their families is constructive and that the gains from the process outweigh the difficulties that can occur. However, it is also important that this approach should not be used to mask the reasons why difficulties occur. Loxley (1997: 70–1) helpfully reminds us that:

> The appeal of teamwork, just as the appeal of collaboration, enables policy makers to avoid the crucial issues of irreconcilable structures and limited resources by laying on practitioners the responsibility of mitigating their effects, and practitioners can accept it without fully understanding or recognising that it contains unresolved contradictions. The myth serves to disguise the reality with an appealing ideology.

However, if we are to progress, these issues need acknowledging so that participants in the process do not become resentful, resulting in inaction by those involved. Rather, issues need to be aired openly and dealt with, thus freeing up the participants to focus on the specific task. This level of openness and honesty may not only help to improve the interpersonal relationships within the collaboration but enable a greater understanding of the positioning of those involved. It is in developing this understanding that degrees in early childhood can really make a difference, as they can provide an arena in which students are able to develop their knowledge and understanding of the different professional roles in relation to children and their families. They are also afforded the opportunity to develop key skills to take with them into the workplace, as the final section of this chapter will illustrate.

So how can we work towards effective collaboration? In order for the collaborative process to be successful, there needs to be some common understanding between the participants. There also needs to be 'respect, reciprocity, realism and risk-taking' (Harrison et al., 2003: 26). Harrison et al. also usefully suggest the framework of 'SMART' (specific, measurable, achievable, relevant, timed) has a positive role to play. This allows purpose to be placed on the agenda by the participants at the start – they are then able to consider how they will work together and how this can be measured. Harrison et al. (2003: 15) also liken the start of partnership to 'the first date', and they provide a useful list of issues that participants need to consider (see Table 11.2).

Table 11.2   The first date

Before the meeting	At the meeting	After the meeting
Researching	Clarifying purpose	Finding the decision-makers
Sharing the idea	Recognizing mutual advantage	Gaining internal commitment
Planning an agenda	Identifying potential barriers	Drafting an agreement
Exploring the pros and cons	Anticipating how to get over the difficulties	Funding formula
Cost–benefit analysis	Drafting a proposal	Keeping an open mind

Source: Harrison et al., 2003: 15

Leeson and Griffiths (2004: 140) provide further insights into the ingredients for successful collaboration, including the importance of 'strengthening the emotional content of the relationship and interactions both inside and outside the working environments'. They also highlight management support, training and the importance of 'breaking down the power struggles among professionals'. I would suggest that the other important ingredient is the importance of a shared vision, a commitment to working together for the benefit of children and their families. In the early years, this is in relation to a holistic approach to the child where professionals value and understand each other's positioning and relationship with the child and their families. Furthermore, the role of the 'consumers', whether a child or adult, of our services is valued and integrated into the collaboration process.

THE ROLE OF TRAINING IN THE EARLY YEARS

Along with government policy to alleviate child poverty and improve early years provision by working collaboratively, comes the need for a trained workforce (Abbott and Hevey, 2001; DfES, 2004e). At the time of writing the first edition, it was argued that over the following 10 years, there could be workforce reforms and the growth in interest in the early years could mean that the early years courses becoming established in universities would have a pivotal role to play. This has indeed become a reality with the development of the previously mentioned, new Early Years Professional Status (see Chapter 14). There is also a growing recognition of the importance of developing professionals that understand integrated children's services, and the Higher Education Academy has been leading on a project exploring higher education courses that focus on integrated children's services (Higher Education Academy, 2008). Early Childhood Studies degrees are seen as an excellent base from which to achieve the Early Years Professional Status and provide a workforce who are able to embrace the current integrated agenda.

The growth in Early Childhood Studies degrees provides a real opportunity for students to engage in the widest debates about the early years from a health, social care and educational perspective. It affords students the opportunity of observing professionals from different working and organizational cultures, with a different professional body of knowledge, different roles, different qualifications and salary scales, coming together to model good multiprofessional collaboration. The agenda is also shifting within other professional training courses and initiatives at two Midlands University support interprofessional learning across the Schools of Education and the School of Health. There are now established programmes of learning interprofessionally (LIP) where students come together from the range of courses in the two schools to work together over two days as part of their first year of study (see case study below).

 Case Study

Early Childhood Studies students are engaged in a variety of learning experiences aimed at developing their knowledge, understanding and practical application of integrated working. In Year 1, they participate in the LIP project which is part of a collaboration between the Schools of Health at two Midlands Universities. The project involves interprofessional learning opportunities over a three-year period. At one of the universities, the project has

(Continued)

(Continued)

been extended to include students from the School of Education in the first year of their degrees. It involves students being placed in groups with students from other courses and working collaboratively together on a two-day project, developing a leaflet for service users that they may all be involved with, explaining the services available and the roles of the different professionals.

Part of the experience is sharing with their peers what their respective roles are in working with children and families. This sharing has raised some interesting issues in relation to the development of professional identity and how, even in the first year of studies, different professions in health, social care and education are viewed. For the students studying early childhood studies, their reflections highlighted some interesting insights into power issues between different health professionals, about whose role was the most important and how other students on professional health and social work courses perceived students who planned to work with the youngest children.

In Year 2, students participate in a role play of a child protection case conference. They are given the details of a complex safeguarding case, are allocated a role which they have to research, then participate in the conference which is chaired by a professional conference chair. Research into the student experience (Lumsden, 2006) reports that students find the experience challenges and changes their perception of families in child protection cases and that there is greater understanding of and commitment to multiprofessional working. Former students indicate that the learning is sustained and transferred to the workplace.

Both these learning activities provide students with insights into the importance of collaboration in work with children, young people and families, and the importance of challenging misconceptions about different roles in health, social care and education, especially if the professionals of the future are going to support better outcomes and allow the *Every Child Matters* outcomes to be met.

The case study above illustrates how different learning activities can be embedded in courses to support an understanding of the importance of collaboration. In relation to early childhood studies students, their preferred first destination for employment is teaching, though it is hoped this will change as the Early Years Professional Status becomes established, but there are numerous issues around pay and conditions which need to be resolved if this shift is to take place.

Students from one Early Childhood Studies degree clearly indicate that they have found the holistic nature of the study programme, where different perspectives are represented, invaluable in preparing them for their future careers (Murray and Lumsden, 2004). Indeed, historically, many early years courses are based within a School of Education; however, having a multidisciplinary approach to teaching means that staff from different backgrounds are coming together and working through the difficulties of their different roles and responsibilities for the child. It is also raising important questions about the balance of delivery of different perspectives, and as students are engaging with health and social care, they are becoming more vocal about the need for a balance between the three in the curriculum, regardless of their final career destinations. While this is an ongoing process, the impact of the partnership has led to health and social care issues being integrated into other traditional education courses, and this can only lead to a better understanding of our respective positioning and roles in a child's journey into adulthood.

SUMMARY

As this chapter has illustrated, working together is not a new concept and there are numerous examples of professionals already working together. However, the language of collaboration is complex, both in relation to terminology and the players in the process. What is clear is that for effective collaboration, those involved need to have a shared vision and a willingness to move beyond the complexities to enable a clear understanding of what each individual collaboration is aiming to achieve, how it is going to achieve it and how it will know when it has got there.

Every Child Matters means that the next 10 years will see collaboration and partnership more evident in practice. Professionals can no longer afford to stay within the comfort zone of their own professional boundaries; they need to move beyond looking through the lens of their own professional training. Stepping outside and embracing other professionals, children and families is essential to develop a shared meaning for our engagement together and a workable process for successful collaboration.

One of the most important ways that this process will be facilitated is through improved training across professional boundaries. There needs to be a range of training initiatives that address the needs of a diverse workforce in education, health and social care. Degrees in early childhood provide one pathway; students develop knowledge and understanding about the different roles professionals play in a child's life. From this base of shared knowledge and understanding, students then have the opportunity to specialize in careers in education, health or social care.

The government needs practically to recognize the importance of valuing all those involved in the process, through ongoing, properly funded training, parity in pay scales and, indeed, pay incentives that value training undertaken. Every child does matter but in order to bring this vision to life, training has to address the issues and provide practical ways in which children, their families and those working with them can develop effective collaborative practice.

 ## QUESTIONS FOR REFLECTION AND DISCUSSION

1. What do you think are the issues that prevent professionals working together?
2. How do you think that training can promote positive collaborative practice?
3. Can children and their carers ever be equal partners in the collaborative process?

Recommended reading

Anning, A., Cottrell, D., Frost, N., Green, J. and Robertson, M. (2006) *Developing Multiprofessional Teamwork for Integrated Children's Services*. Maidenhead: Open University Press.

Fitzgerald, D. and Kay, J. (2007) *Working Together in Children's Services*. Abingdon: Routledge.

Harrison, R., Murphy, M., Taylor, A. and Thompson, N. (2003) *Partnership made Painless: A Joined Up Guide to Working Together*. Dorset: Russell House.

Weinstein, J., Whittington, C. and Leiba, T. (eds) (2003) *Collaboration in Social Work Practice*. London: Jessica Kingsley.

Recommended websites

Centre for Advancement of Interprofessional Education: www.caipe.org.uk/;
Every Child Matters: Change for Children: www.everychildmatters.gov.uk/

12 WORKING WITH FAMILIES

Eunice Lumsden and Celia Doyle

Chapter objectives

- To consider the diversity of children's home lives.
- To discuss early years policy initiatives in relation to children and their families.
- To acknowledge the relationship between the statutory and the private, voluntary and independent sectors in work with families.
- To recognize the importance of home–school/setting liaison.
- To identify what the parent/carer and school/setting partnership actually means.

The family has a significant place in the lives of children and enhancing family life and the role of parents in children's lives is an important aspect of British social policy. However, in order to work effectively with young children and their families, early years practitioners need to appreciate what is meant by 'family' within a diverse society and why family is important for children. They also need to consider how they can work with and support families within legal and policy parameters.

In addition, practitioners need to understand the implications of what it means for children when they do not have an identifiable 'family', as the following example illustrates.

 Case Study

A play therapist had started working with Lily aged 6 and her brother, Lee aged 5. Three days earlier, they had been taken into care and placed with foster carers. The two children were asked by the therapist to draw their family. Lily drew a line of figures. When asked who they were, Lily indicated: Lee, her 'gran', a neighbour, a new teacher, a neighbour's dog, her mother and a worker at a women's refuge. Lee drew his new foster family.

As a child, Lily and Lee's own mother had had no example of secure family life and it was therefore understandable that she was unable to create one for her children. They, in their short lives prior to coming into care, and under the ad hoc arrangements made by their mother, had experienced over 20 different 'homes' and a vast array of casual carers.

> 〰 **Reflection**
>
> This case study of Lily and Lee shows that for some children, 'family' is a remote or confusing concept. It also illustrates how important it is for children to grow up within some form of recognizable family. Researchers such as Rutter (1981) and Clarke and Clarke (2000) have demonstrated that, while children are not totally dependent on a single mother figure, they do need to be able to form attachments to a consistent group of carers in order to thrive (Schore and Schore, 2008). The family, alongside consistent alternative carers such as childminders or key nursery staff, form the secure base from which children can start to explore the wider world.

Despite the clear indications that in order to develop satisfactorily, children need an identifiable, reliable family in the early years, the form it takes can vary. Diverse cultural traditions or socio-economic and geographical factors can mean that families may live as isolated nuclear ones or as large extended families with several generations sharing the same accommodation. Some children have reconstituted families following the death or divorce of a parent and subsequent remarriage or new partnership. Others are in care and have substitute families. Those from traveller or armed services families may well experience a number of different locations or homes but most have a stable, core family. It is through the experience of a 'stable' family life that the family members are able to grow, flourish and meet their full potential.

An understanding and framework of how human needs can be satisfied is provided by the theorists, Maslow (1970) and Alderfer (1972). Their theories have been modified and adapted to ensure their relevance to children's development by researchers such as Doyle (1997) and Thompson et al. (2001). Basically, whatever its nature, as long as a family meets their physical requirements and provides love, care, security, safety and a sense of belonging, children will develop well and reach their potential.

Because of the importance of family, most of the world religions and many cultural traditions provide guidelines on how family life and relationships should be conducted; in some states these are adopted or ratified by national governments. In societies such as the UK, there is a wide variety of religions and cultures and a significant proportion of the population espouses no religion, therefore the government intervenes in order to ensure optimum family lives for children. The following section looks more closely at the diverse experiences of family life for young children. The chapter will then discuss some of the government initiatives. Finally, it addresses the relationships between families and those who work with young children and provide services for them.

FAMILY LIFE

Children's experience of family life in the twenty-first century is one of diversity. There have been many changes to family structure, views about marriage have altered and the composition of society reflects differences of culture, ethnicity and religion (Cleaver,

2006; Gittins, 1993). More recently, there have also been changes in migration patterns to the UK, bringing with them new challenges as children accessing early years services have either had to adapt to a multitude of new experiences or they are the first of their family to be born in their parents' newly-adopted country (Crawley, 2006).

This changing demography heightens the importance for those working with children of reflection on what is meant by family life and early childhood. The following activity aims to assist in reflections about changes in families and the diversity of family structures.

 ## Activity 1 – The Nature of Family

Think about a family that you have known for many years:

- What is the structure of the family (e.g. do the children have one mother and one father or do they have several mother or father figures or only one parent. Is the extended family – aunts, uncles, grandparents – in close contact or rarely involved)?
- How do you think family life has changed?
- What do you think about the changes?

How do you think other people would answer these questions?
Why not ask some of your friends their views on these questions.

While the above activity highlights the diversity in families, the next activity examines children's situations in families. The experience of living in a family will vary from child to child. An eldest sibling may even have a different extended family. A grandparent may be alive during the lives of the older children but have died before the birth of a younger one. Some children have a different set of relatives compared to their siblings. Half-siblings will only share one set of grandparents.

 ## Activity 2 – The place of children in families

Think about what being a child in a family means. Focus on one young child, either from the family you thought of in Activity 1 or another child known to you.

Is he or she an only child?
If not, how many brothers and sisters does the child have? Are they 'full' siblings or are they step, adoptive, foster or half-siblings?
What position in the family is your chosen child – youngest, middle or oldest?
How many parent figures does the child have?
Are the key parent figures birth parents, or are they step, adoptive or foster carers? Or is there some other guardianship arrangement in place?

(Continued)

(Continued)

Are the key parents married? Are they in a civil partnership?
Have they divorced? If divorced, have they remarried?
What are the position and key roles of the mother figure/s in the household?
What are the position and key roles of the father figure/s in the household?
What roles do grandparents, aunts and uncles or other relatives play in the child's life?
Try to draw a 'family tree' for your chosen child. Is it straightforward and easy to draw or is it very complicated with a number of criss-crossing lines?

These activities highlight that while we all share the fact that we have been a child and experienced 'childhood', our experience of being a child is unique, and so is our experience and understanding of being parented and what family life entails. It is an experience that is impacted on by how a society socially constructs childhood as the following discussion will illustrate.

The way that childhood is constructed is fluid and can be different in different cultures and has also changed over time within cultures (Hendrick, 1992, 1997). In some societies, 'childhood' is a limited concept (see Chapter 1). In Medieval Europe, for example, children were simply seen as small adults with no particular distinction made between adult and child (Aries, 1962; Postman, 1983). However, in most societies, there is a concept that the youngest children require some special provision and protection. This special consideration in the majority of societies extends to at least seven years of age, by which time most children will have achieved full mobility and coordination and an ability to communicate efficiently.

In some belief systems, young children are seen as innocents in a Garden of Eden, living in bliss until knowledge of the real world with all its damage and distress intrudes (Ennew, 1986). Similarly, Rousseau (translated Cole, 1913: 222) argued that children are born innocent and that 'man (sic) is naturally good'. In contrast, others, such as some seventeenth-century English Puritans, believed that children were born in sin, and were consorts of devils who needed evil beaten out of them. In some societies, children are seen as objects belonging to their parents. Others challenge this, as exemplified by the words of the Arab philosopher, Kahlil Gibran (1923: 81) who wrote:

Your children are not your children.

They are the sons and daughters of Life's longing for itself.

They come through you but not from you,

And though they are with you yet they belong not to you.

In modern times, there have been moves towards the concept that children are individuals with rights to voice their views, to participation and to be protected. This idea is enshrined in the United Nations Convention on the Rights of the Child. On 20 November 1989, the governments, including the UK, represented at the General Assembly agreed to adopt the convention into international law. It came into force in

September 1990. A further consequence of this is that governments signing up to the UNCRC have introduced policies to provide appropriate services for children. The preamble to the articles in the Convention (UNESCO, 1989: 1) states:

> Convinced that the family, as the fundamental group of society and the natural environment for the growth and well-being of all its members and particularly children, should be afforded the necessary protection and assistance so that it can fully assume its responsibilities within the community, recognizing that the child, for the full and harmonious development of his or her personality, should grow up in a family environment, in an atmosphere of happiness, love and understanding.

Within early years settings, recognizing and valuing the importance and uniqueness of family life will help early years workers to work with parents, carers and other family members to support the child in the transition into education, maximize their opportunities within it and form a solid foundation to assist them with the next stage of their education.

Government statistics continually reflect the changes that are taking place in family life. There are a diminishing number of marriages in England and Wales with 244,710 recorded in 2005 compared to 480,285 in 1972 (National Statistics, 2008a). Since 1971, the number of children living in lone families has tripled. In 2006, 24 per cent of children were living in lone parent families and the number of households rose by 30 per cent in the same period (National Statistics, 2008b). Additionally, society is more diverse in its composition and all of this impacts on the experience of being a child. For example, for some children, the experience of family life is living with one parent during the week and another at weekends.

As the case example of Lily and Lee at the start of this chapter illustrates, not all children live in families with their birth parents. On 31 March 2007, 60,000 children were looked after by the local authority in England, and a further 4640 in Wales, (National Statistics, 2008c), 2356 in Northern Ireland (Northern Ireland Government, 2008) and 14,060 in Scotland (Scottish Government, 2008). These 'looked after' children will live predominantly with foster carers, though some will be placed with extended family members (Kinship Care), and over 3000 were adopted (DCSF, 2007c).

Children living away from their families of origin may have experienced a variety of different types of family life. Some might also have been deemed 'in need' under the terms of the Children Act 1989 (DoH, 1989) or have been subject to a care order. For them, their early lives might well comprise frequent moves between their primary caretaker and foster placements; they thus experience repeated separation, loss and the need to develop multiple new attachments. Fawcett et al. (2004) note that, proportionally, more children with disabilities are in care, compared to those without. They may face additional barriers to satisfactory alternative care. For example, Fawcett et al. (2004) point out that those children 'regarded as having communication difficulties were found to be excluded from participating in discussions about their needs' (2004: 125).

This section has provided an introduction to concepts of 'family' and 'children', the diversity of family structures and changing trends in family life. To illustrate this further, the cases of Sam and Alexander below afford an opportunity to reflect on how children's early life experiences may impact on their capacity for learning and growth and the role of the early years workers in the lives of young children.

 Case Study

Sam is four years old and has just started school. His parents are separated and he spends the weekdays with his mother and weekends with his father. His father collects him from the After-School Club at school on Friday night and brings him to the Breakfast Club at school on Monday morning, with his weekend bag. After school, Sam stays at the After-School Club until he is collected by his mother at 5pm.

In class, Sam is withdrawn and often appears tired. He is having difficulty making friendships and is prone to angry outbursts.

 Discussion Point

What do you think the role of an early years practitioner could be in this situation?

Sam has just started school and has a very long day which may make him tired. He also may or may not find it difficult living in two separate homes. His experiences are impacting on how he is settling into school and making relationships with his peers. His frustration appears to be making him angry and all these circumstances will impact on his receptiveness to learning. For the early years practitioner, supporting Sam is really important, as is good communication with the practitioners running the breakfast and after-school clubs. They also need to be talking to Sam's parents about how Sam is presenting in the setting.

 Case Study

Alexander is four years old and has just started in nursery school, his fifth early years setting. He will only be in the nursery for one term as he is due to move into a primary school reception class. He is the subject of a care order and is living in a foster placement. He has been with his current carers since he was three years old and an adoptive home is being sought for him.

Alexander and his mother have been known to social services since his birth. At the age of 16 weeks, he spent his first period in the care of the local authority; he returned to live with his mother when he was 19 weeks old but went back into care two weeks later.

Unfortunately, he could not go to the same foster placement so he was placed with new foster carers. He stayed there for a month and then returned to live with his mother. He remained with her for the next year, but spent regular periods in respite care because of her mental health difficulties.

At the age of 18 months, he spent a prolonged period in care with another new set of foster carers. He remained there until he was two years old, when he returned to live with his mother. Respite care was provided again but with different carers. At the age of three, he returned into the care of the local authority, was placed with yet another new foster carer and a care order was granted. He is currently awaiting matching with an adoptive family.

 Discussion Point

What do you think the impact of Alexander's life experiences will have on his transition into a nursery setting?

Alexander's early years are marked by frequent moves from his mother to foster and respite care. By the age of four, he has had seven different people responsible for his care and has lived in six different homes. He has also been in five different early years settings. His mother has had mental health difficulties which would have impacted on her capacity to parent Alexander. His experiences could have led to attachment difficulties because of the number of primary carers he has experienced. This amount of change would have made him insecure and impacted on his well-being. When considering the *Every Child Matters* agenda, it is clear that Alexander has not been safe and his capacity for enjoyment and achieving has been compromised. It is important that his transition into the nursery setting is handled sensitively and that he is fully supported, especially as he is likely to move again when an adoptive placement is found for him. It would also be beneficial if all his pictures, photographs and observations were kept to support his understanding of his life story. Early years practitioners need to ensure that they are working as part of the multiprofessional team around Alexander to ensure that there are excellent levels of communication to support improved life chances.

EARLY YEARS POLICY INITIATIVES AND THE FAMILY

The growth of policies in the early years has happened, as Pugh (2005: 31) argues, as a result of the Labour Government putting 'services for children and families higher on the national agenda than at any time in living memory'. She continues to argue that the policies have transpired for three reasons: improved services for children, to support working mothers and the need to support parents and carers. Underpinning these policy developments is the drive for social justice – as Brooker (2005: 9) argues, measures being put into place by the government are aimed at:

> better provision for young children, along with tax credits and other financial measures, [this] would enable more young parents to study, train and work; as a result they would become higher earners (and hence, higher tax payers) and better parents; in the process they would become more integrated into society and feel more committed to their communities and perhaps also the national interest.

The last decade therefore has seen considerable government investment across the UK in improving outcomes and services for children, families and the community by providing a full range of services to support them that are easily accessible. Initially, this was through Early Excellence Centres and then Sure Start local programmes (Sure Start, 2008). Following on from these initiatives is the commitment to provide a children's centre in every community and push forward the Extended Schools programme (DfES, 2007e) which by 2010 aims to work with the local authority and other partners to offer access to a range of services and activities which support and motivate children and young people to achieve their full potential. These services and activities will provide:

- a varied menu of activities, combined with childcare in primary schools
- community access to school facilities
- swift and easy access (referral) to targeted and specialist services
- parenting support.

In England, the government has also put forward their view of proactive support, in *Aiming High for Children: Supporting Families* (DfES, 2007b). There, they argue for the need for proactive support packages for families. They also argue that we need to develop children's resilience and be more responsive to children assessed as 'at risk'.

Alongside these developments has been a growing recognition of the importance of the first five years of life. Government statistics indicate that the number of three-and four-year-olds receiving early years education has tripled between 1970/71 and 2005/6, from 21 per cent to 64 per cent (National Statistics, 2008c).

From 1997, when the new Labour Government came to power, there has been a commitment to improving the early years. The Foundation Stage (DfEE, 2000) for 3–5-year-olds was welcomed as an ongoing demonstration of the government's commitment to improving outcomes for children. There was then a focus on birth to three (Sure Start, 2002) and a growing realization that the curriculum for the youngest children should be seamless. In September 2008, the Early Years Foundation Stage (DfES, 2007a) in England was implemented. This brings together these two areas to provide one curriculum for 0–5 years old.

The legal framework for the new foundation stage is the Childcare Act 2006 (HMG 2006a). This also places a duty on local authorities to secure, in partnership with the private and voluntary sector, sufficient childcare provision for all parents who choose to work or are in training in preparation for work and a duty to provide information and advice to parents on childcare and other services to support parents.

In order to meet these provisions, there needs to be considerable investment in developing the workforce (see Chapter 14). As part of the government's vision is the development of the Integrated Qualifications framework in England (Children's Workforce Network, 2006). It has always been challenging to map the vast number of jobs involved in working with children and families, and by 2010 the framework purports to offer greater transparency for employers and career progression for those working in this area. Hopefully, it will also bring clarity to those wanting to use the services so that they know at what level those working in services for children and families are qualified.

Finally, registered childcare providers need to ensure that they are meeting Ofsted National Care Standard 3: Care, Learning and Play, Standard 9: Equal Opportunities and Standard 12: Working in Partnership with Parents (Ofsted, 2001). In order to do this, it is essential for childcare providers to offer support to ethnic minority children and their families and generally meet the challenges of working in partnership with families, which is discussed in the next section.

In reviewing the previous case studies of Sam and Alexander, the aim of these initiatives is to provide them with better outcomes through the provision of high quality services based (usually) in one place. For example, Alexander's mother would have been able to access the full range of services offered by a children's centre, including support for herself, parenting classes and early years provision for her son.

For both Alexander and Sam, the provision may also have enhanced their development of *resilience* (DfES 2007a; Rutter, 1999). Understanding this concept is important for those working with children and families as it helps understand the different ways in which children manage their life experiences. Why is it that some adults and children are able to manage situations and others seem far less able to do so? There is no one answer to this question as it depends on a range of interacting factors and is unique to the individual. Members of the same family can all face the same situation but can each handle it very differently. However, early years professionals can support and lead practice in this area. For example, it is evident from Sam's case study that he is having difficulty in coping with the nature of the divided care he is receiving from his parents. Early intervention in this case could help both his parents see the impact of his shared care and support them in looking at alternative arrangements that are more sensitive to his needs as a four-year-old making the transition into school. They could also look at work that can be done with Sam to promote his resilience to the changes in his life.

HOME–SCHOOL/SETTING PARTNERSHIPS

The rapidly changing landscape of provision in the early years has had an effect upon early years practitioners' relationships with other professionals, the family and the child. Ideas of partnership are integral to how policies are translated into practice and to the role of the early years practitioner in supporting children and families within a variety of settings. Central to this is the importance of seeing that the family and early years settings have complementary roles in the provision of early childhood education and care (ECEC), as the following discussion emphasizes.

Vygotsky (1956, 1978) highlighted the importance of the child's 'culture' which is far more than ethnicity – it embraces the child's total physical and emotional environment, history and relationships. 'Enculturation is not something that happens to children; it is something that children do' (Miller, 2002: 373). The implications of this are that if the child's home (or homes) and early years settings do not have shared approaches, are distant from each other or are in conflict, the child's environment will be confusing and could delay rather than enhance development. Rogoff (1990), in extending Vygotsky's ideas, uses the analogy of an apprenticeship between the child, who is learning to solve problems, and the adult or older child who provides implicit or explicit instruction (see Chapter 3). However, if children are constantly having to adapt to very different forms of 'instruction', that apprenticeship will be disjointed and perplexing rather than enlightening. For this reason, home/setting links and partnership with parent figures are essential.

Rowan and Honan (2005) provide examples of the difficulties of working in partnership, such as the use of 'book boxes'. Here, children take home books from a range of reading schemes and the parents are expected to read these with their children and sign to affirm they have done so. This appears to be the setting/school working with the home. But as Rowan and Honan (2005: 212) remark, 'school reading practices and processes are taken into the home while the home literary practices are ignored'. Brooker (2005: 128) similarly highlights that there are barriers between parents and early years settings, particularly where families are from minority or socio-economically disadvantaged groups. These barriers however can be overcome by 'serious and respectful listening and not by a home–school dialogue which assumes the school is always right'.

Despite these concerns and warnings, there are many examples of effective home–setting partnerships. An example of close links between setting and home is the Pen Green Centre in Corby. This is an early years provision for families focusing on community regeneration, together with family support and education for young children, including those in need and with special needs. From its inception in 1983, it has highlighted the importance of finding out from parents what is needed rather than 'imposing a predetermined "neat and tidy" plan' (Whalley, 2001: 128). It operates on the basis of inclusion of parents with parent groups and meetings to inform policy. Parents were encouraged to record their children at home and share these with the staff, while they were also involved in curriculum development at the Centre.

An example provided by Anning (1998) endorses the Pen Green philosophy of respecting the expertise of parents, even in the case where parents are struggling or seem vulnerable. Anning describes how the manager of an inner-city early years centre focused on communication between vulnerable mothers and their babies. She wanted to ensure that her staff gained insights into ways of working with parents and children which avoided de-skilling the parents. Jointly with a speech therapist, the manager introduced relaxed but carefully planned workshops and modelled 'motherese' through play with mothers as well as their babies. The mothers learned that their ability to parent was validated rather than being distrusted.

One of the issues highlighted by Draper and Duffy (2001) is the need to address parents' own expectations. They worked at the Thomas Coram Early Excellence Centre, which like Pen Green encouraged parental involvement and engagement. However, they found that at another centre, a proportion of parents had very different ideas about 'what is good for children' and were resistant to involvement in the centre. Some came from cultures where nursery provision was extensive but where nursery staff expected the parents to disappear quickly at the start of the session in order to avoid 'upsetting' their children who would then, in the staff's opinion, not be able to concentrate and learn. Parental involvement appeared to them to mean they were questioning the expertise of the centre staff.

Another issue highlighted by Draper and Duffy (2001, 2001) is the involvement of fathers in early years provision. They experienced the inevitable issue of working fathers who were unable to attend daytime activities. Nevertheless, they found that fathers were committed to their children's development and education and felt the staff were welcoming. However, centre activities and the attitudes of other parents meant that they were reluctant to become directly involved in the centre. A Scottish Government document (2003: para 72) also highlighted that:

> fathers reported that they found family support services almost entirely staffed and attended by women, and however welcoming the service or other users, they felt very isolated. Some of the professionals we interviewed were dismissive of the men they came into contact with.

Fathers of young children face problems which are not an issue for mothers. For example, when out and about with children still needing help with toileting, it is easy for a mother to take her pre-school son into a female public convenience but it is not so acceptable for a father to take his young daughter into the men's toilets. Clearly, when setting policies, practitioners need to ensure that working in partnership extends to fathers as well as mothers. Fathers can usefully be given opportunities to discuss their concerns openly, preferably with other men facing the same issues. In the longer term, the encouragement of more men into early years occupations might help fathers to feel more included.

The case study of Alexander further highlights some of the issues for children with substitute families. For Alexander, joining the nursery setting will not be his first transition. He is used to frequent changes, has lived in a number of different families and has had some very challenging early life experiences. He might be aggressive or withdrawn, and have difficulty trusting adults and forming relationships with his peers. Although he has every right to be angry, actions which harm, distress or alienate others will need to be addressed. His early experiences will impact on his learning and any practitioners involved in his education will have to assess his needs to ensure that his learning opportunities are maximized to the full and that early gaps in his learning are identified and addressed. Indeed, part of the role of the early years worker will be to contribute to the Common Assessment

Framework (DfES, 2007c) that will assess the needs of children from a multiprofessional perspective.

The other issue for early years workers is to recognize that Alexander has different families. He will probably continue to have contact with his mother and his maternal grandparents and any aunts or uncles. Even if there is no mention of a father, Alexander might have a father and a set of relatives on his father's side. He has been with his current foster carers for over a year and at such a crucial stage in his life – the transition from baby/toddler to schoolboy – they form an important family for him. However, early years workers may also have to relate to the new adoptive parents. Even if Alexander has not moved in with them during his time in the nursery school or reception class, he may well be starting to form a relationship with his potential adoptive parents which he might talk about as his 'forever' parents. Recognizing and respecting Alexander's divided loyalties and acknowledging the importance of each of these families in his life require skill and understanding on the part of early years workers.

There is one final point to make in relation to home–school/setting partnerships which relates to child protection. Involving parents in their children's learning is hugely beneficial. However, early years workers need to guard against putting their relationship with the parents before the child's welfare in those, albeit few, instances where children are being neglected, physically or emotionally abused or sexually exploited by their carers.

SUMMARY

Family life for children can be very diverse and early years practitioners need to be careful of making assumptions about families and to see each child as unique.

As the previous discussion has illustrated, partnership with parents is integral to the government's vision of developing services for children and their families. Links between the home and school are therefore very important. However, it is not just because policies dictate this approach, but because children's development will be adversely affected if there is no harmony between the various spheres of a child's life, especially the key domains of family and early years settings.

QUESTIONS FOR REFLECTION AND DISCUSSION

1. In what ways do you think your own family life impacts on you as a person?
2. Why do you think it is important for workers in the early years to understand the diversity of family life?
3. How do you think settings can support children who are being looked after and/or are in local authority care?

Recommended reading

Aldgate, J., Jones, D., Rose, W. and Jeffery, C. (2006) *The Developing World of the Child.* London: Jessica Kingsley.

Guishard-Pine, J., Mccall, S. and Hamilton, L. (2007) *Understanding Looked After Children: Psychology for Foster* Care. London: Jessica Kingsley.

Scott, J., Treas, J. and Richards, M. (2007) *The Blackwell Companion to the Sociology of Families.* Oxford: Blackwell.

Whalley, M. (2007) *Involving Parents in Their Children's Learning.* London: Paul Chapman.

Recommended websites

Department for Children, Schools and Families: www.dfes.gov.uk/index.shtml;
Joseph Rowntree Foundation: www.jrf.org.uk/

13 CHILD HEALTH

Sharon Smith and Tania Morris

Chapter objectives

- To explore an holistic perspective of child health.
- To consider the application of relevant health and social policy affecting child health.
- To focus on obesity as a public health issue and the impact of a multi-agency approach.
- To consider the significance of resilience factors in the promotion of child mental health.

Evidence (Blair et al., 2003) suggests that children are generally healthier than ever before, although this improving picture is marred by stark and persistent inequalities in health between children from advantaged families and those who are poor; across different ethnic groups and across different parts of the country. Healthy mothers produce healthy babies who become healthy children and adults; much preventable adult ill health and disease has its roots during gestation, infancy and childhood. Recent research has illuminated the contribution which physical and emotional factors in infancy and childhood make to adult health and disease.

Children's health has been a major focus of recent government policy and is a priority not only in relation to health services, but also with respect to social services and education (Hill and Morton, 2003). Rising obesity levels in childhood have significant implications for health in later life, as well as impacting adversely on children's peer relationships and self-esteem. Almost one third of children are either overweight or obese and without clear action, this could rise to two thirds by 2050 (Foresight, 2007). In addition, there are concerns over the appropriateness of their diet and the amount of exercise taken. *Healthy Weight, Healthy Lives: A cross-government strategy* (DCSF, 2008b) aims to provide local areas with guidance on how to promote healthy weight and tackle obesity. It is well documented that children and young people learn best and thrive when they are healthy, safe and engaged. Much interest in child health is due to the desire to influence later adult health. Many serious and life-threatening illnesses in adulthood are now seen as having their roots in life-style choices with respect to diet, exercise, alcohol and substance use, which originate in childhood (Rigby, 2002). Changing patterns of eating, playing, working, travel and leisure activities have together led to an unhealthy lifestyle for some children that continues into adolescence and adulthood (DoH, 2004a).

Children and young people are frequent users of all types of health care compared with adults. In a typical year, a pre-school child will see their general practitioner about

six times, while a child of school age will go two or three times. Up to half of all infants aged less than 12 months and one-quarter of older children will attend a hospital accident and emergency department. However, 80 per cent of all episodes of illness in children are managed by parents without reference to the professional health care system. This is important to note in relation to health promotion and support for parents.

The National Service Framework (NSF) for Children, Young People and Maternity Services (DoH, 2004b) is a 10-year programme intended to stimulate long-term and sustained improvement in children's health. It is part of the government's overall plan for tackling child poverty which will be discussed further in this chapter. It is intended to lead to a cultural shift, resulting in services which are designed and delivered around the needs of children and families using those services, not around the needs of organizations. There are three key objectives:

1. To put children and their families at the centre of care.
2. To develop effective partnership working.
3. To deliver needs-led services.

The NSF will have a key role in helping to achieve the outcomes identified by *Every Child Matters* (DfES, 2004e):

- be healthy
- stay safe
- enjoy and achieve
- make a positive contribution
- achieve economic well-being.

These outcomes are linked and mutually reinforcing, crucial to every child's life chances and well-being. Too often, services neglect to see the child as the 'whole' person with basic developmental, physical, mental and social needs that are very different from those of an adult. Seeing the whole child also means recognizing that health protection and promotion and disease prevention are integral to their care in any setting. The child exists in a context – family, friends, and school – and, therefore, it is essential to remember that if care is optimal, the child will avoid missing school to avoid problems with social functioning, friendships, etc.

This chapter will examine key aspects of child health promotion and disease prevention. The role of primary health care practitioners and educationalists will be discussed in the belief that education and health go hand in hand, with both impacting on children's current and future well-being. The support of families, especially those in special circumstances, and effective parenting interventions will be explored. There is increasing evidence to suggest that there is a strong association between aspects of family relationships, parenting behaviour and child behaviour problems (Johnston et al., 2004). It is widely recognized that early intervention is more effective and that health visitors and school nurses are in a strategically important position to deliver behaviour treatment, often more acceptable to families than a mental health service.

THE ROLE OF PRIMARY HEALTH CARE PRACTITIONERS

As key public health and primary care practitioners, health visitors and school nurses have an important role to play in improving child health and tackling inequalities. Promoting health and well-being and preventing illness means tackling the root causes of inequalities. This requires a multi-agency approach. The Children's NSF (DoH, 2004b) sets out a vision and range of national standards for children and young people's health and social services, outlining what support should be available to children and their parents in managing and preventing problems.

Health needs can be responded to in a variety of ways, including individual and family health, programmes – for example, breastfeeding support or counselling for post-natal depression. The provision and promotion of access to information services such as Sure Start programmes, Parentline and health-related websites can have a positive impact on family health need. Community development initiatives can meet local health needs and promote community participation, such as smoking cessations, healthy schools projects and safety schemes. The following case study demonstrates the effectiveness of a multi-agency approach within child health promotion.

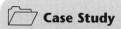 **Case Study**

A teacher identified that a pupil with eczema was reluctant to attend swimming lessons at school because he complained that he felt uncomfortable afterwards. The school nurse identified in his child health plan how swimming was irritating the condition and making it difficult for him to concentrate at school. The school nurse, parent and teacher discussed how they could offer more time and support to enable him to be able to dry his skin carefully and reapply protective lotions. They agreed to assess the effect of the agreed plan over the following two weeks.

When discussing family issues, the parent revealed that an older sibling was missing appointments at the local hospital's enuresis clinic. From a number of child health plans, the school nurse knew that this was a problem as the clinic was difficult to reach and young people did not want to miss school in order to go for treatment. Further investigation suggested venues in their local community would be accessible. As a result, a nurse-led service has been developed locally offering advice, periodic review and the reordering of clinical supplies more conveniently (DoH, 2001a).

THE ROLE OF HEALTH VISITORS

Health visitors have a strong tradition of working with individuals, families and communities to promote health. Cowley and Houston (2003) recognize the different elements:

- public health programmes at community level
- community development
- group work
- health prevention and promotion with families and individuals.

They maintain a caseload of all families in a local area who have children under the age of five years, delivering their service through a combination of individualized home visiting, clinic contacts and community-based activities.

The family in all its diverse forms is the basic unit of society and the place where the majority of health care and preventative work takes place. Health visitors have always played a vital role in promoting family health and supporting parents. The Acheson Report (1998) and the NHS Plan (DoH, 2000b) recognize the importance of working with families with young children to improve the lifetime chances of those in the poorest sections of the population. *Supporting Families* (Home Office, 1998) also highlighted the importance of health visitors' support role in improving child and family health and well-being.

The Family Health Plan (DoH, 2001b) supports this work and provides a tool to assess family health needs and plan services to meet those needs. A family health plan is a core tool for enabling a family to think about their health and parenting needs.

The plan should identify:

- the family's health needs
- how they wish to address them
- an action plan (including multiprofessional support).

Health visitors aim to balance an assessment of health need from both the community and individual health perspective, working with other agencies and sectors to plan services and promote well-being. The content of this plan will form the framework for key health promotion areas to be explored.

THE ROLE OF SCHOOL NURSES

School nurses have an important role to play in improving health and tackling inequalities. They are involved in a wide range of health-promoting and public health activities. Like health visitors, school nurses are registered nurses with additional training (usually at graduate level), skills and knowledge that enable them to work competently with school-age children in a variety of settings, including schools.

School nurses can provide a unique insight into the health needs of the school community and have been pivotal in the implementation of the ECM agenda and in the promotion of the Healthy Schools Status. They can provide a range of health improvement activities including:

- immunization and vaccination programmes
- support and advice to teachers and other school staff on a range of child health issues
- support and counselling in positive mental health
- personal health and social education programmes and citizenship training
- advice on relationships and sex education
- working with parents and other professionals to meet a range of health and social needs.

The development of National Service Frameworks (NSF) Primary Care Trusts and new models of service delivery, such as the National Healthy School Standard (NHSS), give school nurses opportunities to focus on the most important issues affecting children and young people's health and to work with the population groups in greatest need. The National Healthy School Standards (1999) are part of the government's strategy to raise educational achievement and address inequalities.

The Primary Schools/Primary Care Health Links Project aims specifically to promote the involvement of primary health care professionals in supporting children's learning and development in the context of the local healthy schools programme.

WHAT IS A HEALTHY SCHOOL?

By 2009, all schools should be participating in the programme with at least 75 per cent having achieved National Healthy School Status DCSF (2007b).

> A healthy school understands the importance of investing in health to assist in the process of raising levels of pupil achievement and improving standards. It promotes physical and emotional health by providing accessible and relevant information and equipping pupils with the skills and attitudes to make informed decisions about their health. It also recognizes the need to provide both a physical and social environment that is conducive to learning. (DfEE, 2001: 6)

A systematic review of healthy schools (Lister-Sharp et al., 1999) concluded that school-based health promotion initiatives can have a positive impact on children's health and development. For an example, see the case study below.

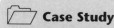 **Case Study**

To increase the number of pupils making healthy lifestyle choices about diet and exercise, 'a Healthy School' middle school employed a supervisor to promote and develop their established 'Huff and Puff' programme. This aims to increase physical activity before and after school, and at lunch and break times. The supervisor planned lunch-time and break activities and oversaw Year 7 pupils who ran the 'equipment loan shop'. The organization of lunch-time activities, particularly football, was restricted so that pupils could deal more effectively with competitive aspects that led to arguments.

Playground work was supported by the behaviour support services, including a 'life skills' project, so that breaks and lunch times were seen as part of the learning that took place each day. Other changes were introduced, including a reward system for pupils who reached set activity targets, giving them play equipment bought through sponsorship from local business. Pupils recorded their progress in their school diary, enabling parents to share their success.

A school nurse ran drop-in sessions and encouraged pupils to join in out-of-hours sports activities. The tuck shop also underwent a transformation, with a local supplier agreeing to supply a variety of fruit and vegetables for a trial period. If pupils bought 'unhealthy' options, they also had to buy five pence worth of fruit, a move that was supported by parents and encouraged pupils to eat fruit on a regular basis.

〰 Reflection

A key factor was helping pupils to make the link between eating well, physical activity and feeling good about themselves. The 'Huff and Puff' scheme appealed to pupils who were not previously engaged, including several who were overweight. The number of serious incidents of negative behaviour was halved with the introduction of structure, purpose and rewards to lunch-time play. Pupils were noticeably more tolerant of each other and there was less disruption in lessons. Teachers and midday supervisors noticed greater cooperation between pupils, and senior staff spent less time dealing with negative behaviour (*Healthy Weight, Healthy Lives* – DCSF, 2008b: 16).

CHILD HEALTH PROMOTION

A variety of factors affect health in children, not only the biological and lifestyle problems of the parents, including unemployment, low income and poor housing. Health promotion can be defined as 'any planned and informed intervention which is designed to improve physical or mental health or to prevent disease' (Hall and Elliman, 2004).

Nutrition

There is increasing concern regarding the relationship between the current state of childhood nutrition and adverse health outcomes in adult life (Hall and Elliman, 2004). What we eat in childhood affects our health – for example, coronary heart disease, diabetes, cancer and bowel disorders in adults can be attributed to the effects of poor diet in the early years, combined with reduced activity levels (Gregory, 2000). Almost two thirds of adults and a third of children are either overweight or obese (NICE, 2006) and the Government Office for Sciences Foresight Programme (Foresight, 2007) suggests that, without clear action, these figures will rise to almost nine in ten adults and two-thirds of children in 2050. Being overweight or obese can have a severe impact on adult and children's physical weight, and is associated with diabetes, cancer, heart and liver disease. It can also have an impact on mental health and put many pressures on families and society. The Children's Plan (2007) recognized child obesity as one of the most serious challenges for children and is linked to a number of poor outcomes – physical, social and psychological. The Department of Health is responsible for overall policy on obesity and is jointly responsible with the DCSF for tackling child obesity, working with other government departments as appropriate.

A cross-government strategy: *Healthy Weight, Healthy Lives* (DCSF, 2008b) has been commissioned to focus the prevention and management of excess weight around five themes. These are:

1. Children: healthy growth and healthy weight
2. Promoting healthier food choices
3. Building physical activity into our lives
4. Creating incentives for better health
5. Personalized support for overweight and obese individuals.

FRAMEWORK FOR LOCAL ACTION – HEALTHY WEIGHT, HEALTHY LIVES (DCSF, 2008B)

Children: Healthy Growth and Healthy Weight
Success is demonstrated by:

- as many mothers breastfeeding up to six months as possible, with families knowledgeable about healthy weaning and feeding of their young children
- all children growing up with a healthy diet, e.g. eating at least five portions of fruit and vegetables a day
- all children growing up with a healthy weight, e.g. by doing at least one hour of moderately intensive physical activity each day
- parents having the knowledge and confidence to ensure that their children eat healthily and are active and fit
- all schools being Healthy Schools, and parents who need extra help being supported through children's centres, health services and their local community.

There has been a major drive by the DCSF to promote healthy eating in schools. The establishment of a School Food Trust in 2005 was designed to transform school food and food skills. Evidence suggests that this improvement is slow and the quality of provision varied (Ofsted, 2006b). There is currently an ongoing debate around the issues of children's diet and the implications of a poor diet both in terms of health and educational attainment. There is a substantial body of evidence that links childhood nutrition to cognitive function and learning ability (Nelson, 2000). School nurses can improve nutrition among school-age children. Nutrition is a key theme within the National Healthy School Standard with, for example, the National Fruit School Scheme enabling access to fruit at school for all children. Easier access to drinking water in schools is promoted as part of the 'Water is cool in school' campaign.

Hall and Elliman (2004) support the need to encourage food-related initiatives in schools – for example, breakfast clubs and food-growing schemes that involve children in their planning.

Alderton and Campbell-Barr (2005) suggest that the nutrition requirement of children in early years settings is largely overlooked and only considered where the child has a cultural or medical condition. They argue that this lack of nutritional knowledge among early years providers leads them to treat the selection, preparation and serving of food as a stand-alone activity outside the early years curriculum. From September 2008, all early years providers, from childminders to schools, have had to deliver the Early Years Foundation Stage (EYFS). They must promote the good health of children by making healthy food choices and engaging in physical activity. These requirements on providers include meals, snacks and drinks provided for children being healthy, balanced and nutritious, and fresh drinking water being available at all times. Along with general practice, children's centres can promote breastfeeding, support parents and empower them to find strategies to adopt healthier lifestyles.

PROMOTING PHYSICAL ACTIVITY

There appear to be declining levels of activity among children, particularly girls. The National Healthy School Standard (NHSS) recommends two hours' of physical activity a week per pupil, whatever their age or ability, within or outside the national curriculum. Pryke (2006) argues that modern living uses up less energy for daily activities (due to changes in transport, central heating, entertainment and environmental concerns) so children need to find ways to actively boost exercise in order to avoid health problems. Pryke (2006) identifies the following opportunities for physical activity:

- Most schools allow children to be dropped off at least ten minutes before the bell rings. If a child likes charging around the playground with other early friends, this can add almost an hour of extra activity each week.
- Some supermarkets have a crèche or ball area that will entertain a child while their parents get on with the shopping.
- An organizational approach might help, e.g. a regular stop-off at the park each Wednesday, or try a school walking bus (see www.walkingbus.com).
- Send the children along with an outdoor toy when they are invited out for tea.
- Consider leaving a fold-up scooter, football or skipping rope in the boot of the car for opportunistic activity when out and about.
- Use a family approach to getting fitter.
- Make exercise enjoyable.

It is suggested (Hall and Elliman, 2004: 188) that measures could be implemented to enhance exercise levels and reduce the risk of obesity. These include:

- making school playgrounds safer and more enjoyable so that children can be more active
- increasing access to exercise (e.g. investment in road safety schemes to promote walking and cycling, free or low-cost sports facilities)
- promoting reduced traffic speeds and introducing traffic calming or diversion so that children can play outside
- reducing television viewing
- increasing the accessibility and affordability of facilities for children and young people outside the home (swimming pools, skating rinks and clubs).

THE EMOTIONAL AND MENTAL WELL-BEING OF CHILDREN

All children from time to time feel sad, anxious, angry or upset – this is part and parcel of growing up. Some children will be able to talk about the way they feel, while others may express their feelings through moody behaviour or by becoming difficult to control. However, sometimes abnormalities of emotions, behaviour or social relationships may lead to potentially serious difficulties, risking the child's optimal physical, psychosocial development, which can result in the child's family unit being disturbed and in some cases can impact upon their local community (DoH, 2004c). Statistics suggest that 10 per cent of 5-to 10-year-old children may be suffering from some degree of mental or emotional problem (Meltzer et al., 2000), with many of those children needing professional help, and a proportion of these children experiencing continuing problems into adulthood (Caspi et al., 1996).

Resilience and its Promotion

It is likely that all children and young people at some time will have to deal with a range of factors which put their emotional well-being at risk – for example, bereavement, divorce, separation or trauma. Of special interest to researchers is the child's ability to cope with difficulties or problems, leading to the question: what makes one child cope against the odds and another unable to? By researching such phenomena, we can learn from the child who is coping and determine common resilience or protective factors that children can possess. Then in our professional work with children and families, we can begin to promote resilience and the child's strengths, thereby enhancing their emotional well-being and ensuring they have the best possible start in life (DfES, 2004e). Resilience factors determined by researchers are outlined in the table opposite (DfES, 2001b).

FACTORS THAT PUT THE CHILD MORE AT RISK

As well as factors that promote resilience, there are factors that put a child more at risk of emotional problems. These are often varied and complex. For example, there

Table 13.1 Resilience factors

Resilience Factors in the Child	Resilience Factors in the Family	Resilience Factors in the Community
Secure early relationships	At least one good parent–child relationship	A supportive extended family
Higher intelligence	Clear, firm and consistent discipline	Good housing
An easy temperament when an infant	Support for education	Successful school experiences Attending a highly moral a
A positive attitude with good problem-solving approach	Parental harmony	school with positive policies for behaviour, attitudes and anti-bullying
A planner who has a belief that they are in control	An absence of severe discord or family conflict	Attending a school with strong academic and non-academic opportunities
Humour		Access to a range of positive sport and leisure activities
Religious faith		Being a member of a religious faith community
The capacity to reflect or ponder Better social skills and a good ability to convey empathy to others		

Source: DfES (2001)

may be factors that make a child more susceptible or more predisposed to mental health problems, such as brain injury prior, during or after birth, previous physical illness, or a genetic or biological vulnerability. Other factors may precipitate or bring on the child's mental health problems – these may include: parental conflict, family breakdown, physical, sexual or emotional abuse, bereavement/loss of a family member or friend, rejecting or hostile relationships or discrimination (Public Health Institute of Scotland, 2003). Research also suggests that some factors may perpetuate or exacerbate the child's emotional difficulties – for example, economic disadvantage (Rodgers et al., 1999), low self-esteem (Emler, 2001), parental psychiatric illness (Carr, 2000) and domestic violence (Abrahams, 1994; Webb, 2001). However, of note is that in some cases, less obviously traumatic events, such as moving house, the arrival of a new baby or being left for a long time with someone a child does not know, can cause long-term distress.

THE PRESENTATION OF MENTAL ILLNESS

Mental illness in children exhibits itself in varied ways. For example, some of the common manifestations of psychological problems are appetite, sleep and elimination problems. These include: excessive 'clinginess', crying, loss of confidence and withdrawal and an inability to concentrate. Psychosomatic problems may be manifested such as headaches or stomach pains. Behavioural problems may occur, for example, demanding or destructive behaviour, clumsiness, carelessness or irritability, temper tantrums or hyperactivity, with the child being very hard to control. Learning difficulties may be detectable. All these signs are indications of possible psychological distress. Many children experiencing this type of distress find it hard to talk and will often show their feelings through behaviour. For example, a school-age child may lose interest in work and play and refuse to go to school – playing truant may be a sign that the child is unhappy.

Notably, babies do not exhibit the classic symptoms of mental illness and disorder; however, they may exhibit poor sleep patterns, difficulties with feeding, restlessness and gastric disturbance; these signs may indicate that the baby is anxious and tense, distressed and fearful (Young Minds, 2003). Researchers suggest that these emotions need to be responded to with love and empathy by those on whom they depend for survival (Dwivedi and Harper, 2004).

As with adults, mental illness in children is diagnosed by noting signs and symptoms that suggest a particular disorder. Behaviours become symptoms when they occur very often, last a long time, occur at an unusual age or cause significant disruption to the child's and/or the family's ability to function. First, physical illness must be ruled out by the child's doctor, and then depending on the child's symptoms, the illness is classified or diagnosed in order that a treatment programme may be planned. Outlined briefly below are some common classifications of children's mental health problems (please note that this list is not exhaustive):

- *Emotional disorders* – excessive anxiety concerning separation from home or from those to whom the child is attached (attachment difficulties). Children with anxiety disorders respond to certain things or situations with fear and dread as well as with physical signs of anxiety or nervousness such as a rapid heart beat and sweating (panic or phobic disorders). Children may also experience mood disorders, where mood may be abnormally lowered as in the case of depression or abnormally elevated as in the case of manic depression.
- *Attention deficit and disruptive behaviour disorders* – children with these disorders tend to defy rules and are often disruptive in structured environments such as school. They include behaviours related to inattention that are maladaptive (attention deficit or hyperactivity disorder) and behaviours that include the violation of the basic rights of others (conduct disorders or oppositional defiant disorder).
- *Pervasive development disorders* – children with these disorders are confused in their thinking and generally have problems understanding the world around them (autistic disorders).
- *Feeding and eating disorders of infancy and early childhood* – these involve intense emotions and attitudes as well as unusual behaviours associated with food and/or weight.
- *Elimination disorders* – these affect behaviour related to the elimination of body waste – faeces (encopresis) and urine (enuresis).

- *Tic disorders* – these disorders cause a person to perform and repeat sudden involuntary and often meaningless movements and sounds called tics (Tourette's disorder).

In order to treat the child, the psychological, social and educational aspects of the child's problems must be addressed (DoH, 2004c). The child's psychiatrist, counsellor, child psychotherapist, educational and clinical psychologists, social workers and other professional workers work together to formulate a treatment package that emphasizes evidence-based treatments that aim to provide a flexible individualized service tailored to the unique needs of the child and their family (Carr, 2000). The treatment approaches vary; psychotherapy, which can include cognitive behavioural therapy, group therapy or family therapy, may be used to address emotional responses to the mental illness. Creative therapies such as art therapy or play therapy may be helpful, especially with the child who has trouble communicating thoughts and feelings. Medication is sometimes used and is effective with some childhood mental health problems. In many cases, a successful treatment intervention will ensure that the distressing and disabling effects of mental illness can be minimized and ultimately prevented.

The promotion of emotional well-being and the prevention of mental health difficulties involve good multiprofessional partnership and collaboration. This ensures that mental health needs are detected early, thereby allowing professionals such as teachers, health visitors, school nurses and youth workers to support the child's resilience and work with their strengths. This also facilitates the child's emotional literacy or their ability to express feelings using specific feelings words. Another important aspect is supporting the family in order that they can support their child. This may involve such interventions as positive parenting programmes, which aim to promote the family's own strengths through empowering parenting strategies.

SUMMARY

This chapter has provided an overview of the activities involved in promoting child physical and emotional health. It stresses the importance of an holistic approach to working with children and their families. A range of health professional roles are considered in trying to encompass three main health targets:

- the promotion of holistic health and development
- the identification of defects and disorders
- a public health approach to the prevention and management of obesity.

A variety of skills and a wide range of activities are undertaken to promote the health of children. Central to this work is the need to support parents. This is often achieved through early intervention, home-visiting programmes and 'parenting programmes' being incorporated into primary care delivery.

QUESTIONS FOR REFLECTION AND DISCUSSION

1. How can we provide children with the skills they need to be confident about leading a healthy lifestyle?
2. How can we promote an understanding of the full range of issues and behaviours which impact upon lifelong health?
3. What role do you play in promoting healthy diets in your setting?
4. Do you regard physical activity as a vital part of the curriculum and provide a range of options?
5. In what way can we promote children's emotional or mental health and well-being?

Recommended reading

Department of Health (2004) *National Service Framework for Children, Young People and Maternity Services*. London: HMSO.

Department of Health and the Department for Children, Schools and Families (2008) *Healthy Weight, Healthy Lives*. London: HMSO

Dwivedi, K. N. and Harper, B. P. (2004) *Promoting the Emotional Well-Being of Children and Adolescents and Preventing their Mental Ill Health: A Handbook*. London: Jessica Kingsley.

Hall, D. and Elliman, D. (2004) *Health for All Children*, 4th edition. Oxford: Oxford University Press.

Recommended websites

Department of Health (Obesity): www.dh.gov.uk/obesity;
Harlow Health Care: www.health-for-all-children.co.uk

14 PROFESSIONAL WORK IN EARLY CHILDHOOD

Denise Hevey

Chapter objectives

By the end of this chapter, you should be able to:

- To distinguish between mothering/informal caring and professional roles with young children.
- To explain the historical context of training and qualifications in childcare.
- To understand the difference between teachers, social pedagogues and Early Years Professionals.
- To describe the pathways and processes towards achieving Early Years Professional Status.
- To identify and debate the characteristics of professionalism.

WHO NEEDS QUALIFICATIONS?

> A baby's best option is to be cared for by someone who loves and responds to it ... That person does not need 'qualifications'. It may be a parent or relative or a childminder in her own home or a paid nanny who is stable, kind and committed. (Libby Purves, *Times*, 14 February 2006)

This quote from an article in the *Times*, entitled 'Baby, you deserve better', highlights one of the persisting problems in relation to professionalizing the childcare workforce – many people who should know better still believe that education and training are not necessary. The 'myth of motherhood' is so pervasive that it is widely assumed that all you need is love and that the experience of being a mother yourself is sufficient to equip anyone (or at least any female) to work with children. 'This ideology of mothering is so widespread, ancient and powerful that it remains, even if one's lived experience does not validate or even correspond to it' (French, 2003: 760). Yet there is substantial evidence to show that good 'mothering' does not come instinctively and can be learned and that looking after other people's children is considerably different from caring for your own (Clarke and Clarke, 1976; Rutter, 1972; Scarr and Dunn, 1984). Further, when it comes to promoting children's development to its full potential, the level of education and training of staff really makes a difference, as was clearly demonstrated by the findings of the EPPE project:

> There was a significant relationship between the quality of a centre and improved outcomes for children. There was also a positive relationship between the qualification levels of the staff and ratings of centre quality. The higher the qualifications of the staff, particularly the manager of the centre, the more progress children made. (Sylva et al., 2003: 4)

For as long as childcare is seen exclusively as women's work for which they are genetically predisposed and instinctively pre-programmed, it will continue to be undervalued and underpaid and, worse, children will be denied the benefits of highly-trained, professional staff.

> The perpetuation of low pay undermines efforts to raise the quality of the early years workforce and the services it provides ... Low pay, low status and a high proportion of females in the workforce interact and reinforce one another ... Market failures and gendered conceptions of care work mean that the material reward given to the early years workforce undervalues its economic and social importance. (Cooke and Lawton, 2008: 6)

THE HISTORY OF CHILDCARE

To understand how these myths have been created it may be useful to take an historical perspective. As Scarr and Dunn (1984: 52) point out: 'Ideas about motherhood have swung historically with the roles of women.' In pre-industrial societies, work and home were largely combined. Childcare was largely women's work but in the context of extended families who would all take their share. Babies would be taken out to the fields with their mothers, and older children put to work on simple tasks or minding younger ones as soon as they were able (Aries, 1962). 'Mothers with many children often gave responsibility for a newborn to a daughter of four or five – the only children put to work that early. Most had no regular chores until they were about eight' (French, 2002: 21).

Industrialization brought change because factories separated work from home and extended families were often left behind as people moved from the countryside into towns and cities. Older children (as young as eight or nine) were put to work in the mines, mills and factories, younger children were left to fend for themselves on the streets and babies and toddlers were farmed out to wet nurses or minding schools where up to 75 per cent died (French, 2003). Charles Dickens, a great social commentator of the nineteenth century, described the practice of 'baby farming' in his book *Our Mutual Friend*, when Mrs Boffin, seeking to adopt an orphan, visits Betty Higden:

> 'These are not his brother and sister?' said Mrs Boffin. 'Oh dear no, Ma'am. Those are minders.' 'Minders?' the secretary repeated. 'Left to be minded, Sir. I keep a minding-school. I can take only three on account of the mangle. But I love children and four pence is four pence.' (*Our Mutual Friend*, cited in Jackson and Jackson, 1981: 172)

When universal education was introduced in 1870, it wasn't so much to promote children's development and education as to keep working-class children off the streets where they might join gangs and engage in crime. 'Schools were like education factories for poor children. It kept them from being idle and a public nuisance' (Penn 2005: 114).

By 1900, more than 50 per cent of three- and four-year-olds were in school – a level that was not to be achieved again until the 1990s. However, the extent to which they benefited from education was debatable.

> A certified teacher has 60 babies to instruct many of whom are hungry, cold and dirty … They are heavy eyed with unslept sleep … What possible good is there in forcing a little child to master the names of letters and numbers at this age? (Board of Education Inspector's Report 1905, in Penn, 2005: 119)

As a result, the under fives were excluded from state primary schools, nursery schools were founded by pioneers such as Margaret Macmillan, day nurseries were established largely by enlightened mill owners and the split between nursery education and daycare became entrenched. Furthermore, organized childcare was still not available for the majority of working-class families so the gap was plugged by an army of unseen and untrained childminders.

This state of affairs persisted until the Second World War when women were needed to take over men's jobs, childcare was suddenly pronounced by the Ministry of Health as good for children as well as the war effort, and 1450 wartime nurseries were rapidly established (Scarr and Dunn, 1984). It was during this war that the National Nurseries Examination Board was set up to guarantee basic standards of training (the NNEB Certificate) for the thousands of young, inexperienced and childless girls who were drawn in to work in the wartime nurseries.

It was not until 1948 that the first legislation was introduced to curb the worst excesses of baby farming and to regulate standards of childcare through a registration process (Nurseries and Childminders Regulation Act 1948). By this time, the number of former wartime nurseries had been slashed by half and the government of the day, needing women to give up their jobs to make way for returning soldiers, had conveniently discovered experts to reverse the previous view and declare that childcare was bad for children. Foremost among those experts was John Bowlby whose work contributed to a damning indictment of childcare by the World Health Organization in 1951. The Report claimed that the use of day nurseries and crèches would inevitably cause 'permanent damage to the emotional health of a future generation' (cited in Rutter, 1976: 154). The history of childcare still resonated in outmoded ideas about early years education and care into the 1990s which had consequences in attitudes to provision of children's services and to training. To caricature: education is good in small doses and is provided by an elite of highly-trained teachers; and childcare is bad – really what young children need is the constant presence of their mothers. If they can't have that, then the next best thing is a 'mother substitute' and, of course, you don't need training to be a mother.

THE ADVENT OF NATIONAL/SCOTTISH VOCATIONAL QUALIFICATIONS

In 1986, a small booklet was published, appropriately entitled *The Continuing Under Fives Muddle* (Hevey, 1986) that tried for the first time to provide an overview of the much neglected area of education and training for work with the under fives. It concluded that the concept of the child reflected in professional training was partitioned into bits to be educated (teachers), bits to be vaccinated (health visitors) and bits to be cared for (social workers). While the highest level and best known qualification available to the majority of childcare workers was the Certificate of the NNEB – pitched at what we would now call level 2 in academic terms – there existed a plethora of other qualifications, some of dubious value, aimed at 16–19 year olds in schools and colleges. However, there was little in the way of accredited training opportunities for mature students with relevant experience who made up a large section of the workforce. The report was published in the same year as the National Council for Vocational Qualifications was established for England and Wales, holding out the hope of some rationalization of qualifications (Jessup, 1991). (NCVQ was later transmuted into the Qualifications and Curriculum Authority and, in Scotland, the Scottish Qualifications Authority performs a similar role.) By 1989, the 'Working with Under Sevens Project' had been set up, based at the National Children's Bureau, to develop National Occupational Standards for all those working with young children and their families throughout the UK as a basis for new qualifications at levels 2 and 3 in Childcare and Education. These standards were multidisciplinary, based on articulated values and principles and centred on a core reflecting the active promotion of children's development (rather than passive notions of caretaking). They were quickly adopted by a range of awarding bodies including SCOTVEC in Scotland. As a result, the NNEB widened its membership base and was transformed into the Council for Awards in Children's Care and Education (CACHE) and the level of its flagship qualification was raised to a level 3 diploma. BTEC/Edexcel also introduced a level 3 diploma in Nursery Nursing for 16–19-year-olds. Perhaps of most significance, the National/Scottish Vocational Qualification (N/SVQ) system of competence-based assessment in the workplace for the first time opened up access to qualifications to thousands of mature women working in playgroups and as childminders (Hevey, 1991).

THE ROLE OF REGISTRATION AND INSPECTION

The registration of childminders and other childcare providers under the 1948 Act was originally the responsibility of 150 individual local authorities in England which were each empowered to set their own criteria. (Similar arrangements pertained to Wales and Scotland but with devolution, the regulatory systems have since diverged. The main differences will be identified in this chapter but the detail of variations is too complex to include.) Standards inevitably varied and in some areas registration meant just that – being added to a register. There were no set requirements for the qualification levels of staff and follow-up inspection rarely happened. In 2000, the then Department for Education and Employment issued the first set of National Standards for Under Eights Day Care and Childminding under Part X of the Children Act 1989 (DfEE, 2000.) (National Care Standards followed from the Scottish Executive in 2002.) This included for the first time standardized qualification requirements set at level 3 for the 'registered person', with an additional requirement for a minimum of 50 per cent of other staff to be qualified at least to level 2. In 2001, responsibility for the regulation and inspection of childcare across England was transferred to the Office for Standards in Education (Baldock et al., 2007; Ofsted, 2002). Changes were also happening in Wales and Scotland where responsibility for funded nursery education stayed with the Education Inspectorates (ESTYN for Wales and HMIE for Scotland), whereas daycare became the responsibility of the new Care Commissions. (A more detailed discussion of the curriculum and regulatory frameworks for Early Years Education and Care for each of the nations of the UK is available in Clark and Waller, 2007.)

In England, a programme of 'transitional inspections' was put in place to ensure that all settings were visited by an Ofsted inspector within 18 months and, where the qualification requirements were not met, actions with the force of law were imposed on settings (Ofsted, 2002). Though not without its critics (Dahlberg et al., 1999), the involvement of Ofsted had a major impact on the sector. It was seen as a strong enforcer that was firmly rooted in education standards, and the promise of publication of inspection reports acted as a powerful lever on private sector settings that operated in the childcare market place. The transition was far from painless and, even though the qualification requirements were relatively low, this was the second important step towards the professionalization of the early years workforce.

THE ADVENT OF FOUNDATION DEGREES

Meanwhile, the impact of the outcomes-based approach and the vocational relevance initiated by N/SVQs were being extended into Higher Education (HE). N/SVQs were developed at level 4 but there were few incentives for higher level training of this sort and N/SVQs did not carry academic credit or sit easily with the independent nature of HE institutions. In the end, in England and Wales, a new type of vocational/academic hybrid award was developed, with a strong work-based component, equivalent in academic terms to the first two years of an undergraduate degree programme. This became known as a Foundation Degree and could be designed and awarded by individual Higher Education Institutions in collaboration with local colleges or with support from local employers. (In Scotland, the strong tradition of Higher National Diplomas awarded through SQA continues.) The danger was that local responsiveness and diversification would result in a lack of comparability across the country. In 2001, the Sure Start Unit took a strong lead by devising a National Statement of Requirements and an endorsement package for the Foundation Degree in Early Years that would confer Senior Practitioner status and guarantee some standardization of content and quality in return for additional support for students.

Early years provision had begun a rapid expansion in the late 1990s in order to meet government targets for a million extra childcare places and to provide part-time pre-school education for all three- and four-year-olds (Baldock et al., 2007). A Nursery Education Grant was payable to a wide range of settings deemed capable of delivering the Foundation Stage (3–5) curriculum, not just primary and nursery schools and classes. (Again, parallel but different curriculum frameworks exist in Wales, Northern Ireland and Scotland – see Clark and Waller, 2007). By 2002, the Foundation Degree in Early Years provided a work-based route to a higher education qualification for the expanding number of experienced staff who were leading the curriculum but did not hold Qualified Teacher Status.

 Case Study

Terri left school at 16 with four GCSEs and no idea what sort of career she wanted. She worked for a while as a shop assistant and then got pregnant. By the age of 21, she found herself married with two children and no prospects. The one thing that she did know was that she loved being with young children.

As soon as her eldest was school age, she got work as a nursery assistant in a community day nursery. She followed their internal training programme and gained NVQ2 in Childcare and Education within 12 months. Gaining the NVQ gave her more confidence in herself as well as in her job.

She soon took on extra responsibility and the manager suggested she should do NVQ3 as Ofsted now required this of room supervisors. When the manager left a couple of years later, she took over as the person in charge.

Amongst the training information that she regularly received from the local authority, she spotted an advert for a Foundation Degree in Early Years by day release and the LA adviser said she would get her fees paid. Terri had never really thought of going to university before but she knew she was good at her job and the entrance requirements were an NVQ3 plus GCSE in English, which she had. She applied and was called for interview which made her very nervous but the tutor was reassuring.

Terri had never written formal essays before but study skills were a core part of the early stages of the course. She soon discovered that one day per week was only the half of it. She had to put in another six to eight hours a week of background reading and work on her assignments but thankfully these were all very relevant to her day-to-day work and helped build up her evidence for the Ofsted inspection. She found that when she sat down in the evenings at her kitchen table and opened her books, her two children often joined her to do their homework. It gave her a real kick to think that they were all studying together and that her children now took their own education much more seriously than she had ever done. After two years of hard work, Terri emerged with a Foundation Degree of which she is justly proud and so were her partner and children when they attended the graduation ceremony and saw her in her gown.

THE CHILDREN'S WORKFORCE DEVELOPMENT COUNCIL

N/SVQs and Foundation Degrees were part of the wider national strategy for up-skilling the workforce with employer involvement through a succession of coalescing Industry Lead Bodies and National Training Organizations, leading finally to Sector Skills Councils such as SkillsActive for the play, sport and leisure sector. Most of the Sector Skills Councils have a UK-wide remit. Early Years and Childcare was unusual as an 'industry sector' as it was characterized by a mixed economy of provision through the maintained sector (local authority schools and nursery schools), independent schools, voluntary and community groups and private day nurseries and childminders. Within this mix, there were few large-scale employers which made achieving employer representation challenging. For several years, the industry sector was represented through the Early Years National Training Organization which included national voluntary organizations (such as the Pre-school Learning Alliance and the National Childminding Association) that were membership organisations rather than employers. EYNTO covered an estimated 350,000 to 500,000 workers in England and Wales but on its own, this workforce 'footprint' was not considered big enough to warrant the designation of Sector Skills Council. So, in line with the extended responsibilities of the DfES for children's social care under the *Every Child Matters* agenda, provision was made in the Children Act 2004 to establish a new arrangement for England covering most forms of children's services outside of schools to be known as the Children's Workforce Development Council. In turn, this links up with comparable bodies for Scotland and Wales and with related Sector Skills Councils (including SkillsActive for play work and the Training and Development Agency for Schools for the wider schools workforce) via the Children's Workforce Network (Owen, 2006).

CHILDREN'S WORKFORCE STRATEGY

Meanwhile, the findings of one of the first large-scale, longitudinal studies of Effective Provision of Pre-school Education (EPPE) had been published which demonstrated conclusively that better quality provision led to better outcomes for children and that in turn the quality of provision was largely dependent on the qualification levels of staff, especially those of the setting leader/manager (Sylva et al., 2003) (see quote at the beginning of this chapter). The quality of provision was highest in nursery schools and in integrated settings that were led by a graduate (normally a teacher). The government published a workforce strategy consultation document early in 2005, which, among other things, set out ideas about graduate leadership of early years and childcare settings and invited comments on whether this leader should be a teacher or a broader-based type of professional akin to the European model of a 'social pedagogue' (Boddy et al., 2007).

INTERNATIONAL COMPARISONS

The role of social pedagogues with graduate level education and training is well established in Europe, particularly in Scandinavian countries such as Denmark and Sweden

---

(Einarsdottir and Wagner, 2006). Social pedagogues have a broad-based education and are trained to engage with all aspects of human development and learning and with all age groups from the youngest children, to adolescents and the elderly (Petrie et al., 2005). They work in social and residential care settings as well as in daycare and in the community where they may be supporting independent living for adults with disabilities or learning difficulties. As such, their training has a particular focus on social–emotional development and life skills and, although they may understand the principles of learning to read and phonics, for example, and they may be employed in classrooms alongside teachers, they are concerned with promoting holistic development rather than with the delivery of a particular curriculum. In Denmark, formal schooling does not begin until the age of six and, although some teachers are also employed in kindergarten, social pedagogues (and pedagogue assistants) dominate services for young children (Eurybase, 2006/07). The word 'pre-school' is anathema in Danish eyes because the ethos of childcare and kindergarten is to value the child's experience of the present rather than to see their present experience as a preparation for school (a human being not a 'human becoming' – Qvortrup, 1994).

In contrast, New Zealand decided as recently as 2006 to aim not just for graduate leadership but for a largely graduate workforce in early years settings, with those graduates being qualified teachers. The tradition and philosophical approach of teacher education is very different from that of social pedagogy and, despite the extended age range and greater breadth in the New Zealand model of 'new teacher', it has a primary focus on education through delivering a structured curriculum and on preparing children for formal schooling as the next stage in the education process (MoE, 2002). This policy has not been without its problems, not least because of the huge expense of employing an all-graduate workforce on teachers' terms and conditions. Early Years suddenly became one of the major issues in the New Zealand general election of 2007 (see Chapter 5).

EARLY YEARS PROFESSIONAL STATUS

Over recent years, with the devolution of responsibility for education and care services, the nations of the UK have increasingly diverged in relation to early years policy and in relation to education and training. So, for example, in Wales and Scotland, the schools' inspectorates (ESTYN and HMIE respectively) retain a responsibility for the inspection of nursery education while the responsibility for regulation of childminding and daycare is separately located with their respective care councils, rather than being integrated under a single regulator like Ofsted (Clark and Waller, 2007). The policy direction for England was confirmed in the government's response to the Children's Workforce Strategy Consultation issued in 2006 (HMG, 2006b) which set out proposals for a new form of multidisciplinary Early Years Professional Status (EYPS) to be conferred on graduates with relevant knowledge and experience across the birth-to-five age range who will: 'lead practice in the Early Years Foundation Stage (EYFS), support and mentor other practitioners and model the skills and behaviours that safeguard and promote good outcomes for children' (CWDC, 2006: 6). This has since been followed by the publication in Scotland of the Standard for Childhood Practice (Quality Assurance Agency for Higher Education, 2007) and the launch of new graduate-level qualifications for early years and childcare practitioners in May 2008 (Scottish Social Services Council, 2008)

In England, EYPS is intended to be broadly equivalent to Qualified Teacher Status for those working in the private, voluntary and independent sector but taking an holistic approach covering the age band 0–5. There are four different pathways to achieving EYPS depending on previous qualifications and experience, but all culminate in the same assessment against the 39 national standards for Early Years Professional Status.

- EYPS Validation – (four months) for those with a relevant degree plus experience across the whole of the 0–5 age band.
- EYPS Short pathway – (six months) consisting of three months part-time training preceding validation for those with a broadly relevant degree and experience in part of the age band (for example, primary teachers).
- EYPS Long Pathway – (12–15 months) an academically accredited education and training programme designed primarily as a top-up for those with an Early Years Foundation Degree.
- EYPS Full Pathway – (36 weeks full time, including 18 weeks of placement) for those with non-relevant degrees who wish to take up work with young children as newly qualified graduates or who are looking for a career change.

All pathways culminate in the same validation process which is made up of three stages:

- **Stage 1:** Gateway review of skills – a type of management centre-style assessment of the candidate's ability to communicate, negotiate and deal with problems under pressure. This is formative rather than summative and candidates are given feedback to help them improve their presentation style, negotiation skills, etc.
- **Stage 2:** Written tasks – candidates are required to submit seven separate written accounts, demonstrating how they have met the 39 national standards for EYPS through aspects of their day-to-day practice with babies, toddlers and pre-school children.
- **Stage 3:** Setting visit – A trained assessor spends a whole day in the candidate's setting during which he/she has a guided tour of the setting, interviews supervisors and co-workers (witnesses) about the candidate's practice, examines the setting records, policies and other documentary evidence and interviews the candidate in relation to the standards.

This whole process is rigorously recorded and moderated to ensure an effective audit trail of evidence. However, the assessor's judgement is on the basis of what the candidate and others claim and write – at no stage does the assessor undertake formal observation of the candidate's practice with children or families.

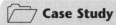 **Case Study**

Terri is coming back to university for a third year to do the EYPS Long Pathway, which is fully funded by the CWDC, and will lead to an ordinary degree plus EYPS status. Both she and her setting will benefit from the Graduate Leader Fund and she will have a professional qualification – something that she would never have dreamed of at 16, and something that would not have been possible for her personally without work-based routes to qualification which enabled her to go on earning while she studied.

THE RELATIONSHIP BETWEEN EYPS AND TEACHING

The role of qualified teachers appears to remain largely unchanged by the development of EYPS. Although every daycare setting and children's centre in England will be required to achieve graduate leadership of the Early Years Foundation Stage (EYFS) by employing someone with Early Years Professional Status by 2015, nursery and reception classes in maintained schools will still be led only by teachers with Qualified Teacher Status – normally with early years (3–8) or primary (5–11) training. At the time of writing, there is no formal requirement for teachers to undertake additional training in the birth-to-three age band, in child health and well-being or in multi-agency working that are key features of the holistic approach to children's development incorporated in the EYFS (DfES, 2007a). However, the issue has at least been recognized in the recommendations of the early years curriculum review in Northern Ireland (Sproule et al., 2005, cited in Walsh, 2007). Teachers in maintained schools and nurseries in England are not currently eligible to be trained and validated as Early Years Professionals. However, many experienced primary teachers who are taking up roles in children's centres do see the need to broaden their training and are undertaking the EYPS short course.

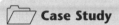 **Case Study**

Praksha has been a nursery and reception class teacher for eight years, working in a primary school in an area of social disadvantage with a high proportion of children for whom English is an additional language. Three years ago, the school became host to a Sure Start local programme and developed a range of additional services for families and children. Last year, they decided to bring the two aspects together within a children's centre including full daycare provision for children from six months. Praksha was the first to recognize that her own training as a teacher had not covered working with babies or working as part of a multi-professional team so she enrolled on the EYPS short course. Praksha felt she learnt as much from colleagues with backgrounds in family support work and childminding as she did from the tutor. She was able to get hands-on experience in the baby room and came to understand the importance of flexible routines, of standing back and letting the child explore, of responding to the child's initiations and the particular importance of the consistency of the key worker to pre-verbal children. As a result of her experience, she found herself questioning her practice with the pre-school group as well. Praksha thinks that there are many advantages to holding both QTS and EYPS if you are a teacher in a children's centre.

Initial teacher training in the UK is either through a first degree at Honours level with integrated professional (QTS) training over a three to four-year period or through a one-year intensive Professional Graduate Certificate in Education following on from a first degree in a relevant area such as Early Childhood Studies or a curriculum subject such as English. In both cases, students undergo extensive and varied placements and are visited and observed and have their practice assessed on a regular basis. In their first year before registration is confirmed, Newly Qualified Teachers (NQTs) have a special status and entitlement to ongoing supervision and support. Teachers are employed on distinct terms and conditions of service which make them better paid than other workers in the early years sector, and they may be deployed in reception (four- and five-year-olds) and later stages of primary schools not just in nursery classes which gives added flexibility in small schools.

One consequence of the exclusion of teachers from EYPS training is that, with the new Early Years Foundation Stage becoming statutory in England, many teachers in the maintained sector may be leading a curriculum stage for which they are not fully trained, most having received only a couple of days of in-service training on the EYFS as a whole. On the other hand, in the private, voluntary and independent sector, the EYFS will be led (in time) solely by Early Years Professionals – graduates with multi-disciplinary training that covers the whole of the EYFS and with at least some experience of working across the full 0–5 age range. (Similarly in Scotland, early years and childcare settings will be led by those with the new Childhood Practice Award.) However, despite the latest government incentives in the form of the Graduate Leader Fund, EYPs currently have no guarantee of the pay and conditions commensurate with a graduate role. Unfortunately, confidence in their status may be undermined by the fact that, unlike teachers, the training and validation process that EYPs undergo does not require direct observation and assessment of their practice with children.

SUMMARY

So what does it mean to be a professional in early years? Rather than thinking about professionalism as a quality of some elite group of graduates that have been through a particular form of training, one could argue that professionalism is an attribute that one would want to see in practitioners at all career grades from novice to expert and from nursery assistant to manager – an 'inclusive' model rather than the traditional 'exclusive' approach (Nurse, 2007).

This chapter has shown that attitudes to work with young children are changing over time and that a range of qualifications are now available to validate knowledge, skills and competence at a variety of levels. Graduate leadership is increasingly seen as essential for all early years settings, much in the same way that the professionalization of teachers, nurses or social workers has progressed from largely unqualified through certificate/diploma to graduate-level requirements. The main difference is that, in the case of the early years sector, professionalization has started to happen much later and much faster than in comparable areas with requirements for leaders changing from level 3 N/SVQ to level 5

(Continued)

(Continued)

Foundation Degree/SQA HND and then to level 6 EYPS (or in Scotland CPA at level 9 in the Scottish Curriculum and Qualifications Framework) in less than a decade. Whether the process will be successfully achieved to meet the target of graduate leadership of every day-care setting by 2015, and whether this alone will be enough to drive up quality, have already been questioned. A recent report by the Institute of Policy Studies of the early years workforce identified low pay, lack of progression routes other than into management and the alienating effect of the current approach to professionalization which fails to recognize long-standing experience, as serious blockers to achieving the ultimate policy goals (Cooke and Lawton, 2008). They make a number of recommendations including:

- setting level 3 as the minimum qualification for early years practitioners
- increasing the number of Senior Practitioners at level 5
- developing an integrated careers structure across children's services
- creating a Practitioner Board to represent the views of the workforce
- using that board to develop a mechanism for agreeing wage floors for practitioners with different levels of qualification.

Government intervention is justified, they argue, because of the constraints on the market (dependent on fees charged to parents) and the importance of childcare both directly and indirectly to the economy and future well-being of society. On the other hand, encouraging professionalization through the establishment of a professional association which allowed for different levels of membership would be an alternative approach to giving practitioners a voice and government a body with whom to negotiate.

Professional associations have traditionally restricted their membership to those with the highest qualifications in their field. The term 'professional' brings with it a lot of historical baggage. Historically, the only reputable professions were the church and the law – these were the basis on which the original mediaeval universities were founded. Medicine (originally the province of quacks and surgeon–barbers) took time to be recognized and it was not until the twentieth century that teaching, nursing and social work became graduate professions and were then brought into regulation. EYPS is in an intermediate position where it is now a nationally recognized status but as yet does not have a professional association or chartered status through a professional body (such as the British Psychological Society) or registration through a regulator (like the General Social Care Council in England or the Scottish Social Services Council in Scotland which in time will register all care workers). Whereas no one can take a qualification (such as a degree) away once it has been awarded, regulation requires professionals to abide by a code of conduct, and breach of the code can lead to someone being 'struck off' and barred from practice or having their professional status removed. This higher level of scrutiny is characteristic of all the more established professions and is put in place to protect the public from malpractice by those in positions of trust. So, at best, we can say that early years now has a fledgling profession in England that is aspiring to recognition and regulation on a par with established professions.

But if only the most highly qualified are described as professionals, what does that say about others working in related subsidiary roles? Are they at best *para*-professional (such as paramedics) or *non*-professional workers and at worst *un*-professional? No one who takes their job seriously, whatever their role or status, would wish to be described as unprofessional, so a corollary of professionalization of the workforce must be the promotion of a professional and reflective approach across all job roles and levels within the sector, not just at graduate leadership level (Paige-Smith and Craft, 2008).

For me, a professional approach to work in early years means recognizing and accepting that:

- working with young children and their families is skilled work for which you need education and training
- skills alone are not enough – you need the underpinning knowledge to know when and how to apply them
- many different roles and agencies are involved in work with children and families – you need to understand, respect and value their different contributions
- children and families are all different and your business is to know them well enough to respond appropriately in meeting their needs and wishes – equity and equality do not mean treating everyone the same
- a professional approach means taking responsibility for the quality of your own work, reflecting on what you have done and working out what could be done better
- as a professional, you can never know it all and you never stop learning.

Professionalizing the early years workforce starts with debunking the 'myth of motherhood' and moving to a situation in which everyone is expected, and expects, to take a professional approach to their work – engaging in education, training, reflective practice and personal development in ways that are appropriate to their roles (Paige-Smith and Craft, 2008). It means introducing a climbing frame of qualifications through which individuals can progress and develop or broaden their knowledge and skills (Abbott and Hevey, 2001). And it does not end with the achievement of one particular professional qualification or status.

QUESTIONS FOR REFLECTION AND DISCUSSION

1. If most of all babies need carers who are sensitive and responsive to their needs, why should anyone need training?
2. In what ways is looking after other people's children different from caring for your own?
3. What are the similarities and differences between a teacher, a social pedagogue and an Early Years Professional?
4. Should all those who work in early years be considered professionals? If not, why not?
5. What do you think are the most important characteristics of a profession?

Recommended reading

Abbott, L. and Hevey, D. (2001) 'Training to work in the early years; developing the climbing frame.' In G. Pugh (ed.), *Contemporary Issues in Early Years,* 2nd edition. London: Paul Chapman.

Baldock, P., Fitzgerald, D. and Kay, J. (eds) (2007) *Understanding Early Years Policy.* London: Paul Chapman.

Einarsdottir, J. and Wagner, J. T. (eds) (2006) *Nordic Childhoods and Early Education.* Greenwich, CI: Information Age Publishing.

Paige-Smith, A. and Craft, A. (2008) 'What does it mean to reflect on our practice?' In A. Paige-Smith and A. Craft (eds) *Developing Reflective Practice in the Early Years.* Maidenhead: Open University Press.

Sylva, K. Melhuish, E., Sammons, P., Siraj-Blatchford, I., Taggart, B. and Elliott, K. (2003) *The Effective Provision of Pre-School Education (EPPE) Project: Findings from the Pre-School Period.* Research Brief RBX15–03. Nottingham: DfES Publications.

Recommended websites

Children's Workforce Development Council: www.cwdcouncil.org.uk/early-years;
Ofsted (Office for Standards in Education and Childcare for England): www.ofsted.gov.uk

GLOSSARY

ACCAC   Awdurdod Cwricwlwm, Cymwysterau ac Asesu Cymru (Wales Curriculum, Qualifications and Assessment Authority). ACCAC became part of the WAG's Department for Education, Lifelong Learning and Skills (DELLS) on 1 April 2006.

Agency   Children's capacity to understand and actively influence their world.

ALN   Additional learning needs – is gradually replacing SEN as the preferred term in Wales (see Wyn Siencyn and Thomas, 2007).

BERA   British Educational Research Association.

CACHE   Council for Awards in Children's Care and Education

CAF   Common Assessment Framework An assessment tool that is intended to be used across the children's workforce to assess the additional needs of children and young people holistically at the first signs of difficulty. The framework provides a mechanism that any practitioner working with children can use (or have access to) to identify unmet needs, so as to prevent a child's needs becoming more serious.

CAFCASS   The Child and Family Court Advisory Service – CAFCASS was established in April 2001 as a non-departmental public body for England and Wales. CAFCASS advises the court so that any decisions they take are in the best interests of children. Specifically, its role is to safeguard and promote the welfare of the child; advise the court about any application made to it; make provision for children to be represented; and to provide information, advice and support for children and their families.

CCEA   Council for the Curriculum, Examinations and Assessment, Northern Ireland.

Child development   The study of children – which has mainly focused on individual development in Western society as a natural progress towards adulthood.

Childminder   Childminders look after under-fives at any time and school-age children outside school hours and in the school holidays. The children are usually cared for in the childminder's home.

Children in Scotland   Children in Scotland is the national agency for voluntary, statutory and professional organizations and individuals working with children and their families in Scotland.

Children in Wales   Children in Wales is the national umbrella organization for those working with children and young people in Wales. It aims to promote the interests of these groups and take action to meet their needs. Children in Wales is a registered charity and an independent non-governmental organization.

Children's Centres   Children's Centres in England provide childcare integrated with early learning, family support, health services and support for parents wanting to return to work or training.

Children's Commissioner   A Children's Commissioner has been established in all four countries of the UK to be an advocate for children's and young people's rights and to promote awareness of the views and interests of children. However, the mandates, independence and funding arrangements of each Commissioner vary considerably. There are concerns over whether some Commissioners are sufficiently independent from government to allow full autonomy. In England, for example, the Commissioner may be directed by the government to undertake a specific inquiry (see UK Children's Commissioners' Report to UN Committee on the Rights of the Child, 2008).

Children's Plan   The Children's Plan was published by the DCSF in England in December 2007. It outlines a ten-year vision 'to make this country a better place for children and young people. It aims to raise attainment and aspirations for this and future generations, closing gaps in educational achievement and ensuring standards of educational excellence for everyone'.

Children's trusts   Children's trusts bring together all services for children and young people in an area, underpinned by the Children Act 2004 duty to cooperate, to focus on improving outcomes for all children and young people.

CRAE   Children's Rights Alliance in England.

CSIE   Centre for Studies on Inclusive Education.

Curriculum for Excellence   The curriculum in Scotland for 3–18 years.

CWDC   Children's Workforce Development Council (England).

Daycare Trust   A national childcare charity, campaigning for quality, accessible, affordable childcare for all and promoting the voices of children, parents and carers. The Trust also provides advice for parents and carers, providers, employers, trade unions and policymakers on childcare issues.

DCSF   Department for Children, Schools and Families.

DENI   Department for Education in Northern Ireland.

DES   Department of Education and Science.

DfEE   Department for Education and Employment.

DfES   Department for Education and Skills.

DoH   Department of Health.

DWP   Department for Work and Pensions.

Early childhood   Internationally recognized as the period of childhood from conception to around eight years of age.

Early years   This is a term used within education, generally to refer to children (or provision for children) within the age range of 0–7. However, it is also sometimes used more narrowly to refer to the under-fives, or to those settings, such as nurseries, where pre-school children are cared for and educated.

ECM   Every Child Matters – the government's vision for improving the lives and well-being of children and young people from birth to age 19. Published in 2003 as a green paper, and followed by the Children Act in 2004, Every Child Matters (ECM) aims to achieve better outcomes for all children by ensuring all organizations and professionals that provide services to children, such as schools, social workers, the police and health professionals, work together in a more effective way. This multi-agency approach places the child as the focus of attention, and a key feature of the ECM agenda is to give children and young people far more say about issues that affect them as individuals and collectively. The five ECM outcomes are: being healthy, staying safe, enjoying and achieving, making a positive contribution to society and achieving economic well-being, and were identified by children themselves.

ECS   Early Childhood Studies.

EDCM   Every Disabled Child Matters – a campaign to get rights and justice for every disabled child.

EECERA   European Early Childhood Education Research Association.

EPPE   Effective Provision of Pre-School Education – a longitudinal study funded by the DfES since 1997. The research focuses on the progress and development of 3000 children from entering pre-school to the end of Key Stage 3 in secondary school from age 3 to 14 years old.

ESTYN   The government agency responsible for the inspection of schools in Wales.

ETI   Education and Training Inspectorate (Northern Ireland).

Extended schools   A range of services and activities, usually outside the school day, to help meet the needs of children and young people, their families and the wider community, including: breakfast and after-school clubs; summer schools and holiday clubs; sport, music, artistic and drama clubs; support for family learning; access to ICT equipment and software outside school hours for adults and children; health care, family support and other training, advice and personal help.

EYDCP   Early years and childcare partnerships.

EYFS   Early Years Foundation Stage (the curriculum for 0–5 in England as of September 2008).

EYP   Early years practitioner.

EYPS   Early Years Practitioner Status (England).

Flying Start   A programme in Wales targeted at supporting families with children under 4.

Foundation Phase A play-based curriculum for schools in Wales for children aged 3–7 introduced in September 2008.

Foundation Stage The foundation stage was introduced in September 2000 as a distinct phase of education for children aged three to five. It provides a framework for children's learning in nursery or reception class. The Foundation Stage Curriculum for 3–5-year-olds is based on learning through play and on six areas of learning. These areas of learning are based on the skills and understanding that children will need to participate in formal education when they start school at the age of five. The Education Act 2002 extended the National Curriculum to include the foundation stage.

Good Childhood Inquiry A report commissioned by the Children's Society in 2007 to elicit views about what constitutes a good childhood.

HMIE Her Majesty's Inspectorate of Education (Scotland).

IEP Individual Education Plan – an individual learning programme devised by a school for a child who has been identified as having special educational needs. It sets out key individual short-term targets for the child, the teaching strategies to be used, and any extra support that may be needed.

Inclusion Inclusion (or inclusive education, inclusive schooling or educational inclusion) is a term used within education to describe the process of ensuring equality of learning opportunities for all children and young people, whatever their disabilities or disadvantages or social exclusion.

Integrated Centres Integrated Children's Centres in Wales provide integrated education, care, family support and health services.

Integrated practice Collaboration between a number of education, health and social care professionals in children's services (also interagency collaboration).

Interprofessional Where there is a willingness to share and give up exclusive claims to specialist knowledge if the needs of service users can be better met by members of other professional groups (see Banks, 2004).

IQF Integrated Qualifications Framework – a framework proposed in England to coordinate approved qualifications, progression and continuing professional development across the children's workforce.

LA Local Authority – a body responsible for providing education for children of school age in its area. It also has responsibility for children's services (including early years), the youth service and adult education.

Learning stories Learning stories are structured narrative documentation based on critical incidents of children's learning, including the child's own comments (see Carr, 2001).

LTS Learning and Teaching Scotland – LTS provides advice, support, resources and staff development to the education community, throughout Scottish education.

MDG Millenium Development Goals – the MDGs are eight targets to be achieved by 2015 that respond to the world's main development challenges. The MDGs are drawn from the actions and targets contained in the Millennium Declaration that was adopted during the United Nations Millennium Summit in September 2000.

Multiple intelligences A theory by Howard Gardner (1983) who argued that people learn in different ways and that there are different types of intelligences. He suggested that everyone possesses each type of intelligence to varying degrees. Gardner identified seven different types of intelligence and a key element of Gardner's theory is that learning and intelligence are not fixed. They can and do change throughout each individual's lifetime.

Multiprofessional working Where the traditional forms and divisions of professional knowledge and authority are retained.

NAEYC National Association for the Education of Young Children (USA) – a professional organization which promotes early childhood education and provides information for practitioners and parents.

National Childcare Strategy Launched in 1998 and updated in 2004, the strategy aims to provide access to affordable childcare and early years services, remove barriers to parental employment and alleviate child poverty.

NCB National Children's Bureau – founded in 1963, NCB is a charitable organization that acts as an umbrella body for organizations working with children and young people in England and Northern Ireland. NCB coordinates a membership and multi-agency network of child education, health and social care, youth, early years and other children's services professionals. NCB also works in partnership with Children in Scotland and Children in Wales.

Neuroscience The study of the brain and nervous system using computer technology and brain imaging techniques, to measure activity in the brain and map the growth of the brain.

NHSS The National Health School Standards (England).

NIPPA An early years organization in Northern Ireland

(formerly Northern Ireland Pre-School Play Groups Association).

NNEB National Nurseries Examination Board – established to guarantee a basic standard of training for those working in nurseries.

NSF National Service Framework for Children, Young People and Maternity Services (DoH, 2004c) is a 10-year programme intended to stimulate long-term and sustained improvement in children's health.

NVQ National Vocational Qualifications.

OECD Organization for Economic Cooperation and Development – an organization that collects and shares economic and social data across more than 100 countries throughout the world.

OFSTED Office for Standards in Education (England) – a government agency responsible for the inspection of schools and the regulation of early years childcare, including childminders in England. Under the Children Act 2004, Ofsted will take the lead in developing a framework for integrated inspections of children's services.

Participation Children's right to participate in the processes and decisions that affect their lives.

Practitioner The generic term for an adult who works with young children in any setting or capacity.

QAA The Quality Assurance Agency for Higher Education reviews the quality and standards of higher education in universities and colleges across the UK.

QCA Qualifications and Curriculum Authority (England) – its remit is to maintain and develop the national curriculum and associated assessments, tests and examinations.

Scaffolding The process by which an adult (or another child) assists a child to carry out a task beyond the child's individual capability.

Scottish Executive The devolved Government for Scotland – responsible for health, education, justice, rural affairs and transport.

SEN Special Educational Needs – the needs of children who have learning difficulties or disabilities which significantly affect access to the curriculum. Approximately one in five children may have a special educational need at any one time.

Setting The generic term for all forms of early years provision where a child may be cared for and educated, including childminding, LA nurseries, playgroups, independent provision and voluntary groups.

Social justice Social justice is linked to principles of equality and equal worth. This perspective argues that everyone should have the chance and opportunity to make the most of their lives and use their talents to the full and that unjust inequalities should be eradicated.

Socio-cultural A perspective that views learning as socially constructed through joint activities leading to shared knowledge.

SOWC State of the World's Children – a report produced annually by UNICEF.

SQA Scottish Qualifications Authority.

Stockholm syndrome The Stockholm syndrome is a recognized range of protective processes with relevance to abused children. The syndrome was first identified when bank employees were held hostage in Stockholm, and it has been observed in hostage, kidnap, concentration camp, domestic violence and other abuse situations. There are a number of stages that victims experience. However, as with grief processes, these stages are not experienced by everyone nor in a clearly defined order.

Sure Start A government programme first launched in 1999 with the specific objective of eradicating child poverty. Sure Start centres were established in economically deprived areas to improve the health and well-being of families and children from before birth to age four. All Sure Start local programmes became Sure Start Children's Centres by 2006.

The policies and programmes of Sure Start apply in England only. Responsibility for early education and childcare in Scotland, Wales and Northern Ireland rests with the separate devolved administrations.

UK United Kingdom – the UK comprises four nations: England, Northern Ireland, Scotland and Wales. Policy relating to education, health and children's services is devolved but England is under the full jurisdiction of the UK Parliament in Westminster, with no separate devolved administration. The UK Parliament continues to legislate on matters which affect the UK as a whole and these matters, which are reserved to Westminster, include immigration and nationality.

UNCRC United Nations Convention on the Rights of the Child.

UNESCO United Nations Educational, Scientific and Cultural Organization – UNESCO promotes international cooperation among its 193 Member States and six Associate Members in the fields of education, science, culture and communication. Through its strategies and activities, UNESCO is actively pursuing the Millennium Development Goals.

UNICEF The United Nations Children's Fund – UNICEF works for children's rights, their survival, development and protection, guided by the Convention on the Rights of the Child (UNCRC).

WAG Welsh Assembly Government.

Well-being A complex concept involving feelings and actions relating to physical, psychological, cognitive, social and economic domains.

WHO World Health Organization.

REFERENCES

Aasen, W. and Waters, J. (2006) 'The new curriculum in Wales: a new view of the child?', *Education 3–13,* 34 (2): 123–9.

Abbott, L. and Hevey, D. (2001) 'Training to work in the early years: developing the climbing frame.' In G. Pugh (ed.), *Contemporary Issues in the Early Years: Working Collaboratively with Children,* 3rd edition. London: Sage.

Abrahams, C. (1994) *'The Hidden Victims' – Children and Domestic Violence.* London: NCH Action for Children. Available from: www.nch.org.uk (Accessed 17 October 2004).

ACCAC (Curriculum and Assessment Authority for Wales) (2000) *Desirable Outcomes for Children's Learning before Compulsory School Age.* Cardiff: ACCAC.

ACCAC (Curriculum and Assessment Authority for Wales) (2004) *The Foundation Phase in Wales: a draft framework for children's learning.* Cardiff: ACCAC.

Acheson, D. (1998) *Independent inquiry into inequalities in health.* Report of the committee chaired by Donald Acheson. London: HMSO.

Ainscow, M., Booth, T., and Dyson, A. (eds) (2006) *Improving Schools, Developing Inclusion (Improving Learning).* London: Routledge.

Alderfer, C.P. (1972) *Existence, Relatedness and Growth: Human Needs in Organizational Settings.* New York: Free Press.

Alderson, P. (1995) *Listening to Children: Children, Ethics and Social Research.* London: Barnardo's.

Alderson, P. (2001) 'Research by children.' *International Journal of Social Research Methodology,* 4 (2): 139–53.

Alderson, P. (2005) 'Children's rights: a new approach to studying childhood.' In H. Penn, *Understanding Early Childhood: Issues and Controversies.* Maidenhead: Open University Press and McGraw-Hill Education.

Alderson, P. and Morrow, G. (2004) *Ethics, Social Research and Consulting with Children.* London: Barnardo's.

Alderton, T. and Campbell-Barr, V. (2005) 'Quality Early Education – quality food and Nutritional practices? Some initial results from a pilot research project into food and nutrition practices in early years settings in Kent, UK', *International Journal of Early Years Education,* 13 (3): 197–213.

Alexander, R.J. (2008) *Towards Dialogic Teaching: Rethinking classroom talk,* 4th edition. York: Dialogos.

Alwin, D.F. (1990) 'Historical changes in parental orientations to children', *Sociological Studies of Child Development,* 3: 65–86.

Anning, A. (1998) 'The Co-construction by Early Years Care and Education Practitioners of Literacy and Mathematics Curricula for Young Children.' Paper presented at the British Educational Research Association Annual Conference (BERA), Queen's University of Belfast, Northern Ireland, August 27th–30th.

Anning, A. and Edwards, A. (1999) *Promoting Children's Learning from Birth to Five.* Buckingham: Open University Press.

Anning, A. and Edwards, A. (2006) *Promoting Children's Learning from Birth to Five.* 2nd edition. Maidenhead: Open University Press.

Anning, A., Cullen, J. and Fleer, M. (eds), (2004) *Early Childhood Education.* London: Sage.

Anning, A., Aubrey, C., Calder, P., David, T., (eds) (2003) *Early Years Research: Pedagogy, Curriculum and Adult Roles, Training and Professionalism.* Available from: www.bera.ac.uk/pdfs/BERAEarlyYears Review31May03.pdf (Accessed 19 July 2008).

Aries, P. (1962) *Centuries of Childhood.* London: Cape.

Arnold, C. (2003) *Observing Harry: Child Development and Learning 0–5.* Maidenhead: Open University Press.

Arnstein, S.R. (1969) 'A ladder of Citizen Partnership', *Journal of the American Institute of Planners,* 35 (4): 216–24.

Athey, C. (1990) *Extending Thought in Young Children: A Parent–Teacher Partnership.* London: Paul Chapman.

Athey, C. (2007) *Extending Thought in Young Children: A Parent–Teacher Partnership,* 2nd edition. London: Paul Chapman.

Aubrey, C., Quick, S., Lambley, C. and Newcomb, E. (2002) *Implementing the Foundation Stage in Reception Classes.* London: DfES.

Aylott, M. (2006) 'Developing Rigour in Observation of the Sick Child', *Paediatric Nursing,* 18 (8): 38–44.

Badham, B. (2004) 'Participation – For a Change: Disabled Young People Lead the Way', *Children and Society,* 18 (2): 143–54.

Bailey, D. and Martin, A. (1994) 'Physical activity and skeletal health in adolescents', *Paediatric Exercise Science* 6 (4): 330–47.

Baldock, P., Fitzgerald, D. and Kay, J. (eds) (2007) *Understanding Early Years Policy.* London: Paul Chapman.

Ball, D. (2002) *Playgrounds – Risks, Benefits and Choices.* Norwich: Health and Safety Executive, HMSO.

Ball, S.J. and Vincent, C. (2005) 'The childcare champion? New Labour, social justice and the childcare market', *British Educational Research Journal,* 31(5): 557–70.

Banks, S. (2004) *Ethics, Accountability and Social Professions.* Basingstoke: Palgrave Macmillan.

Barnardo's (1995) *Playing it safe.* London: Barnardo's.

Barnardo's and Transport 2000 (2004) *Stop, Look and Listen: Children Talk about Traffic.* London: Barnado's.

Ben-Arieh, A. (2005) 'Where are the children? Children's role in measuring and monitoring their well-being.' *Social Indicators Research,* 74: 573–96

Ben-Arieh, A. and Frones, I. (2007) 'Indicators of Children's Well-being: What should be Measured and Why?', *Social Indicators Research,* 84: 249–50.

Bennett, J. (2001) 'Goals and curricula in early childhood.' In, S. Kammerman (ed.), *Early Childhood Education and Care: International Perspectives.* New York: The Institute for Child and family Policy at Columbia University.

Bennett, J. (2003) 'Starting Strong – the persistent division between education and care', *Journal of Early Childhood Research,* 1 (1): 21–48.

Bennett, J. (2004) 'Curriculum Issues in National Policy Making'. Paper presented at the EECERA Annual Conference, Malta (September).

Bennett, N., Desforges, C., Cockburn, A. and Wilkinson, B. (1984) *The Quality of Pupils' Learning Experiences.* London: Lawrence Erlbaum.

Berk, L. (2000) *Child Development,* 5th edition. Boston, MA: Allyn and Bacon.

Berk, L. and Winsler, A. (1995) *Scaffolding Children's Learning: Vygotsky and Early Childhood Education.* Washington, DC: NAEYC.

Bertram, T. and Pascal, C. (2002) *Early Years Education: An International Perspective.* London: QCA/NfER.

Bichard, M. (2004) *Final Report: An Independent Inquiry arising from the Soham Murders.* London: Home Office.

Bilton, H. (2002) *Outdoor Play in the Early Years: Management and Innovation,* 2nd edition. London: David Fulton.

Bird, J. and Gerlach, L. (2005) *Improving the Emotional Health and Wellbeing of Young People in Secure Care: Training for Staff in Local Authority Secure Children's Homes.* London: National Children's Bureau.

Blair, M., Brown, S., Waterson, T. and Crowther, R. (2003) *Child Public Health.* Oxford: Oxford University Press.

Blakemore, S.J. (2000) *Early Years Learning.* (Post Report 140) London: Parliamentary Office of Science and Technology.

Blakemore, S.J., and Frith, U. (2005) *The Learning Brain: Lessons for Education.* Oxford: Blackwell.

Blakemore Brown, L. (2001) *Reweaving the Autistic Tapestry.* London: Jessica Kingsley.

Blanchet-Cohen, N. and Rainbow, B. (2006) 'Partnership between children and adults? The experience of the International Children's Conference on the Environment', *Childhood,* 13: 113–26.

BMA (2001) *Consents, Rights and Choices in Health Care for Children and Young People.* London: BMJ Books.

Boddy, J., Cameron, C., Moss, P., Mooney, P., Petrie, P. and Statham, J. (2007) *Introducing Pedagogy into the Children's Workforce*. London: Thomas Coram Research Institute.

Bodrova, E. and Leong, J. (2007) *Tools of The Mind*, 2nd edition. Colombus, OH: Pearson.

Bondy, B., Ross, D., Sindelar, P., and Griffin, C. (1995) 'Elementary and special educators learning to work together: team building processes', *Teacher Education and Special Education*, 18 (2): 91–102.

Booth, T. and Ainscow, M. (eds) (1998) *From them to us: an international study of inclusion in education*. London: Routledge.

Boushel, M. (2000) 'Child rearing across Cultures'. In M. Boushel, M. Fawcett and J. Selwyn (eds), *Focus on Early Childhood: Principles and Realities*. Oxford: Blackwell.

Bowlby, J. with Ainsworth, M. (1965) *Child Care and the Growth of Love*, 2nd edition. Harmondsworth: Penguin.

Bransford, J.D., Brown, A.L., and Cocking R.R. (2000) *How People Learn: Brain, Mind, Experience and School*. Washington, DC: Academy Press.

Braye, S. (2000) 'Participation and involvement in social care: an overview.' In H. Kemshall and R. Littlechild (eds), *User Involvement and Participation in Social Care: Research Informing Practice*. London: Jessica Kingsley.

Brierley, J. (1994) *Give Me a Child until he is Seven: Brain Studies and Early Education*, 2nd edition. London: The Falmer Press.

British Educational Research Association Early Years Special Interest Group (BERA SIG) (2003) *Early Years Research: Pedagogy, Curriculum and Adult Roles, Training and Professionalism*. Southwell, Notts: BERA.

British Educational Research Association (BERA) (2004) *Revised Ethical Guidelines for Educational Researchers*. Southwell: British Educational Research Association.

Broadhead, P. (2004) *Early Years Play and Learning: Developing Social Skills and Cooperation*. London: RoutledgeFalmer.

Bronfenbrenner, U. (1977) 'Toward an experimental ecology of human development', *American Psychologist*, 32: 513–31.

Bronfenbrenner, U. (1979) *The Ecology of Human Development: Experiments by Nature and Design*. Cambridge, MA: Harvard University Press.

Brooker, E. (2002) *Starting School: Young Children Learning Cultures*. Buckingham: Open University Press.

Brooker, L. (2005) 'Learning to be a child: cultural diversity and early years ideology.' In N. Yelland (ed.), *Critical Issues in Early Childhood Education*. Maidenhead: Open University Press.

Brooker, L. and Broadbent, L. (2003) 'Personal, social and emotional development: the child makes meaning in the world.' In J. Riley (ed.), *Learning in the Early Years: A Guide for Teachers of 3–7*. London: Paul Chapman.

Brown, A. (1987) 'Metacognition, executive control, self-regulation and other more mysterious mechanisms.' In F.E. Weinert and R.H. Kluwe (eds), *Metacognition, Motivation and Understanding*. Hillsdale, NJ: Erlbaum Associates.

Brown, B. (1998) *Unlearning Discrimination in the Early Years*. Stoke-on-Trent: Trentham Books.

Brown, B. (2001) *Combating Discrimination: Persona Dolls in Action*. Stoke-on-Trent: Trentham Books.

Bruce, T. (2001) *Learning Through Play – Babies,Toddlers and the Foundation Years*. London: Hodder Stoughton.

Bruce, T. (2005) *Early Childhood Education*, 3rd edition. London: Hodder & Stoughton.

Bruer, J.T. (1997) 'Education and the brain: A bridge too far' *Educational Researcher*, 26 (8): 4–16.

Bruner, J.S. (1978) 'The role of dialogue in language acquisition.' In A. Sinclair, R. Jarvella, and W.J.M. Levelt (eds), *The Child's Conception of Language*. New York: Springer.

Bruner, J.S. (1986) *Actual Minds, Possible Worlds*. Cambridge, MA: Harvard University Press.

Bruner, J.S. (1990) *Acts of Meaning*. Cambridge, MA: Harvard University Press.

Bruner, J.S. (1996) *The Culture of Education*. Cambridge, MA: Harvard University Press.

Burke, C. (2005) 'Play in focus: children researching their own spaces and places for play', *Children, Youth and Environments* 15 (1): 27–53. Available from: www.colorado.edu/journals/cye/. (Accessed 7 July 2005).

Burr, R. (2002) 'Global and local approaches to children's rights in Vietnam', *Childhood,* 9 (1): 49–61.

Burr, R. (2004) 'Children's rights: international policy and lived practice.' In M.J. Kehily (ed.), *An Introduction to Childhood Studies.* Maidenhead: Open University Press.

Butcher, T. (2002) *Delivering Welfare,* 2nd edition. Buckingham: Open University Press.

Calder, M. (2003) 'The assessment framework: a critique and reformulation.' In M.C. Calder and S. Hackett (eds), *Assessment in Child Care: Using and Deveoping Frameworks for practice.* Lyme Regis: Russell House Publishing.

Calder, M. C. and Hackett. S. (eds) (2003) *Assessment in Child Care: Using and Developing Frameworks for Practice.* Lyme Regis: Russell House Publishing.

Cameron, C. (2006) 'Men in the nursery revisited: issues of male workers and professionalism,' *Contemporary Issues in Early Childhood, 7* (3): 68–79.

Cameron, C. (2007) 'Understandings of Care Work with Young Children: Reflections on children's independence in a video observation study', *Childhood* 14: 467–86.

Cannella, G.S. (1997) *Deconstructing Early Childhood Education: Social Justice and Revolution.* New York: Peter Lang.

Cannella, G.S. (1999) 'The scientific discourse of education: predetermining the lives of others – Foucault, education and children', *Contemporary Issues in Early Childhood, 1* (1): 36-84.

Cannella, G.S. and Greishaber, S. (2001) 'Identities and possibilities.' In S. Greishaber and G. Cannella (eds), *Embracing Identities in Early Childhood Education: 'Diversity and Possibilities'.* New York: Teachers College Press.

Carmichael, E. and Hancock, J. (2007) 'Scotland'. In M.M. Clark and T. Waller (eds) *Early Childhood Education and Care.* London: Sage.

Carnwell, R. and Buchanan, J. (eds) (2005) *Effective Practice in Health and Social Care: A Partnership Approach.* Maidenhead: Open University Press.

Carr, A. (ed.) (2000) *What Works With Children and Adolescents? A Critical Review of Research on Psychological Interventions with Children, Adolescents and their Families.* London: Routledge.

Carr, M. (2001) *Assessment in Early Childhood Settings.* London: Paul Chapman.

Carr, M. and Claxton, G. (2002) 'Tracking the development of learning dispositions', *Assessment in Education* 9 (1): 9–37.

Carrier, J. and Kendall, I. (1995) *Interprofessional Relations in Health Care.* London: Edward Arnold.

Casey, T. (2007) *Environments for Outdoor Play. A Practical Guide for Making Space for Children.* London: Paul Chapman.

Caspi, A., Newman, D.L, Moffitt, T.E. and Silva, P.A. (1996) 'Behavioural Observations at age 3 yrs predict adult psychiatric disorders', *Archives of General Psychiatry*, 53: 1033–99.

Catherwood, D. (1999) 'New views on the young brain: offerings from developmental psychology to early childhood education', *Contemporary Issues in Early Childhood*, 1 (1): 23–35.

Central Advisory Council for Education (CASE) (1967) *Children and their Primary Schools* (the Plowden Report). London: HMSO.

Chand, A. (2008) 'Every Child Matters? A critical review of child welfare reforms in the context of minority ethnic children and families', *Child Abuse Review* 17 (1): 8–22.

Children's Rights Alliance in England (CRAE) (2008) Listen and Change: A Guide to Children and Young People's Participation Rights. London: CRAE.

Children's Workforce Development Council (CWDC) (2006) *Early Years Professional Prospectus.* Leeds: CWDC.

Children's Workforce Development Council (CWDC) (2008) *Clear Progression 2008: The Next Steps Towards Building an Integrated Qualifications Framework for the Children and Young People's Workforce.* Leeds: CWDC.

Children's Workforce Network (2006) *Clear Progression: Towards an Integrated Qualifications Framework.* Leeds: CWDC.

Christensen, P. and James, A. (2008) *Research with Children: Perspectives and Practices,* 2nd edition. London: Falmer Press.

Christensen, P. and Prout, A. (2005) 'Anthropological and sociological perspectives on the study of children.' In S. Green and D. Hogan (eds), *Researching Children's Experiences.* London: Sage.

Clark, A. (2004) 'The mosaic approach and research with young children.' In V. Lewis, M. Kellet, C. Robinson, S. Fraser and S. Ding (eds), *The Reality of Research with Young Children*. London: Sage Publications with the Open University.

Clark, A. and Moss, P. (2001) *Listening to Young Children: The Mosaic Approach.* London: National Children's Bureau.

Clark, A. and Moss, P. (2005) *Spaces to Play: More Listening to Young Children Using the Mosaic Approach.* London: National Children's Bureau.

Clark, A. and Statham, J. (2005) 'Listening to young children: experts in their own lives', *Adoption and Fostering*, 29 (1): 45–56.

Clark, M.M. and Waller, T. (eds) (2007) *Early Childhood Education and Care: Policy and Practice*. London: Sage.

Clark, A., Kjorholt, A. and Moss, P. (eds) (2005) *Beyond Listening: Children's Perspectives on Early Childhood Services*. Bristol: The Policy Press.

Clarke, A. and Clarke, A. (2000) *Early Experience and the Life Path*. London: Jessica Kingsley.

Clarke, A.M. and Clarke, A.D.B. (eds) (1976) *Early Experience: Myth And Evidence*. London: Open Books.

Clarke, J.N. and Fletcher, P.C. (2004) 'Parents as advocates: stories of surplus suffering when a child is diagnosed and treated for cancer', *Social Work in Health Care*, 39 (1–2, 27): 107–27.

Claxton, G. (1990) *Teaching to Learn.* London: Cassell.

Claxton, G. and Carr, M. (2004) 'A framework for teaching learning: the dynamics of disposition', *Early Years*, 24 (1): 87–97.

Cleaver, H. (2006) 'The influence of parenting and other family relationships.' In J. Aldgate, D. Jones, W. Rose and C. Jeffery, *The Developing World of the Child*. London: Jessica Kingsley.

Clements, R. (2004) 'An investigation of the status of outdoor play', *Contemporary Issues in Early Childhood*, 5 (1): 68–80.

Clothier, C., MacDonald, C.A. and Shaw, D.A. (1994) *The Allitt inquiry: independent inquiry relating to deaths and injuries on the children's ward at Grantham and Kesteven General Hospital during the period February to April 1991.* London: HMSO.

Cohen, S. Humphreys, B. and Mynott, E. (2001) *From Immigration Controls to Welfare Controls*. London: Routledge.

Cohen, B., Moss, P., Petrie, P., and Wallace, J. (2004) *A New Deal for Children? Re-forming Education and Care in England, Scotland and Sweden*. Bristol: The Policy Press.

Cole, M. (1996) *Cultural Psychology: A Once and Future Discipline*. Cambridge, MA: The Belknap Press of Harvard University Press.

Connell, R. (1987) *Gender and Power*. Sydney: Allen & Unwin.

Cooke, G. and Lawton, K. (2008) *For Love or Money: Pay, Progression and Professionalisation in The 'Early Years' Workforce*. London: Institute for Public Policy Research.

Coombe, V. and Little, A. (1986) *Race and Social Work: A Guide to Training*. London: Tavistock Publications.

Corsaro, W.A. (2005) *The Sociology of Childhood,* 2nd edition. Thousand Oaks, CA: Pine Forge Press.

Council for the Curriculum, Examinations and Assessment (CCEA) (2006) *The Revised NI Primary Curriculum*. Belfast: DENI.

Council of Europe (1950) *European Convention on Human Rights*. Rome: Council of Europe.

Cousins, J. (1999) *Listening to Four Year Olds.* London: The National Early Years Network.

Cowley, S. and Houston, A. (2002) 'An empowerment approach to needs assessment in health visiting practice', *Journal of Clinical Nursing*, 11 (5): 640–50.

Crawley, H. (2006) *Child First, Migrant Second: Ensuring that Every Child Matters*. London: ILPA. Available from: www.ilpa.org.uk/publications/ilpa_child_first.pdf (Accessed 20 May 2008).

Crimmens, D. and West, A. (2004) *Having Their Say – Young People and Participation: European Experience*. Lyme Regis: Russell House Publishing.

CSIE (2000) *Index for Inclusion*. Bristol : Centre for Studies on Inclusion.

Csikszentmihalyi, M. (1979) 'The concept of flow.' In B. Sutton-Smith, *Play and Learning,* New York: Gardner.

Cullen, J. (1996) 'The challenge of *Te Whāriki* for future development in early childhood education', *Delta* 48 (1): 113–25.

Cunningham, H. (1995) *Children and Childhood in Western Society since 1500*. Harlow: Longman Group.

Curry, N. and Johnson, C. (1990) *Beyond Self-Esteem: Developing a Genuine Sense of Human Value*. Washington, DC: NAEYC.

Curtis, A. and O'Hagan, M. (2003) *Care and Education in Early Childhood*. London: Routledge.

Dagis, M. (2006) 'The first rule states "Don't interfere with our play"', *Nursery Children*, Täby, Sweden.

Dahlberg, G. (1985) *Context and the Child's Orientation to Meaning: A Study of the Child's Way of Organising the Surrounding World in Relation to Public Institutionalised Socialisation*. Stockholm: Almqvist and Wiskell.

Dahlberg, G. and Moss, P. (2005) *Ethics and Politics in Early Childhood Education*. London and New York: RoutledgeFalmer.

Dahlberg, G., Moss, P. and Pence, A. (1999) *Beyond Quality in Early Childhood Education and Care: Postmodern Perspectives*. London and New York: RoutledgeFalmer.

Dahlberg, G., Moss, P. and Pence, A. (2007) *Beyond Quality in Early Childhood Education and Care: Postmodern Perspectives,* 2nd edition. London and New York: RoutledgeFalmer.

David, T. (ed.) (1999) *Young Children Learning*. London: Paul Chapman.

David, T. (2006) 'The world picture.' In G. Pugh and B. Duffy (eds), *Contemporary Issues in the Early Years,* 4th edition. London: Sage.

Daycare Trust (2001) 'Call for children's centres', *Childcare Now*, 15 (Summer), p. 3.

Department for Children, Education, Lifelong Learning and Skills (DCELLS) (2008) *Foundation Phase: Framework for Children's Learning for 3 to 7-year-olds in Wales*. Cardiff: Welsh Assembly Government.

Department for Children, Schools and Families (DCSF) (2007a) *The Children's Plan: Building Brighter Futures*. Norwich: HMSO.

DCSF (2007b) A Study into Children's Views On Physical Discipline and Punishment [online]. Available from: www.dcsf.gov.uk/publications/section58review/pdfs/Section% 2058%20Children%20and% 20Young%20People%20Survey.pdf (Accessed 11 May 2008).

Department for Children Schools and Families (DCSF) (2007c) *Children looked after in England* [Online] Available from: www.dfes.gov.uk/rsgateway/DB/SFR/s000741/SFR27-2007v2.pdf (Accessed 13 December 2007).

DCSF (2007d) *Guidance on the duty to promote community cohesion*. HMSO. [online] Available from: www.multiverse.ac.uk/viewarticle2.aspx?contentId=13955 (Accessed 13 May 2008).

Department for Children, Schools and Families (DCFS) (2008a) *Children's Play Consultation*. Available from: www.dfes.gov.uk/pns/DisplayPN.cgi?pn_id=2008_0067 (Accessed 4 April 2008).

Department for Children, Schools and Families and Department of Health (2008b) *Healthy Weight, Healthy Lives*. London: HMSO.

Department for Children, Schools and Families (DCFS) (2008c) *The Inclusion of Gypsy, Roma and Traveller Children and Young People*. London: HMSO.

Department for Children, Schools and Families (DCFS) (2008d) *About Personalised Learning*. [online] Available from: www.standards.dfes.gov.uk/personalisedlearning/about/ (Accessed 12 August 2008).

Department for Constitutional Affairs (2004) *Freedom of Information Act* (2004). Available online at: www.dca.gov.uk (Accessed 12 December 2004).

Department for Education (DfE) (1994) *Code of Practice on the Identification and Assessment of Special Educational Needs*. London: DfE.

Department of Education and Science (DES) (1978) *Special Educational Needs: Report of the Committee of Enquiry into the Education of Handicapped Children and Young People (The Warnock Committee)*. London: HMSO.

Department of Education and Science (DES) (1985) *Education for All (The Swann Report)*. London: HMSO.

Department for Education and Employment (DfEE) (1997) *Excellence for All Children: Meeting Special Educational Needs*. London: DfEE.

Department for Education and Employment (DfEE) (1998a) *Meeting the Childcare Challenge.* Sudbury: Department for Education and Employment.

Department for Education and Employment ((DfEE) 1998b) *The National Literacy Strategy.* London: Department for Education and Employment.

Department for Education and Employment (DfEE) (1999a) *The National Curriculum.* London: Department for Education and Employment and Qualifications and Assessment Authority.

Department for Education and Employment (DfEE) (1999b) *The National Numeracy Strategy.* London: Department for Education and Employment.

Department for Education and Employment (DfEE) (2000a) *Curriculum Guidance for the Foundation Stage.* London: Qualifications and Curriculum Authority.

Department for Education and Employment (DfEE) (2000b) 'National Standards For Under Eights Day Care and Childminding.' In *Department For Education And Employment* (ed.). Nottingham: DfEE Publications.

Department for Education and Employment (DfEE) (2001) *NHSS Guidance.* London: DfEE.

Department of Education for Northern Ireland (DENI) (2006) *Outcomes of the Review of Pre-school Education in NI.* Belfast: DENI.

Department for Education and Skills (DfES) (2001a) *Special Educational Needs Code of Practice.* London: DfES Publications.

Department for Education and Skills (DfES) (2001b) *Promoting Children's Mental Health within Early Years and School Setting.* London: HMSO.

Department for Education and Skills (DfES) and Department of Health (DoH) (2003) *Together From the Start – Practical Guidance for Professionals Working with Disabled Children (Birth to Third Birthday) and their Families.* Nottingham: DfES.

Department for Education and Skills and Qualifications and Curriculum Authority. (2003) *Foundation Stage Profile.* London: Qualifications and Curriculum Authority.

Department for Education and Skills (DfES) (2003) *Every Child Matters.* Green Paper. London: The Stationery Office.

Department for Education and Skills (DfES) (2004a) *Meeting the Childcare Challenge.* Available online at www.standards.dfes.gov.uk (Accessed 13 December 2004).

Department for Education and Skills (DfES) (2004b) *Removing Barriers to Achievement.* Available from: www.standards.dfes.gov.uk/thinkingskills/resources/565178?view=get-24k–(Accessed 12 December 2004).

Department for Education and Skills (DfES) (2004c) *Birth to Three Matters.* Available online at: www.surestart.gov.uk (Accessed 13 December 2004).

Department for Education and Skills (DfES) (2004d) *Children Act 2004.* London: HMSO.

Department for Education and Skills (2004e) *Every Child Matters: Change for Children.* London: HMSO. Available on: www.everychildmatters.gov.uk/ (Accessed 17 December 2004).

Department for Education and Skills (DfES) (2004f) *Five Year Strategy for Children and Learners.* London: the Stationery Office.

Department for Education and Skills (DfES) (2005) *Children's Workforce Strategy* Available online from: www.everychildmatters.gov.uk/childrensworkforcestrategy/ (Accessed 12 May 2006).

Department for Education and Skills (DfES) (2006a) *Education Outside the Classroom Manifesto consultation.* Available from: www.dfes.gov.uk/consultations/index.cfm (Accessed 11 February 2006).

Department for Education and Skills (DfES) (2006b) *Exclusion of Black Pupils: Priority Review. Getting it right.* London: DfES.

Department for Education and Skills (DfES) (2006c) *Childcare Act 2006.* London: HMSO. Available on: www.everychildmatters.gov.uk (Accessed 3 February 2007).

Department for Education and Skills (DfES) (2006d) *A Short Guide to the Education and Inspections Act 2006.* London: DfES.

Department for Education and Skills (DfES) (2007a) *Curriculum guidance for the Foundation Stage.* Available from www.standards.dfes.gov.uk/resources/downloads (Accessed 13 May 2008).

Department for Education and Skills (DfES) (2007b) *Aiming High for Children: Supporting Families* London: The Stationary Office. Available online from: http://www.everychildmatters.gov.uk/_files/HMT%20YOUNG%20CHILDREN.pdf (Accessed 20 May 2008).

Department for Education and Skills (DfES) (2007c) *Common Assessment Framework for Children and Young People: Practitioners' Guide – Integrated Working to Improve Outcomes for Children and Young People.* Leeds: Children's Development Workforce Council.

Department for Education and Skills (DfES) (2007d) *Aiming High for Disabled Children: Better Support for Families.* Runcorn: DfES/HM Treasury.

Department for Education and Skills (DfES) (2007e) *Extended Schools: Access to Opportunities and Services for All.* Nottingham: DfES.

Department for Education and Department of Health (1999) *National Healthy School Standards Document.* London: HMSO.

Department of Health (DOH) (1989) *Children Act 1989.* London: HMSO.

Department of Health (DOH) (1991) *Working Together Under the Children Act 1989: A Guide for Inter-Agency Co-Operation for the Protection of Children from Abuse.* London: HMSO.

Department of Health (DOH) (1998) *Working Together to Safeguard Children: New Proposals For Inter-Agency Co-operation.* London: HMSO. Available on: www.doh.gov.uk (Accessed 17 December 2004).

Department of Health (DOH) (2000a) *Framework for the Assessment of Children in Need and their Families.* London: HMSO.

Department of Health (DOH) (2000b) *The NHS Plan.* London: HMSO.

Department of Health (DOH) (2001a) *School Nurse Development Pack.* London: HMSO.

Department of Health (2001b) *Health Visitor Development Pack.* London: HMSO.

Department of Health (DoH) (2004a) *Best Practice Guidance for Doctors and Other Health Professionals on the Provision of Advice and Treatment to Young People Under 16 on Contraception, Sexual and Reproductive Health* [online]. Available from: www.dh./gov/uk/PublicationsAnd Statistics/PublicationsPolicyAnd Guidance/fs/en (Accessed 28 December 2004).

Department of Health (DoH) (2004b) *National Standards, Local Action: Health and Social Care Standards and Planning Framework.* London: Department of Health.

Department of Health (DoH) (2004c) *National Service Framework for Children, Young People and Maternity Services: The mental health and psychological wellbeing of children and young people.* London: Department of Health.

Department of Health (DoH) Department for Education and Skills (DfES), Home Office. (2004) *Framework for the Assessment of Children in Need and their Families.* London: The Stationery Office.

Department of Health (2005) [Online] *Report of the Ad Hoc Advisory Group on the Operation of NHS Research Ethics Committees.* Available at: www.dh.gov.uk/en/Publicationsandstatistics/Publications/PublicationsPolicyAndGuidance/DH_4112416 (Accessed: 24 May 2008).

Department of Health and Social Security (DHSS) (1973) *Report on the Working Party on Collaboration Between the NHS and Local Government.* London: HMSO.

Department of Health and Social Security (DHSS) (1984) *Report of Joint Working Group on Collaboration between Family Practitioner Committees and District Health Authorities.* London: DHSS.

Dockett, S. and Fleer, M. (1999) *Play and Pedagogy in Early Childhood:Bending the rules.* Marrickville, NSW: Harcourt Brace & Co.

Dominelli, L. (2002) *Anti-oppressive Social Work Theory and Practice.* Basingstoke: Palgrave Macmillan.

Donaldson, M. (1978) *Children's Minds.* Harmondsworth: Penguin.

Donaldson, M. (1993) 'Sense and sensibility: some thoughts on the teaching of literacy.' In R. Beard (ed.), *Teaching Literacy Balancing Perspectives.* London: Hodder & Stoughton.

Dowling, M. (2005) *Young Children's Personal, Social and Emotional Development,* 2nd edition. London Paul Chapman

Doyle, C. (1987) 'Sexual abuse – giving help to children,' *Childhood and Society,* 1 (3): 210–23.

Doyle, C. (1994) *Child Sex Abuse: A Guide for Health Professionals.* London: Chapman and Hall.

Doyle, C. (1997) 'Emotional abuse of children: issues for intervention', *Child Abuse Review,* 6: 330–42.

Doyle, C. (1998) 'Emotional abuse of children: issues for intervention.' Unpublished PhD Thesis, University of Leicester.

Doyle, C. (2001) 'Surviving and coping with emotional abuse in childhood', *Clinical Child Psychology and Psychiatry* 6 (3): 387–402.

Doyle, C. (2006) *Working with Abused Children,* 3rd edition. Basingstoke: Palgrave Macmillan.

Draper, L. and Duffy, B. (2001) 'Working with Parents.' In G. Pugh (ed.), *Contemporary Issues in the Early Years.* London: Paul Chapman.

Drifte, C. (2001) *Special Needs in Early Years Settings: A Guide for Practitioners.* London: David Fulton.

Dumfries and Galloway Child Protection Committee (2000) *Child Protection Inquiry into the Circumstances Surrounding the Death of Kennedy McFarlane.* Dumfries: Dumfries and Galloway CPC.

Dunn, J. (1988) *The Beginnings of Social Understanding.* Oxford: Basil Blackwell.

Durant, S. (2003) *Outdoor Play.* Leamington Spa: Step Forward Publishing.

Dweck, C. and Leggett, E. (1988) 'A social-cognitive approach to motivation and personality'. *Psychological Review,* 95 (2): 256–73.

Dwivedi, K.N. and Harper, B.P. (2004) *Promoting the Emotional Well-being of Children and Adolescents and Preventing Their Mental Ill Health: A Handbook.* London. Jessica Kingsley.

Dyson, A. and Millward, A. (2000) *Schools and Special Needs: Issues of Innovation and Inclusion.* London: Paul Chapman.

Early Childhood Forum (2003) *Definition of Inclusion.* Available online from http://www.ncb.org.uk/Page.asp?sve=819 (Accessed 12 April 2008).

Edgington, M. (2004) *The Foundation Stage Teacher in Action: Teaching 3, 4 and 5 year olds.* London: Paul Chapman.

Educational and Social Research Council (2005) *Research Ethics Framework.* Swindon: Educational and Social Research Council.

Edwards, D. and Mercer, N. (1987) *Common Knowledge: The Development of Understanding in the Classroom.* London: Methuen.

Eekelaar, J. (1992) 'The importance of thinking that children have rights.' In P. Alston and J. Seymour (eds), *Children's Rights and the Law.* Oxford: Clarendon Press.

Einarsdottir, J. and Wagner, J. (eds) (2006) *Nordic Childhoods and Early Education.* Greenwich, CI: Information Age.

Elfer, P. and Wedge, D. (1996) 'Defining, measuring and supporting quality.' In G. Pugh (ed.), *Working Collaboratively for Children,* 2nd edition. London: National Children's Bureau.

Emilson, A. and Folkesson, A.M. (2006) 'Children's participation and teacher control', *Early Child Development and Care,* 176 (3&4): 219–38.

Emler, N. (2001) *Self-esteem: The Causes and Costs of Low Self-worth.* York: York Publishing Services (for the Joseph Rowntree Foundation).

End Child Poverty (2008) Poverty and Life Chances. Available online from: www.endchildpoverty.org.uk/why-end-child-poverty/the-effects (Accessed 20 June 2008).

Ennew, J. (1986) *The Sexual Exploitation of Children.* Cambridge: Polity Press.

Equality and Human Rights Commission (2007) *Our History.* Available online from: www.equalityhumanrights.com/en/aboutus/history/pages/oldsitelinks.aspx (Accessed 11 July 2008).

Eraut, M. (1999) 'Non-formal learning in the workplace.' Paper presented at Researching Work and Learning Conference, Leeds, September.

European Commission Network on Childcare and Other Measures to Reconcile the Employment Responsibilities of Men and Women. (1996) *Quality Targets in Services for Young Children: Proposals for a Ten Year Action Programme.* University of Toronto: Childcare Resource and Research Unit.

Eurybase (2006/07) General Organisation of the Education System and Administration of Education. Denmark.

Every Disabled Child Matters (EDCM) (2006) *Getting rights and justice for every disabled child.* Available online from: www.edcm.org.uk/page.asp (Accessed 21 April 2007).

Facer, K., Furlong, J., Furlong, R. and Sutherland, R. (2003) *ScreenPlay: Children and Computing in the Home.* London: RoutledgeFalmer.

Farson, R. (1974) *Birthrights.* London: Collier Macmillan.

Fawcett, B., Featherstone, B. and Goddard, J. (2004) *Contemporary Child Care Policy and Practice.* Basingstoke: Palgrave Macmillan.

Fawcett, M. (2000) 'Historical views of childhood.' In M. Boushel, M. Fawcett and J. Selwyn (eds), *Focus on Early Childhood: Principles and Realities.* Oxford: Blackwell.

Fielding, M. (2001) 'Students as radical agents of change', *Journal of Educational Change,* 2: 123–41.

Finkelhor, D. (1984) *Child Sexual Abuse: New Theory and Research.* New York: The Free Press.

Fitzgerald, D. and Kay, J. (2007) *Working Together in Children's Services.* Abingdon: Routledge.

Fjørtoft, I. (2001) 'The natural environment as a playground for children: the impact of outdoor play activities in pre-primary school children', *Early Childhood Education Journal,* 29 (2): 111–17.

Fjørtoft, I. (2004) 'Landscape as playscape: the effects of natural environments on children's play and motor development', *Children, Youth and Environments* 14 (2): 21–44. Available from: www.colorado.edu/journals/cye/ (Accessed 4 January 2005).

Foresight (2007) 'Tackling obesities: future choices.' In DH/DCSF (2008) *Healthy Weight, Healthy Lives.* London: HMSO.

Fortin, J. (2003) *Children's Rights and the Developing Law.* London: Butterworth.

Francis, M. and Lorenzo, R. (2002) 'Seven realms of children's participation', *Journal of Environmental Psychology,* 22: 157–69.

Franklin, B. (ed.) (2002) *The New Handbook of Children's Rights: Comparative Policy and Practice.* London: Routledge.

Fraser, S. (2000) *Authentic Childhood: Experiencing Reggio Emilia in the Classroom.* Scarborough, Ont: Thomas Nelson Learning.

Freeman, M. (1983) *The Rights and Wrongs of Children.* London: Pinter.

French, M. (2002) *From Eve to Dawn: A History of Women Volume II: The Masculine Mystique.* Toronto, Ont: McArthur and Company.

French, M. (2003) *From Eve to Dawn: A History of Women Volume III: Infernos and Paradises.* Toronto: McArthur and Company.

Froebel, F. (1826) *The Education of Man.* Keilhau/Leipzig: Wienbrach.

Frones, I. (1994) 'Dimensions of childhood.' In J. Qvortrup, G. Sgritta and H. Wintersberger (eds), *Childhood Matters: Social Theory, Practice and Politics.* Aldershot: Avebury.

Furedi, F. (2002) *Culture of Fear: Risk Taking and the Morality of Low Expectations.* London: Continuum.

Gabriel, N. (2004) 'Being a child today.' In J. Willan, R. Parker-Rees and J. Savage. *Early Childhood Studies.* Exeter: Learning Matters.

Galton, M., Simon, B. and Croll, P. (1980) *Inside the Primary Classroom* (The ORACLE Report). London: Routledge and Kegan Paul.

Gammage, P. (2006) 'Early Childhood Education and Care', *Early Years* 26 (3): 235–48.

Gardner, H. (1983) *Frames of Mind: The Theory of Multiple Intelligences.* New York: Basic Books.

Gelder, U. (2004) 'The importance of equal opportunities in the early years.' In J. Willan, R. Parker Rees and J. Savage (eds) *Early Childhood Studies: An Introduction to Children's Worlds and Children's Lives.* Exeter: Learning Matters.

Gerhardt, S. (2004) *Why Love Matters: How Affection Shapes a Baby's Brain.* Hove: Brunner-Routledge.

Gewirtz, S. (2000) 'Social justice, New Labour and school reform.' In G. Lewis, S. Gewirtz and J. Clarke (eds), *Rethinking Social Policy.* London: Sage/Open University.

Gewirtz, S. (2001) *The Managerial School: Post-Welfarism and Social Justice in Education.* London: RoutledgeFalmer.

Gibran, K. (1923). *The Prophet* (annotated edition by S. Bushrui 1995). Oxford: Oneworld.

Gill, T. (2007) *No Fear: Growing up in a Risk Averse Society.* London: Calouste Gulbenkian Foundation.

Gittins, D. (1993) *The Family in Question,* 2nd edition. London: Macmillan.

Gittins, D. (1998) *The Child in Question.* Basingstoke: MacMillan.

Gittins, D. (2004) 'The historical construction of childhood.' In, M.J. Kehily (ed.), *An Introduction to Childhood Studies.* Maidenhead: Open University Press and McGraw-Hill Education.

Gloucestershire Area Child Protection Committee (1995) *Part 8 Case Review: Overview Report in Respect of Charmaine and Heather West.* Gloucester: Gloucestershire Area Child Protection Committee.

Goldson, B. (2001) 'The demonization of children: from the symbolic to the institutional.' In P. Foley, J. Roche and S. Tucker (eds), *Children in Society: Contemporary Theory, Policy and Practice.* Basingstoke: Palgrave.

Goldthorpe, L. (2004) 'Every Child Matters: a legal perspective', *Child Abuse Review,* 13: 115–36.

Gopnick, A., Meltzoff, A. and Kuhl, P. (1999) *How Babies Think: The Science of Childhood.* London: Weidenfeld & Nicolson.

Goswami, U. (2004) 'Neuroscience and education', *British Journal of Educational Psychology*, 74: 1–14.

Graham, M. (2007) *Black Issues in Social Work and Social Care*. Bristol: Policy Press.

Great Britain Board of Education Consultative Committee (GBBECC) (1933) *Infant and Nursery Schools* (also known as the Hadow Report). London: HMSO.

Greeno, J. (1997) 'On claims that answer the wrong questions', *Educational Researcher*, 26 (1): 5–17.

Gregory, E., Long, S. and Volk, D. (eds) (2004) *Many Pathways to Literacy*. Abingdon: RoutledgeFalmer.

Gregory, J. (2000) *National Diet and Nutrition Survey: young people aged 4 to 18 years. Vol 1 Findings*. London: HMSO.

Hall, D. and Elliman, D. (2004) *Health for All Children*, 4th edition. Oxford: Oxford University Press.

Hall, J. (1997) *Social Devaluation and Special Education*. London: Jessica Kingsley.

Hallet, C. (1995) 'Child abuse: an academic overview.' In P. Kingston and B. Penhale (eds), *Family Violence and the Caring Professions*. London: Macmillan.

Haralambos, M. and Holborn, M. (2004) *Sociology, Themes and Perspectives*, 6th edition. London: Collins.

Harden, J. (2000) 'There's no place like home. The public/private distinction in children's theorizing of risk and safety', *Childhood*, 7 (1): 43–59.

Hargreaves, L.M. and Hargreaves, D.J. (1997) 'Children's Development 3–7: The learning relationship in the early years.' In N. Kitson and R. Merry (eds), *Teaching in the Primary School: a Learning Relationship*. London: Routledge.

Harms, T., Clifford, M. and Cryer, D. (1998) *Early Childhood Environment Rating Scale, revised edition* (ECERS-R). New York: Teachers College Press.

Harrison, R., Mann G., Murphy, M., Taylor, T. and Thompson, N. (2003) *Partnership Made Painless: A Joined Up Guide to Working Together*. Dorset: Russell House Publishing.

Hart, R. (1979) *Children's Experience of Place*. New York: Irvington Publishers.

Hart, R. (1992) *Children's Participation from Tokenism to Citizenship*. Innocenti Essays No 4. Florence: UNICEF.

Hart, R. (1997) *Children's Participation*. London: Earthscan/UNICEF.

Hendrick, H. (1992) *Child Welfare: England 1872–1989*. London: Routledge.

Hendrick, H. (1997) 'Constructions and reconstructions of British childhood: an interpretative survey, 1800 to the present.' In A. James and A. Prout (eds), *Constructing and Reconstructing Childhood: Contemporary Issues in the Sociological Study of Childhood*. London: RoutledgeFalmer.

Heppell, S. (2000) 'Foreword'. In N. Gamble and N. Easingwood (eds), *ICT and Literacy*. London: Continuum.

Her Majesty's Government (HMG) (1989) *Children Act*. London: The Stationery Office.

Her Majesty's Government (HMG) (1998) *The Data Protection Act 1998* available online at www.opsi.gov.uk/acts/acts1998/19980029.htm (Accessed: 30 January 2008).

Her Majesty's Government (HMG) (2004) *Children Act*. London: The Stationery Office.

Her Majesty's Government (HMG) (2006a) *Childcare Act*. London: The Stationery Office.

Her Majesty's Government (HMG) (2006b) *Children's Workforce Strategy: The Government's Response to Consultation*. Nottingham: DfES Publications.

Hevey, D. (1986) *The Continuing Under Fives Muddle; An Investigation Of Current Training Opportunities*. London: Voluntary Organisations Liaison Council For Under Fives.

Hevey, D. (1991) 'National vocational qualifications in child care and education. Starting Points No.5: A Series of VOLCUF Briefing Papers'. London: Voluntary Organisations Liaison Committee for Under Fives.

Hewlett, B.S. (1991) *Intimate fathers: The Nature and Context of AKA Pygmy Paternal Infant Care*. Ann Arbor, MI: University of Michigan Press.

Higher Education Academy (2008) *Integrating Children's Services in Higher education (ISE-HE): Preparing Tomorrow's Professional*. Available online: icshe.escalate.ac.uk/ (Accessed 5 March 2008).

Hill, D. (2003) 'Global neo-liberalism, the deformation of education and resistance', *Journal for Critical Education Policy Studies*, 1 (1), March. Available from www.jceps.com/?pageID=article&articleID=7 (Accessed 1 August 2003).

Hill, M. (2006) 'Children's voices on the ways of having a voice: children's and young people's perspectives on methods used in research and consultation', *Childhood*, 13 (1): 69–89.

Hill, M. and Morton, P. (2003) 'Promoting children's interest in health: An evaluation of the child health profile,' *Children & Society*, 17 (4): 291–304.

Hillman, M. (1993) *Children, Transport and the Quality of Life*. London: Policy Studies Institute.

Holland, P. (2004) *Picturing Childhood: The Myth of the Child in Popular Imagery*. London: I.B. Taurus.

Holloway, S. and Valentine, G. (eds) (2000) *Children's Geographies: Playing, Living, Learning*. London and New York: Routledge.

Holt, J. (1974) *Escape From Childhood: The Needs and Rights of Childhood*. New York: E.P. Dutton and Co.

Home Office (1998) *Supporting Families: Summary of Responses to the Consultation Document – Report*. London: HMSO.

Hope, G., Austin, R., Dismore, H., Hammond, S. and Whyte, T. (2007) 'Wild woods or urban jungle: playing it safe or freedom to roam', *Education 3–13*, 35 (4): 321–32.

Housley, W. (2003) *Interaction in Multidisciplinary Teams*. Aldershot: Ashgate Publishing.

Hoyles, M. and Evans, P. (1989) *The Politics of Childhood*. London: Journeyman Press.

Hoyuelos, A. (2004) 'A pedagogy of transgression', *Children in Europe* March (6): 6–7.

Hudson, J.A. (1993) 'Script knowledge.' In M. Bennett, *The Child as Psychologist: An Introduction to the Development of Social Cognition*. New York: Harvester Wheatsheaf.

Hunter, M. (2004) *Hearts and Minds Reluctantly Follow as Bill Finally Completes Passage*. Available from: www.communitycare.co.uk/articles (Accessed 16 January 2005).

Huskins, J. (1998) *From Disaffection to Social Inclusion*. Bristol: John Huskins.

Isaacs, S. (1954) *The Educational Value of the Nursery School*. London: British Association of Early Childhood Education.

Jackson, B. and Jackson, S. (1981) *Childminder*. London: Penguin Books.

James, A. and Prout, A. (eds) (1990/1997) *Constructing and Deconstructing Childhood: Contemporary Issues in the Sociological Study of Childhood*. Brighton: Falmer Press.

James, A. and James, A. (1999) 'Pump up the volume: listening to children in separation and divorce', *Childhood*, 6 (2): 189–206.

James, A., Jenks, C. and Prout, A. (1998) *Theorising Childhood*. Cambridge: Polity Press.

James, A., James, A. and McNamee, S. (2004) 'Turn down the volume? Not hearing children in family proceedings', *Child and Family Law Quarterly*, 16 (2): 189–202.

Jans, M. (2004) 'Children as citizens: towards a contemporary notion of child participation', *Childhood*, 11 (1): 27–44.

Jenkinson, J. (1997) *Mainstream or Special: Educating Students with Disabilities*. London: Routledge

Jenks, C. (1982) *The Sociology of Childhood*. London: Batsford.

Jenks, C. (2004) 'Constructing childhood sociologically.' In M.J. Kehily (ed.), *An Introduction to Childhood Studies*. Maidenhead: Open University Press.

Jessup, G. (1991) *Outcomes: NVQs and The Emerging Model Of Education and Training*. London: Falmer.

Johnson, R. (1999) 'Colonialism and cargo cults in early childhood education: does Reggio Emilia really exist?', *Contemporary Issues in Early Childhood*, 1 (1): 61–77.

Johnston, T. and Titman, P (2004) 'A health visitor-led service for children with behavioural problems', *Community Practitioner*, 77 (3): 90–4.

Johnston-Wilder, S. and Collins, J. (2008) 'Children negotiating identities.' In J. Collins and P. Foley (eds), *Promoting Children's Wellbeing: Policy and Practice*. Bristol: The Policy Press.

Jones, E. and Nimmo, J. (1994) *Emergent Curriculum*. Washington, DC: National Association for the Education of Young Children.

Jones, C. (2004) *Supporting Inclusion in the Early Years*. Maidenhead: University Press.

Jordan, B. (2004) 'Scaffolding learning and co-constructing understandings.' In A. Anning, J. Cullen and M. Fleer (eds), *Early Childhood Education*. London: Sage.

Karstadt, L., Lilley, T. and Miller, L. (2000) 'Professional roles in early childhood.' In R. Drury, L. Miller and R. Campbell (eds), *Looking at Early Years Education and Care*. London: David Fulton.

Kaltenborn, K. (2001) 'Family Transitions and Childhood Agency', *Childhood*, 8 (4): 463–98.

Katz, L. (1992) *Five Perspectives on Quality in Early Childhood Program*, Perspectives from ERIC/EECE: A Monograph Series.

Katz, L.G. (1993) *Dispositions as Educational Goals.* ERIC Digest: Urbana, Illinois. ERIC Clearing house on Elementary and Early Childhood Education. EDO PS 93 10 (September).

Katz, L.G. (1995) *Talks with Teachers of Young Children.* Norwood, NJ: Ablex.

Katz, L. (1999) *Another Look at What Young Children Should be Learning.* ERIC digest Available from: www.vtaide.com/png/ERIC/Learning-EC.htm (Accessed 11 January 2005)

Kehily, M.J. (2004) (ed.) *An Introduction to Childhood Studies.* Maidenhead: Open University Press and McGraw-Hill Education.

Kennedy, M. (2002) 'Disability and child abuse.' In K. Wilson and A. James (eds), *The Child Protection Handbook,* 2nd edition. Edinburgh: Harcourt Publishers.

King, M. (1987) 'Playing the symbols – Custody and the Law Commission', *Family Law,* 17: 186–91.

Kirby, P. and Marchant, R. (2004) 'The participation of young children: communication, consultation and involvement.' In B. Neale (ed.), *Young Children's Citizenship: Ideas into Practice.* York: Joseph Rowntree Foundation.

Kjørholt, A.T. (2002) 'Small is powerful: discourses on "Children and Participation" in Norway', *Childhood,* 9 (1): 63–82.

Knobel, M. and Lankshear, C. (eds) (2007) *New Literacies Sampler.* New York: Peter Lang.

Kobayashi, A. and Ray, B. (2000) 'Civil risk and landscapes of marginality in Canada: a pluralist approach to social justice', *The Canadian Geographer,* 44 (4): 401–17.

Krishnamurti, J. (1981) *Education and the Significance of Life.* London: HarperOne.

Kunnskapsdepartementet (2006) *Rammeplan for barnehagens innhold og oppgaver (R-06). (Norwegian Framework Plan for the Content and Tasks of Kindergartens).* Oslo: Kunnskaps department – Akademia.

Labbo, L. and Reinking, D. (2003) 'Computers and early literacy instruction.' In N. Hall, J. Larson and J. Marsh (eds), *Handbook of Early Childhood Literacy.* London:Sage.

Laevers, F. (ed.) (1994) *The Leuven Involvement Scale for Young Children. Manual and Video. Experiential Education Series, No. 1.* Leuven, Belgium: Centre for Experiential Education.

Laevers, F. (2000) 'Forward to basics! Deep-level-learning and the experiential approach', *Early Years,* 20 (2): 19–29.

Laming (2003) *Inquiry into the death of Victoria Climbié.* London: The Stationery Office.

Lane, J. (2007) *Embracing Equality: Promoting Equality and Inclusion in Early Years.* Pre-School Alliance. Available online: www.multiverse.ac.uk/attachments/e45687e4-ae2f-4922-993e 8f3ca94a 47bc.pdf (Accessed 30 June 2008).

Lancaster, Y.P. (2006) 'Listening to Young Children: respecting the voice of the child.' In G. Pugh and B. Duffy (eds), *Contemporary Issues in the Early Years,* 4th edition. London: Sage.

Lansdown, G. (2001) 'Children's welfare and children's rights.' In P. Foley, J. Roche and S. Tucker (eds), *Children in Society: Contemporary Theory, Policy and Practice.* Basingstoke: Palgrave.

Lave, J. (1988) *Cognition in Practice.* Cambridge: Cambridge University Press.

Leadbeater, C. (2004) *Learning about Personalisation: How Can we Put the Learner at the Heart of the Education system?* Annesley: Department for Education and Skills.

Learning and Teaching Scotland (LTS) (2007) *Taking Learning Outdoors: Partnerships For Excellence.* Edinburgh: LTS.

Learning and Teaching Scotland (LTS) (2008) *Curriculum for Excellence.* Available online: www.curriculumforexcellencescotland.gov.uk/(30 January 2008).

Learning Through Landscapes (2005) 'Supergrounds for Schools', *Play Today,* 46.

Leeson, C. and Griffiths, L. (2004) 'Working with Colleagues.' In J. Willan, R. Parker-Rees and J. Savage, *Early Childhood Studies.* Exeter: Learning Matters.

Leiba, T. (2003) 'Mental health policies and inter-professional working.' In J. Weinstein, C. Whittington and T. Leiba (eds), *Collaboration in Social Work Practice.* London: Jessica Kingsley.

Leiba, T. and Weinstein, J. (2003) 'Who are the participants in the collaborative process and what makes collaboration succeed or fail?' In J. Weinstein, C. Whittington and T. Leiba (eds), *Collaboration in Social Work Practice.* London: Jessica Kingsley.

Lepper, M.R., Drake, M.F. and O'Donnell-Johnson, T. (1997) 'Scaffolding techniques of expert human tutors.' In M. Pressley and K. Hogan (eds), *Advances in Teaching and Learning.* New York: Brookline Press.

Lindon, J. (1999) *Too Safe for Their Own Good? Helping Children Learn about Risk and Lifeskills.* London: National Early Years Network.

Lister Sharp, D., Chapman, S., Stewart Brown, S. and Sowden, A. (1999) 'Health-promoting schools and health promotion in schools: two systematic reviews', *Health Technol Assess*, 3 (22): 1–207.

Little H. (2006) 'Children's risk-taking behaviour: implications for early childhood policy and practice'. *International Journal of Early Years Education*, 14 (2): 141–54.

Lloyd, G., Stead, J. and Kendrick, A. (2001) *Interagency working to Prevent School Exclusion*. York: Joseph Rowntree Foundation. Available: www.jrf.org.uk/knowledge/findings/socialpolicy/ 961asp. (Accessed 10 October 2004).

Loxley, A. (1997) *Collaboration in Health and Welfare: Working with Difference*. London: Jessica Kingsley.

Lumsden, E. (2006) 'Safeguarding Children: Developing Confidence in Working Across Professional Boundaries.' Paper presented at XVIth ISPCAN International Congress on Child Abuse and Neglect, York, September.

Lumsden, E. and Murray, J. (2007) 'Wartime Nursery, Nursery, Neighbourhood Nursery, Children's Centre: the Changing Role of Early Years Provision'. Paper presented at European Early Childhood Education Research Association (EECERA) 17th Annual Conference, Prague, Czech Republic, September.

Luke, C. (1999) 'What next? Toddler netizens, playstation thumb, techno-literacies', *Contemporary Issues in Early Childhood*, 1 (1): 95–100.

Lynch, J. (1987) *Prejudice reduction and the schools*. New York: Nichols Publishing.

Macdonald, D., Rodger, S., Abbott, R., Zviani, J. and Jones, J. (2005) ' "I could do with a pair of wings": perspectives on physical activity, body and health from young Australian children', *Sport, Education and Society*, 10 (2): 195–209.

Macormick, N. (1982) *Legal Rights and Social Democracy: Essays in Legal and Political Philosphy*. Oxford: Clarendon Press.

MacNaughton, G. (2003) *Shaping Early Childhood*. Maidenhead: Open University Press.

MacNaughton, G. (2004) 'Exploring critical constructivist perspectives on children's learning.' In A. Anning, J. Cullen and M. Fleer (eds), *Early Childhood Education, Society and Culture*. London: Sage.

Macpherson, W. (1999) *The Stephen Lawrence Enquiry: Report of an Inquiry by Sir William Macpherson of Cluny*. London: HMSO.

Makin, L. (2006) 'Literacy 8–12 months: what are babies learning?', *Early Years*, 26 (3): 267–79.

Makkonen, T. (2006) *European Handbook on Equality Data*. Paris: European Commission.

Malaguzzi, L. (1993) 'For an education based on relationships', *Young Children*, 11/93: 9–13.

Malaguzzi, L. (1996) 'The hundred languages of children.' In *The Hundred Languages of Children*. Reggio Emilia: Reggio Children.

Malina, R. and Bouchard, C. (1991) *Growth, Maturation and Physical Activity*. Champaign, IL: Human Kinetics.

Mandela, N. (1994) *Long Walk to Freedom: The Autobiography of Nelson Mandela*. London: Little, Brown and Co.

Manning-Morton, J. and Thorp, M. (2003) *Key Times for Play: The First Three Years*. Maidenhead: Open University Press.

Marsh, J. (ed.) (2005) *Popular Culture, New Media and Digital Technology in Early Childhood*. London: RoutledgeFalmer.

Marsh, J. (2007) 'Digital Beginnings: Conceptualisations of Childhood.' Paper presented at the WUN Virtual Seminar, 13 February. Available from www.wun.ac.uk/download.php?file=2488_ Childrenpaper13Feb.pdf&mimetype=application/pdf. (Accessed 11 August 2007).

Marsh, J., Brooks, G., Hughes, J., Ritchie, L. and Roberts, S. (2005) *Digital Beginnings: Young Children's Use of Popular Culture, Media and New Technologies*. Sheffield: The University of Sheffied. Available from www.digitalbeginings.shef.ac.uk/. (Accessed 15 March 2006).

Maslow, A.H. (1970) *Motivation and Personality*, 2nd edition. New York: Harper Row.

May, V. and Smart, C. (2004) 'Silence in Court? Hearing Children in Residence and Contact Disputes', *Child and Family Law Quarterly*, 16 (3): 305–20.

Mayall, B. (1996) *Children, Health and the Social Order*. Buckingham: Open University Press.

Mayall, B. (2002) *Towards a Sociology of Childhood: Thinking from Children's Lives*. Buckingham: Open University Press.

Maynard, T. (2007) Adopting the Forest School approach: challenges and changes. In R. Austin (ed.), *Letting the outside in.* Stoke-on-Trent: Trentham Books.

Maynard, T. and Thomas, N. (eds) (2004) *An Introduction to Early Childhood Studies.* London: Sage.

Maynard, T. and Waters, J. (2007) 'Learning in the outdoor environment: a missed opportunity', *Early Years,* 27 (3): 255–65.

McGillivray, G. (2007) 'England.' In M.M. Clark and T. Waller (eds) *Early Childhood Education and Care: Policy and Practice.* London: Sage.

McMahon, L. and Farnfield, S. (1994) 'Infant and child observation as preparation for social work practice', *Social Work Education,* 13 (3): 81–98.

Melhuish, E. (2007) *National Evaluation of Sure Start.* London: Institute for the Study of Children, Families and Social Issues. Available online from: www.ness.bbk.ac.uk/ (Accessed 10th February 2008).

Meltzer, H., Gatward, R. and Goodman. R (2000) *Mental Health of Children and Adolescents in Great Britain.* London: Office of National Statistics.

Mental Health Foundation (1999) *Bright Futures: Promoting Children and Young People's Health.* London: Mental Health Foundation.

Merry, R. (1997) 'Cognitive Development 7–11: the learning relationship in the junior years.' In N. Kitson and R. Merry (eds), *Teaching in the Primary School: A Learning Relationship.* London: Routledge.

Miller, P.H. (2002) *Theories of Developmental Psychology,* 4th edition. New York: Worth Publishers.

Ministry of Education (MoE) (1996a) *Te Whāriki: He Whaariki Matauranga: Early Childhood Curriculum.* Wellington: Learning Media.

Ministry of Education (1996b) Early Childhood Curriculum: Te Whāriki Available online from: www.minedu.govt.nz/index.cfm?layout=document&documentid=3567&data=l (Accessed 10 January 2005).

Ministry of Education (2002) *Pathways to the Future: Nga Huarahi Aratiki. A 10-Year Strategic Plan for Early Childhood Education.* Wellington: Learning Media.

Monk, D. (2004) 'Childhood and the law: in whose best interests?.' In M.J. Kehily (ed.), *An Introduction to Childhood Studies.* Maidenhead: Open University Press.

Montessori, M. (1912–1964) *The Montessori Method.* New York: Schocken.

Moorhead, J. (2007) 'Let's set them free: What would it take to make you happy to let your kids play out alone?', *Guardian,* Saturday 9 June, Family Features Section, p1.

Morss, J. (1992) 'Making waves: deconstruction and developmental psychology', *Theory & Psychology,* 2 (4): 445–65.

Mortimer, H. (2002) *Special Needs Handbook: Meeting Special Needs in Early Years Settings.* Leamington Spa: Scholastic.

Moss, P. (2001a) *Beyond Early Childhood Education and Care.* Report to OECD Conference, Stockholm 13–15 June.

Moss, P. (2001b) 'The otherness of Reggio.' In L. Abbott and C. Nutbrown (eds) *Experiencing Reggio Emilia: Implications for Pre-School Provision.* Oxford: Oxford University Press.

Moss, P. (2001c) 'Policies and Provisions, Politics and Ethics.' In T. David (ed) *Advances in Applied Early Childhood Education, Vol I: promoting evidence based practice in Early Childhood Education.* London JAI 79–96.

Moss, P. (2001d) 'The otherness of Reggio'. In L. Abbot and C. Nutbrown (eds) *Experiencing Reggio Emilia: Implications for Preesschool Provision.* Oxford: Oxford University Press.

Moss, P. (2002) 'From Children's Services to Children's Spaces'. Paper presented at Seminar 1 of the ESRC Seminar Series, Challenging 'Social Inclusion'. Perspectives for and from Children and Young People, University of Edinburgh.

Moss, P. (2006) 'Structures, Understandings and Discourses: possibilities for re-envisioning the early childhood worker', *Contemporary Issues in Early Childhood,* 7 (1): 30–41.

Moss, P. and Petrie, P. (2002) *From Children's Services to Children's Spaces.* London and New York: RoutlegdeFalmer.

Moss, P., Candappa, M., Cameron, C., Mooney, A., McQuail, S. and Petrie, P. (2003) *Early Years and Childcare International Evidence Project: An Introduction to the Project.* London: DfES.

Moyles, J.R. (1997) 'Just for fun? The child as an active learner and meaning maker.' In N. Kitson and R. Merry (eds), *Teaching in the Primary School: a Learning Relationship.* London: Routledge.

Moyles, J.R. (ed.) (2005) *The Excellence of Play,* 2nd edition. Maidenhead: Open University Press.

Murray, J. and Lumsden, E. (2004) 'Joining up the thinking – turning the policy into real practice.' Paper presented at the EECERA Annual Conference, Malta, September.

Murray, R. (2003) *Forest School Evaluation Report: A Study in Wales.* (April to November). London: New Economics Foundation.

Mustard, F. and McCain, J. (1999) *Reversing the Real Brain Drain: Final Early Years Report for Ontario Government.* Ontario: Canada.

National Statistics (2008a) Available online: www.statistics.gov.uk/pdfdir/mar0207.pdf (Accessed 2 February 2008).

National Statistics, (2008b) Available online www.statistics.gov.uk/pdfdir/st0407.pdf (Accessed 2 February 2008).

National Statistics, (2008c) Available online: http://www.statistics.gov.uk/cci/nugget.asp?id=1766 (Accessed 2 February 2008).

Nelson, M. (2000) 'Childhood nutrition and poverty', *Proceedings of the Nutrition Society,* 59: 307–15.

NCH Action for Children (1996) *Factfile 96/97.* London: NCH.

NICE (2006) *Guidance on the prevention, identification, assessment and management of overweight and obesity in adults and children.* Available from: www.nice.org.uk/CG43 (Accessed 24 April 2007).

Nightingale, F. (1859) *Notes on Nursing.* Philadelphia, PA: J.P. Lippincott.

Northern Ireland Government (2008) Department of Health, Social Services and Public Safety. *Looked After Children.* Available from: www.dhsspsni.gov.uk/statistics_and_research-cib_looked-after-children (Accessed 2 February 2008).

Norwich, B. (1997) *Inclusion or Exclusion: future policy for emotional and behavioural difficulties education. SEN Policy Options Steering Group.* Tamworth: NASEN.

Nurse, A. D. (ed.) (2007) *The New Early Years Professional; Dilemmas and Debate.* Abingdon: Routledge.

Nutbrown, C. (1999) *Threads of Thinking.* London: Paul Chapman.

Nutbrown, C. (2006) *Threads of Thinking,* 2nd edition. London: Paul Chapman.

Nutbrown, C. (ed.) (1996) *Children's Rights and Early Education.* London: Paul Chapman.

Nutbrown, C. and Abbott, L. (2001) 'Experiencing Reggio Emilia.' In L. Abbott and C. Nutbrown (eds), *Experiencing Reggio Emilia: Implications for Pre-School Provision.* Oxford: Oxford University Press.

O'Brien, T. (ed.) (2001) *Enabling Inclusion : Blue Skies...Dark Clouds?* London: The Stationcry Office.

Organisation for Economic Co-operation and Development (OECD) (2001) *Starting Strong – Policy challenges for early childhood education and care provision across OECD countries.* Paris: OECD.

OECD Centre for Educational Research and Innovation (CERI) (2007) *Understanding the Brain: The Birth of a Learning Science.* Paris: OECD.

Office for Standards in Education (Ofsted) (2001) *National Standards for Under-Eights Day Care and Childminding: crèches.* London: DfES-0487-2001.

Office for Standards in Education (Ofsted) (2002) *Early Years: Early Days.* In Office For Standards in Education (ed.). London: HMSO.

Office for Standards in Education (Ofsted) (2003) *The Education of Six Year Olds in England, Denmark and Finland: An International Comparative Study.* London: Ofsted.

Office for Standards in Education (Ofsted) (2006a) *Early Years: safe and sound.* HMI 2663. Available from: www.ofsted.gov.uk (Accessed 3 April 2007).

Office for Standards in Education (Ofsted) (2006b) *Healthy Eating in Schools.* HMI 2625. London: Ofsted.

Organisation for Economic Co-operation and Development (OECD) (2004) *Five Curriculum Outlines. Starting Strong: Curricula and Pedagogies in Early Childhood Education and Care.* Paris: OECD.

Organisation for Economic Co-operation and Development (OECD) (2006) *Starting Strong II: Early Childhood Education and Care.* Paris: OECD.

Ouseley, H. and Lane, J. (2006) *Response to the Consulation on a Single Quality Framework for Services to Children from Birth to Five: Every Child Matters: Change for Children* (DfES/DWP). Available from: www.blink.org.uk/docs/EYFS_HO_AN_JL_July%2006.pdf (Accessed 12 May 2007).

Owen, C. (2003) *Men's Work? Changing the Gender Mix of the Childcare and Early Years Workforce.* London: Thomas Coram.

Owen, R. (1813) *A New View of Society: Second Essay on the Principle of the Formation of Human Character.* London: Cadell & Davies.

Owen, S. (2006) 'Training and workforce issues in the early years.' In G. Pugh and B. Duffy (eds), *Contemporary Issues in The Early Years,* 4th edition. London: Sage.

Oxford English Dictionary (2002) Oxford: Oxford University Press.

Paige-Smith, A. and Craft, A. (eds) (2008) *Developing Reflective Practice In The Early Years.* Maidenhead: Open University Press.

Pascal, C. and Bertram, T. (eds) (1997) *Effective Early Learning.* London: Hodder and Stoughton.

Pascal, C. and Bertram, A.D. (1994) 'Defining and assessing quality in the education of children from 4–7 years.' In F. Laevers (ed.), *Defining and Assessing the Quality in Early Childhood Education.* Studia Paedagogica (16). Leuven, Belgium: Leuven University Press.

Pascal, C., Bertram, A.D., Ramsden, F., Georgeson, J., Saunders, M. and Mould, C. (1996) *Evaluating and Developing Quality in Early Childhood Settings: A Professional Development Programme.* Worcester: Amber Publications.

Pascal, C., Bertram, T. and Ramsden, F. (1997) 'The effective early learning research project: reflections upon the action during phase 1', *Early Years,* 17 (2): 40–7.

Paley, V.G. (1990) *The Boy Who Would Be a Helicopter: The Uses of Storytelling in the Classroom.* Cambridge, MA: Harvard University Pres.

Pence, A. (1992) 'Quality care: thoughts on R/rulers.' Paper presented at the Workshop on Defining and Assessing Quality, Seville, September.

Penn, H. (1997) *Comparing Nurseries.* London: Paul Chapman.

Penn, H. (1999) *A Framework for Quality: A European perspective.* London: Institute of Education, London University, May.

Penn, H. (ed.) (2000) *Early Childhood Services.* Buckingham: Open University Press.

Penn, H. (2005) *Understanding Early Childhood: Issues and Controversies.* Maidenhead: Open University Press and McGraw-Hill Education.

Penn, H. (2007) 'Childcare Market Management: how the United Kingdom Government has reshaped its role in developing early childhood education and care', *Contemporary Issues in Early Childhood,* 8 (3): 192–207.

Perry, B.D. (1996) *Maltreated Children: Experience, Brain Development, and the Next Generation.* New York: W. W. Norton.

Pestalozzi, J.H. (1894) *How Gertrude Teaches her Children.* Trans. by L.E. Holland and F.C. Turner. Edited with an introduction by E. Cooke. London: Swan Sonnenschein.

Petrie, P., Boddy, J., Cameron, C., Hepinstall, E., Mcquail, S., Simon, A. and Wigfall, V. (2005) 'Pedagogy – a holistic, personal approach to work with children and young people across services.' *European Models for Practice, Training, Education and Qualifications.* London: Thomas Coram Research Institute, University of London, p. 8.

Phillips, D., McCartney, K. and Scarr, S. (1987) 'Child care quality and children's social development', *Journal of Applied Developmental Psychology,* 23 (4): 537–43.

Piaget, J. (1954) *The Construction of Reality in the Child.* New York: Basic Books.

Piaget, J. and Inhelder, B. (1969) *The Psychology of the Child.* New York: Basic Books.

Pinkerton, J. (2001) *'Developing partnership practice.'* In P. Foley, J. Roche and S. Tucker, *Children in Society: Contemporary Theory, Policy and Practice.* Basingstoke: Palgrave.

Podmore, V.N. (2004) 'Questioning evaluation quality in early childhood'. In A. Anning, J. Cullen and M. Fleer (eds), *Early Childhood Education.* London: Sage.

Pollard, E. L. and Lee, P. D. (2002) 'Child Well-being: A Systematic Review of the Literature', *Social Indicators Research,* 61: 59–78.

Pollock, L. (1983*) Forgotten Children – Parent:Child Relations from 1500–1900.* Cambridge: Cambridge University Press.

Polnay, J., Polnay, L., Lynch, M. and Shabde, N. (2007) *Child Protection Reader.* London: Royal College of Paediatrics and Child Health.

Pont, B., Nusche, D. and Moorman, H. (2008) *Improving School Leadership, Policy and Practice: Preliminary report.* Paris: Organisation for Economic Co-operation and Development.

Postman, N. (1983) *The Disappearance of Childhood.* New York: W.H. Allen.

Powell, A. (2004) 'High Court Challenge to Secret Abortions for under-16s', *Daily Mail,* 15 December, p. 33.

Prout, A. (2003). 'Participation, Policy and the Changing Conditions of Childhood.' In C. Hallett and A. Prout (eds), *Hearing the Voices of Children*. London: Falmer/Routledge.

Prout, A. (2005) *The Future of Childhood: Towards the Interdisciplinary Study of Children*. London: Falmer Press.

Prout, A. and James, A. (1990) 'A new paradigm for the sociology of childhood?' In A. James and A. Prout (eds), *Constructing and Deconstructing Childhood: Contemporary Issues in the Sociological Study of Childhood*. Brighton: Falmer Press.

Pryke, R. (2006) *Weight Matters for Children*. Oxford: Radcliffe Publishing.

Public Health Institute of Scotland (2003) *Need Assessment Report on Child And Adolescent Mental Health*. NHS Scotland

Pugh, G. (2005) 'Policy Matters.' In L. Abbott and A. Langston (eds) *Birth to Three Matters: Supporting the Framework of Effective Practice*. Berkshire: Open University Press.

Pugh, G. and Duffy, B. (2006) *Contemporary Issues in the Early Years*, 4th edition. London: Sage.

Quality Assurance Agency for Higher Education (2007) *The Standard for Childhood Practice 2007: Scottish Subject Benchmark Statement*. Mansfield: QAA Publications.

Qualifications and Curriculum Authority (QCA) (2000) *The National Curriculum Inclusion Statement*. Available online from: www.qca.org.uk/qca_6757.aspx. (Accessed 12 April 2007).

QCA (2007) *Meeting the challenge: Achieving equality for all. Single equality scheme*. Available online from: www.qca.org.uk/qca_15500.aspx (Accessed 10 March 2008).

Qvortrup, J., Bardy, M., Sgritta, G. and Wintersberger, H. (eds) (1994) *Childhood Matters: Social Theory, Practice and Politics*. Aldershot: Avebury.

Raban, B., Ure, C. and Manjula, W. (2003) 'Multiple perspectives: acknowledging the virtue of complexity in measuring quality', *Early Years*, 23 (1): 67–77.

Radford, M. (1999) 'Co-constructing reality: the child's understanding of the world.' In T. David (ed.), *Young Children Learning*. London: Paul Chapman.

Refugee Council (2008) *The Truth About Asylum*. Refugee Council. Available online from: www.refugeecouncil.org.uk/practice/basics/truth.htm (Accessed 13 May 2008).

Reder, P., Duncan, S. and Gray, M. (1993) *Beyond Blame: Child Abuse Tragedies Revisited*. London: Routledge.

Reynolds, P., Nieuwenhuys, O. and Honson, K. (2006) 'Refractions of Children's Rights in Development Practice: a view from anthropology-Introduction', *Childhood* 13: 291–302.

Rickinson, M., Dillon, J., Teamey, K., Young Choi, M., Morris, M. and Benefield, P. (2003) *A Review of Research on Outdoor Learning: Summary of Interim Findings*. Reading: NFER.

Rigby, K. (2002) *New perspectives on bullying*. London: Jessica Kingsley.

Riley, J. (ed.) (2003) *Learning in the Early Years: A guide for teachers of 3–7*. London: Paul Chapman.

Rinaldi, C. and Moss, P. (2004) 'What is Reggio?', *Children in Europe*, March (6): 2–3.

Rivkin, M.S. (1995) *The Great Outdoors: Restoring Children's Rights to Play Outside*. Washington, DC: NAEYC.

Roberts, R. (1998) 'Thinking about me and them.' In I. Siraj-Blatchford (ed.) *A Curriculum Development Handbook for Early Childhood Educators*. Stoke on Trent: Trentham Books.

Roberts, R. (2006) *Self Esteem and Early Learning*, 2nd edition. London: Paul Chapman.

Robinson, K.H. and Diaz, C.J. (2006) *Diversity and Difference in Early Childhood Education*. Berkshire: Open University Press.

Robinson, K.H. (2005) 'Doing Anti-homophobia and Anti-heterosexism in Early Childhood Education: moving beyond the immobilising impacts of "risks", "fears" and "silences" – can we afford not to?', *Contemporary Issues in Early Childhood*, 6 (2): 175–88.

Roche, J. (2001) 'Social Work Values and The Law.' In L. Cull and J. Roche (eds), *The Law and Social Work*. Basingstoke: Palgrave.

Roffey, S. (2001) *Special Needs in the Early Years*. London: David Fulton.

Rodgers, B., Pickles, A., Power, C., Collishaw, S. and Maughan, B. (1999) 'Validity of the Malaise Inventory in general population sample', *Social Psychiatry and Psychiatric Epidemiology*, 34 (6): 333–41.

Rogoff, B. (1990) *Apprenticeship in Thinking: Cognitive Development in Social Context*. New York: Plenum Press.

Rogoff, B. (1997) 'Evaluating development in the process of participation: theory, methods and practice building on each other.' In E. Amsel and K.A. Renninger (eds), *Change and Development: Issues of Theory, Method and Application.* Mahwah, NJ and London: Erlbaum Associates.

Rogoff, B. (1998) 'Cognition as a collaborative process.' In D. Kuhn and R.S. Seigler (eds), *Handbook of Child Psychology,* Vol 2, 5th edition. New York: John Wiley.

Rogoff, B. (2003) *The Cultural Nature of Human Development.* New York: Oxford University Press.

Rose, N. (1990) *Governing the Soul.* London: Routledge.

Rose, R. (2003) 'Encouraging Pupils with Learning Difficulties to Understand and Express their own Learning Needs.' In M. Shevlin and R. Rose, *Encouraging Voices: Respecting the Insights of Young People who Have Been Marginalized.* Dublin: National Disability Authority.

Rose, S. (1989) *From Brains to Consciousness? Essays on the New Sciences of the Mind.* London: Penguin.

Rousseau, J. J. (1913) (trans Cole, G. D. H) *The Social Contract and Discourses.* London: Dent.

Rowan, L. and Honan, E. (2005) 'Literarily lost: the quest for quality literacy agendas in early childhood education.' In N. Yelland, (ed.) *Critical Issues in Early Childhood Education.* Maidenhead: Open University Press.

Rutter, J. (2003) *Working with Refugee Children.* York: Joseph Rowntree Foundation.

Rutter, J. and Hyder, T. (1998) *Refugee Children in the Early Years: Issues for Policy-makers and Providers.* London: Save the Children and the Refugee Council.

Rutter, M. (1972) *Maternal Deprivation Reassessed.* London: Penguin.

Rutter, M. (1976) 'Parent-child separation: psychological effects on the children.' In A.M. Clarke and A.D.B Clarke (eds), *Early Experience: Myth and Evidence.* London: Open Books.

Rutter, M. (1981) *Maternal Deprivation Reassessed,* 2nd edition. London: Penguin.

Rutter, M. (1999) 'Resilience concepts and findings: implications for family therapy'. *Journal of Family Therapy,* 21: 119–44.

Ryder, M. and Wilson, B. (1997) 'From Center to Periphery: shifting agency in complex technical learning environments.' Paper presented at the American Educational Research Association, Chicago, March.

Sainsbury, C. (2000) *Martian in the Playground*: *Understanding the Schoolchild with Asperger's Syndrome.* Bristol: Lucky Duck Publishing.

Sanders, B. (2004) 'Interagency and Multidisciplinary Working.' In T. Maynard and N. Thomas (eds), *An Introduction to Early Childhood Studies.* London: Sage.

Saunders, L. (2006) *A Quiet Revolution? Teachers, research and school improvement.* Paper presented at Topic Conference, 12 July 2006, Slough, UK. Available online at: www.pre-online.co.uk/saunders.pdf (Accessed 30 January 2008).

Sayeed, Z. and Guerin, E. (2000) *Early Years Play: a Happy Medium for Assessment and Intervention.* London: David Fulton.

Schaffer, H.R. (1992) 'Joint involvement episodes as contexts for cognitive development.' In H. McCurk (ed.) *Childhood and Social Development: Contemporary Perspectives*: London Erlbaum Associates.

Schaffer, H.R. (1996) *Social Development.* Oxford: Blackwell.

Schor, J.B. (2004) *Born to Buy: The Commercialized Child and the New Consumer Culture.* New York: Scribner.

Schore J.R. and Schore A. N. (2008) 'Modern attachment theory: the central role of affect regulation in development and treatment', *Clinical Social Work Journal,* 36 (1): 9–20.

Schweinhart, L. (2001) *How the High/Scope Perry Preschool Study has Influenced Public Policy.* Conference paper given at Third International Interdisciplinary Evidence-based Policies and indicator Systems conference, Durham, UK, July.

Schweinhart, L.J., Barnes, H.V. and Weikart, D.P. (1993) 'Significant benefits: The High/Scope Perry Preschool Study through age 27.' *Monographs of the High/Scope Educational Research Foundation,* 10. Ypsilanti, MI: High/Scope Press.

Scott, W. (1996) 'Choices in Learning.' In C. Nutbrown, *Respectful Educators – Capable Learners: Children's Rights and Early Education.* London: Paul Chapman.

Scott, W. (2001) 'Listening and Learning.' In L. Abbott and C. Nutbrown (eds), *Experiencing Reggio Emilia: Implications for pre-school provision.* Buckingham: Open University Press.

Scottish Executive (1999) *Curriculum Framework for Children 3–5.* Glasgow: Learning and Teaching Scotland.

Scottish Executive (2002) *It's Everyone's Job to Make Sure I am Alright: Report of the Child Protection Audit and Review.* Edinburgh: The Stationery Office.

Scottish Executive Curriculum Review Group [SECRG] (2004) *A Curriculum for Excellence.* Edinburgh: Scottish Executive.

Scottish Executive (2005) *A Curriculum for Excellence.* Edinburgh: Scottish Executive.

Scottish Government (2003) *Growing Support: A Review of Services for Vulnerable Families with Young Children.* Available from: www.scotland.gov.uk/Publications/2003/01/15814/13953. (Accessed 23 May 2008).

Scottish Social Services Council (2008) *Investing In Children's Futures: The New Childhood Practice Awards.* Dundee: SSSC.

Scrivens, C. (2002) 'Early childhood education in New Zealand: the interface between professionalism and the New Right.' In L.K.S. Chan and E.J. Mellor (eds), *International Developments in Early Childhood Services.* New York: Peter Lang.

Sharp, R. (2004) 'Risk in outdoor education.' In P. Barnes and B. Sharp (eds), *Outdoor Education.* Lyme Regis: Russell House Publishing.

Shaw, I. (2000) 'Just Inquiry? Research and Evaluation for Service Users.' In H. Kemshall and R. Littlechild (eds), *User Involvement and Participation in Social Care: Research Informing Practice.* London: Jessica Kingsley.

Shuttleworth, D. (2003) *School Management in Transition.* London: Routledge Falmer.

Silin, J. (1995) *Sex, Death and the Education of Children: Our Passion for Ignorance in the Age of Aids.* New York: Teachers College Press.

Sinclair, R. (2004) 'Participation in practice: Making it meaningful, effective and sustainable', *Children and Society,* 18: 106–18.

Singer, E. (1993) 'Shared Care for Children', *Theory and Psychology,* 3 (44): 129–49.

Siraj-Blatchford, I. (1994) *The Early Years. Laying the foundations for Racial Equality.* Stoke-on-Trent: Trentham Books.

Siraj-Blatchford, I. and Wong, Y. (1999) 'Defining and evaluating "Quality" – early childhood education in an international context: dilemmas and possibilities', *Early Years: An International Journal of Research* and Development, 20 (1): 7–18.

Siraj-Blatchford, I. (2004) 'Quality teaching in the early years.' In A. Anning, J. Cullen and M. Fleer (eds), *Early Childhood Education.* London: Sage.

Siraj-Blatchford, I., Sylva, K., Muttock, S., Gilden, R. and Bell, D. (2002) *Researching Effective Pedagogy in the Early Years. RR 356.* London: Department for Education and Skills.

Smidt, S. (2002) *A Guide to Early Years Practice.* London: RoutledgeFalmer.

Smith P.K. and Cowie H. (2003) *Understanding Children's Development.* Oxford: Blackwell.

Smith, S. (1998) *Risk and our Pedagogical Relation to Children.* New York: State University of New York Press.

Snodgrass-Godoy, A. (1999) 'Our Right to be Killed', *Childhood,* 6 (4): 425–42.

Social Exclusion Unit (2003) A *Better Education for Children in Care.* London: Social Exclusion Unit.

Sproule, L., McGuinness, C., Trew, K., Rafferty, H., Walsh, G., Sheehy, N., and O'Neill, B. (2005) *The Early Years Enriched Curriculum Evaluation Project [EYECEP].* Available at: www.nicurriculum.org.uk/docs/foundation/eye_curric_project/v2/year5_full_report_v7.pdf (Accessed 30 January 2008).

Staggs, L. (2004) Cited in Palmer, S. [2004] 'Early Years: The Right Start'. *Times Educational Supplement,* 19 March, pp.14–15.

Stainton Rogers, R. (1992) 'The Social Construction of Childhood'. In W. Stainton Rogers, J. Hevey, J. Roche and E. Ask (eds), *Child Abuse and Neglect: Facing the challenge,* 2nd edition London: Batsford.

Stakes, R. and Hornby, G. (1997) *Meeting Special Needs in Mainstream Schools.* London: David Fulton.

Stenhouse, L. (1975) *An Introduction to Curriculum Research and Development.* London: Heinemann.

Stephenson, A. (2003) 'Physical risk-taking: dangerous or endangered?', *Early Years* 23 (1): 35–43.

Stine, S. (1997) *Landscapes for Learning.* New York: John Wiley & Sons.

Stone, C.A. (1998) 'What is missing in the metaphor of scaffolding?'. In D. Faulkener, K. Littleton and M. Woodhead (eds), *Learning Relationships in the Classroom.* London: Routledge.

Sturge, C. and Glaser, D. (2000) 'Contact and Domestic Violence–The Experts' Court Report', A *Family Law,* (30): 615–29.

Sure Start (2002) *Birth to Three Matters: A Framework to Support Children in Their Earliest Years.* London: Sure Start Unit.

Sure Start (2008) Sure Start Local Programmes. Available at: www.surestart.gov.uk/surestartservices/settings/surestartlocalprogrammes (Accessed 1 February 2008).

Sustainable Development Commission (2007) *Every Child's Future Matters.* London: SDC.

Sylva, K. (2003) *Assessing Quality in the Early Years.* Stoke-on-Trent: Trentham Books.

Sylva, K. and Siraj-Blatchford, I. (2001) 'The relationship between children's developmental progress in the pre-school period and two rating scales.' Paper presented at the International ECERS Network Workshop, Santiago, Chile, 31 July.

Sylva, K., Melhuish, E.C., Sammons, P., Siraj-Blatchford, I. and Taggart, B. (2004) *The Effective Provision of Pre-School Education (EPPE) Project:* Technical Paper 12 – *The Final Report: Effective Pre-School Education.* London: DfES/Institute of Education, University of London.

Sylwester, R. (1995) *A Celebration of Neurones: An Educator's Guide to the Brain.* Alexandra, VA: ASCD.

Tharp, R. and Gallimore, R. (1991) 'A Theory of Teaching as Assisted Performance.' In P. Light, S. Sheldon and M. Woodhead (eds), *Learning to Think.* London: Routledge.

Tassoni, P. (2003) *Supporting Special Needs: Understanding Inclusion in the Early Years (Professional Development).* Oxford: Heinemann.

The Children's Society (2007a) *Good Childhood Inquiry.* London: GfK NOP (Job no: 451311).

The Children's Society (2007b) *The Good Childhood – evidence Summary 1: Friends.* Pdf available from: www.childrenssociety.org.uk/all_about_us/how_we_do_it/the_good_childhood_inquiry/ 1818.html (Accessed 15 December 2007).

The Children's Society (2007c) *The Good – Childhood: evidence summary 2: Family.* Pdf available from: www.childrenssociety.org.uk/all_about_us/how_we_do_it/the_good_childhood_inquiry/1818.html (Accessed 15 December 2007).

The Children's Society (2007d) *The Good – Childhood: evidence summary 3: Learning* Pdf available from: www.childrenssociety.org.uk/all_about_us/how_we_do_it/the_good_childhood_inquiry/ 1818 html (Accessed 15 December 2007).

The Children's Society (2008) '*Good Childhood Inquiry Reveals Mounting Concern Over Commercialisation of Childhood*', 26 February 2008. Available at: www.childrenssociety.org.uk/whats_happening/media_office/latest_news/6486_pr.html (Accessed 1 March 2008).

The Scottish Government (2008) *Statistics: Children Looked After.* Available from: www.scotland.gov.uk/Topics/Statistics/Browse/Children/TrendLookedAfter (Accessed 2 February 2008).

Thomas, N. (2000) *Children, Family and the State.* London: Macmillan.

Thomas, N. (2001) 'Listening to children.' In P. Foley, J. Roche, and S. Tucker (eds) *Children in Society: Contemporary Theory, Policy and Practice.* Basingstoke: Palgrave.

Thomas, N. (2004) 'Law relating to children.' In T. Maynard and N. Thomas (eds) *An Introduction to Early Childhood Studies.* London: Sage.

Thompson, M., Grace, C., and Cohen, L. (2001) *Best Friends, Worst Enemies: Understanding the Social Lives of Children.* New York: Ballantine Books.

Thompson, N. (2003) *Communication and Language: A Handbook of Theory and Practice.* Basingstoke: Palgrave.

Thompson, N. (2006) *Anti-discriminatory Practice,* 4th edition. London: Macmillan.

Thompson, T. (2003) *Learning Disabilities: Effective Partnership and Teamwork to Overcome Barriers in Service Provision.* In J. Weinstein, C. Whittington and T. Leiba, *Collaboration in Social Work Practice.* London: Jessica Kingsley.

Thomson, P. and Gunter, H. (2006) 'From, 'consulting pupils, 'to pupils as researchers', A situated case narrative', *British Educational Research Journal,* 32 (6), December: 839–56.

Thorpe, S. (2004) 'Positive Engagement', *Care and Health Magazine,* 73: 22–3.

Tisdall, E., Kay, M. and Davis, J. (2004) 'Making a difference? Bringing children's and young people's views into policy-making', *Children and Society,* 18 (2): 131–42.

Titman, W. (1994) *Special Places for Special People – Hidden curriculum of School Grounds.* Godalming: World Wide Fund for Nature.

Tizard, B.and Hughes, M. (1984) *Young Children Learning.* London: Fontana.

Tobin, J. Wu, D. and Davidson, D. (1989) *Preschool in Three Cultures: Japan, China and the United States.* New Haven, CT: Yale University Press.

Tomlinson, S. (1982) *A Sociology of Special Education.* London : Routledge Kegan Paul.

Tovey, H. (2007) *Playing Outdoors.* Maidenhead: Open University Press.

Treseder, P. (1997) *Empowering Children and Young People: Training Manual.* London: Save the Children and Children's Rights Office.

Trevarthen, C. (1977) 'Descriptive analyses of infant communicative behaviour.' In H.R. Schaffer (ed.), *Studies in Mother Infant Interaction.* London: Academic Press.

Trevarthen, C. (1993) 'The functions of emotions in early infant communication and development.' In J. Nadel and L. Camaiori (eds), *New Perspectives on Early Communicative Development.* London: Routledge.

UK Children's Commissioners (2008) *UK Children's Commissioners' Report to UN Committee on the Rights of the Child.* London: 11 Milllion, Belfast: NICCY, Edinburgh: SCCYP, Swansea: Children's Commissioner for Wales.

United Nations (1989) *Convention on the Rights of the Child* (UNCRC). New York: United Nations.

United Nations Educational, Scientific and Cultural Organization Almaty Office. (2004). *Six Education For All Goals.* Available from: www.unesco.kz/index.php?lang=&sector=Education&newsid=854 (Accessed 2 August 2004).

United Nations Educational, Scientific and Cultural Organization (UNESCO) (2006) *Strong Foundations: Early Childhood care and education. Education for all Global Monitoring Report.* Paris: UNESCO.

UNICEF (2004) *The State of the World's Children.* New York: UNICEF.

UNICEF (2005) *The State of the World's Children.* New York: UNICEF.

UNICEF (2006) *The State of the World's Children.* New York: UNICEF.

UNICEF (2007a) *The State of the World's Children.* New York: UNICEF.

UNICEF (2007b) *Child Poverty in Perspective: An Overview of Child Well-Being in Rich Countries.* Report card 7. New York: UNICEF, Innocenti Research Centre.

UNICEF (2008a) *The State of the World's Children.* New York: UNICEF.

UNICEF (2008b) *The State of the Africa's Children.* New York: UNICEF.

United Nations Children's Fund. (2003) *The Best Start in Life for Every Child.* Available online from: www.unicef.org/earlychildhood/ (Accessed 24 July 2004).

Valentine, G. and McKendrick, J. (1997) 'Children's outdoor play: exploring parental concerns about children's safety and the changing nature of childhood', *Geoforum* 28 (2): 219–35.

Vandenbroeck, M. and Bouverne-De Bie, M. (2006) 'Children's Agency and Educational Norms: A Tensed Negotiation', *Childhood* 13 (1): 127–43.

Vecchi, V. (1993) 'Role of the *atelierista*.' In C. Edwards, L. Gandini and G. Foreman (eds), *The Hundred Languages of Children – The Reggio Emilia Approach to Early Childhood Education.* Norwood, NJ: Ablex.

Vong, K.I. (2005) 'Towards a creative early childhood programme in Zhuhai-SER and Macau-SER of the People's Republic of China – Unpublished Doctoral Thesis, University of London.

Vygotsky, L.S. (1956) *Selected Psychological Investigations.* Moscow: IAPNSSR.

Vygotsky, L.S. 1966 (1933) 'Play and its role in the mental development of the child', *Voprosy Psikhologii*, 12: 62–76.

Vygotsky, L.S. (1978) *Mind in Society.* Cambridge, MA: Harvard University Press.

Vygotsky, L.S. (1986) *Thought and Language.* Amherst, MA: MIT Press.

Waite, S., Davis, B. and Brown, K. (2006a) 'Current Practice and Aspirations for Outdoor Learning for 2–11 Year Olds in Devon.' Consultation Report, June, University of Plymouth.

Waite, S., Davis, B. and Brown, K. (2006b) 'Five Stories of Outdoor Learning from Settings for 2–11 Year Olds in Devon.' Consultation Report, June, University of Plymouth.

Walkerdine, V. (1984) 'Developmental psychology and the child-centred pedagogy.' In J. Henriques, W. Hollway, C. Urwin, C. Venn, and V. Walkerdine, *Changing the Subject: Psychology, Social Regulation and Subjectivity.* London and New York: Methuen.

Walkerdine, V. (1993) 'Beyond Developmentalism', *Theory & Psychology*, 3 (4): 451–69.

Walkerdine, V. (2004) 'Developmental psychology and the study of childhood.' In M.J. Kehily (ed.), *An Introduction to Childhood Studies.* Maidenhead: Open University Press and McGraw-Hill Education.

Waller, T., Murray, J. and Waller, J. (2004) 'Outdoor learning and well-being: Children's spaces and children's minds.' Paper presented at the *EECERA Annual Conference*, Malta, September.

Waller, T. (2005a) 'Outdoor learning and well-being: recording and evaluating young children's perspectives,' Paper presented at the Fifth Warwick International Early Years Conference, University of Warwick, UK, March.

Waller, T. (2005b) 'Outdoor learning and well-being: recording and evaluating children's perspectives,' Paper presented at the EECERA Annual Conference, Dublin, August–September.

Waller, T. (2005c) 'This is the way we go to the park!' Recording and evaluating young children's knowledge and perspectives of geography Paper presented at the BERA Annual Conference, Glamorgan, September.

Waller, T. (2006) '"Be careful – don't come too close to my Octopus Tree": recording and evaluating young children's perspectives of outdoor learning', *Children, Youth and Environments,* 16 (2): 75–104.

Waller, T. (2007a) '"The swamp monster with 18 heads". Young children's narratives and outdoor spaces: in search of the possible'. Paper presented at the EECERA Annual Conference, Prague, August – September 2007.

Waller, T. (2007b) '"The Trampoline Tree and The Swamp Monster with 18 Heads": outdoor Play in the Foundation Stage and Foundation Phase', *Education 3–13,* 35 (4): 395-409.

Waller, T. (2008) 'ICT and Literacy.' In J. Marsh and E. Hallett (eds), *Desirable Literacies: Approaches to Language and Literacy in the Early Years, 2nd edition.* London: Sage.

Walsh, G. (2007) 'Northern Ireland.' In, M.M. Clark and T. Waller (eds), *Early Childhood Education and Care: Policy and Practice.* London: Sage.

Waters, J. and Begley, S. (2007) 'Supporting the development of risk-taking behaviours in the early years: an exploratory study', *Education 3–13,* 35 (4): 365–78.

Webb, E. (2001) 'The health of children in refuges for women victims of domestic violence: cross-sectional descriptive study', *BMJ,* 323: 210–13.

Weinberger, J., Pockstone, C. and Hannon, P. (2005) *Learning from Sure Start: Working with Young Children and their Families.* Maidenhead: Open University Press.

Weinstein, J., Whittington, C. and Leiba, T. (2003) *Collaboration in Social Work Practice.* London: Jessica Kingsley.

Welsh Assembly Government (WAG) (2002) *Welsh Assembly Government Play Policy.* Cardiff: WAG.

Welsh Assembly Government (WAG) (2003) *The Learning Country: Foundation Phase 3–7 years.* Cardiff: WAG.

Welsh Assembly Government (WAG) (2007) *All Wales Child Protection Procedures* Cardiff: All Wales Child Protection Procedures Review Group.

Wenger, E. (1998) *Communities of Practice: Learning, Meaning and Identity.* Cambridge: Cambridge University Press.

Whalley, M. (2001) 'Working as a Team.' In G. Pugh (ed.), *Contemporary Issues in the Early Years: Working Collaboratively with Children,* 3rd edition. London: Sage.

Whalley, M. (2007) *Involving Parents in Their Children's Learning,* 2nd edition. London: Paul Chapman.

Whalley, M. (2000) *House of Commons Select Committee on Education and Employment Minutes of Evidence: Examination of Witnesses (Questions 320–339).* Available at: www.parliament. the-stationery-office.co.uk/pa/cm199900/cmselect/cmeduemp/386/0061409.htm (Accessed 27 January 2008).

Whittington, C. (2003) 'Collaboration and Partnership in Context.' In J. Weinstein, C. Whittington and T. Leiba, *Collaboration in Social Work Practice.* London: Jessica Kingsley.

Willan, J., Parker-Rees, R. and Savage, J. (2004) *Early Childhood Studies.* Exeter: Learning Matters.

Willey, C. (2000) 'Working with Parents in Early Years Settings.' In R. Drury, L. Miller and R. Campbell(eds), *Looking at Early Years' Education and Care.* London: David Fulton.

Willow, C., Marchant, R., Kirby, P. and Neale, B. (2004) *Young Children's Citizenship.* York: Joseph Rowntree Foundation.

Wilson, H. (2002) 'Brain science, early intervention and 'at risk', 'families: implications for parents, professionals and social policy' *Social Policy and Society,* 1: 191–202.

Wilson, R. (1998) *Special Educational Needs in the Early Years.* London: Routledge.

Wolfendale, S. (2000) 'Special needs in the early years: prospects for policy and practice', '*Support for Learning,* 15 (4): 147–51.

Wolfendale, S. and Robinson, M. (2006) 'Meeting Special Needs in the Early Years: An Inclusive Stance.' In G. Pugh and B. Duffy (2006), *Contemporary Issues in the Early Years.* London: Sage.

Wood, D. (1993) 'Ground to Stand on: Some Notes on Kids' Dirt Play', *Children's Environments*, 10 (1): 1–22. Available online from: www.colorado.edu/journals/cye/ (Accessed 10 June 2005).

Wood, D.J., Bruner, J.S. and Ross, G. (1976) 'The role of tutoring in problem solving,' *Journal of Child Psychology and Psychiatry*, 17 (2): 89–100.

Wood, E. (2004) 'Developing a pedagogy of play.' In A. Anning, J. Cullen and M. Fleer (eds), *Early Childhood Education: Society and Culture.* London: Sage.

Wood, E. (2007) 'New directions in play: consensus or collision?', *Education 3–13*, 35 (4): 309–20.

Wood, E. and Attfield, J. (1996) *Play, Learning and the Early Childhood Curriculum.* London: Paul Chapman.

Wood, E. and Attfield, J. (2005) *Play, Learning and the Early Childhood Curriculum,* 2nd edition. London: PCP.

Woodhead, M. (2003) 'Childhood studies: past, present and future.' Paper presented at the Open University Conference, 'Childhood Reconsidered', Milton Keynes, June.

Woodhead, M. and Montgomery, H. (2003) *Understanding Childhood: An Interdisciplinary Approach* Chichester: John Wiley & Sons.

Wells, G. (1987) *The Meaning Makers.* London: Hodder & Stoughton.

World Health Organization (1948) *Constitution of the World Health Organization.* Geneva: World Health Organization.

World Health Organization. (1999) *A Critical Link – Interventions for Physical Growth and Psychological Development.* Geneva: World Health Organization.

Wray, D. and Medwell, J. (1998) *Teaching English in Primary Schools.* London: Letts.

Wyness, M.G. (1999) 'Childhood, Agency and Education Reform', *Childhood,* 6 (3): 353–68.

Wyness, M.G. (2000) *Contesting Childhood.* London and New York: Falmer Press.

Wyn Siencyn, S. and Thomas, S. (2007) 'Wales.' In, M.M. Clark and T. Waller (eds), *Early Childhood Education and Care: Policy and Practice.* London: Sage.

Wyse, D. (2004) *Childhood Studies: An Introduction.* Oxford: Blackwell.

Yelland, N. (2006) *Shift to the future: Rethinking learning with New Technologies in Education.* New York: RoutledgeFalmer.

Young Minds (2003) *Tuning in to our Babies: The Importance of the Relationship Between Parents and their Babies and Toddlers.* London: Young Minds.

Yr Adran Addysg, Dysgu Gydol Oes a Sgiliau (YAADGOS) [Department for Education, Lifelong Learning and Skills] (2006) *Building the Foundation Phase Action Plan.* Cardiff: Yr Adran Addysg, Dysgu Gydol Oes a Sgiliau (Department for Education, Lifelong Learning and Skills).

Zelitzer, V. (1985) *Pricing the Priceless Child.* New York: Basic Books.

Zaninotto, P., Wardle, H., Stamatakis, E., Mindell, J. and Head, J. (2006) *Forecasting Obesity to 2010.* London: Department of Health.

Zuckerman, M. (1993) 'History and developmental psychology: a dangerous liaison.' In G. Elder, J. Modell and R. Parke (eds), *Children in Time and Space: Developmental and Historical Insights.* Hillsdale, NJ: Erlbaum Associates.

INDEX

Added to a page number 'f' denotes a figure and 't' denotes a table.